TWELVE BOOKS OF THE APOCALYPSE

Including The Apocalypse of Peter, Abraham, Elijah, Paul, Adam, 1st James, 2nd James, Thomas, the Apocryphon of John, Coptic Peter, Thunder: Perfect Mind, and Baruch

by Joseph Lumpkin

TWELVE BOOKS OF THE APOCALYPSE

Including The Apocalypse of Peter, Abraham, Elijah, Paul, Adam, 1st James, 2nd James, Thomas, the Apocryphon of John, Coptic Peter, Thunder: Perfect Mind, and Baruch

by Joseph Lumpkin

Copyright © 2024 by your name here

All rights reserved.

Printed in the United States of America. No part of this book may be used or reproduced in any manner whatsoever without written permission except in the case of brief quotations embodied in critical articles and reviews.

Fifth Estate Publishing, Blountsville, AL 35031

Printed on acid-free paper

Library of Congress Control No:

ISBN: 9798334258662

Fifth Estate Publishing

Fifth Estate, 2024

Table of Contents

Introduction	7
Information on the Apocalypse of Peter	9
The Apocalypse of Peter	16
Information on the Apocalypse of Abraham	21
The Apocalypse of Abraham	25
Information on the Coptic Apocalypse of Elijah	44
The Coptic Apocalypse of Elijah	46
Information on the Apocalypse of Paul	60
The Apocalypse of Paul	63
Gnosticism	100
Information on the Apocalypse of Adam	125
The Apocalypse of Adam	127
Information on the First and Second Apocalypse of James	137
Introduction to The First Apocalypse of James	138
First Apocalypse of James	155
Information on The Second Apocalypse of James	168
Second Apocalypse of James	171

Information on the Apocalypse of Thomas	181
The Apocalypse of Thomas	185
Information of the Apocryphon of John	196
Apocryphon of John	199
Information on The Coptic Apocalypse of Peter	224
The Coptic Apocalypse of Peter	225
Information on Thunder: Perfect Mind	232
Thunder: Perfect Mind	236
Information on The Apocalypse of Baruch	247
The Apocalypse of Baruch	252

Introduction

APOCALYPSE

a ·poc ·a ·lypse

Apocalypse (noun) · the Apocalypse (noun) · apocalypse (noun) · apocalypses (plural noun) (the Apocalypse)

the complete final destruction of the world, as described in the biblical book of Revelation.

(especially in the Vulgate Bible) the book of Revelation.

an event involving destruction or damage on an awesome or catastrophic scale.

Origin

Old English apocalipsin, via Old French and ecclesiastical Latin from Greek apokalupsis, from apokaluptein 'uncover, reveal', from apo- 'un-' + kaluptein 'to cover'.

(Merriam-Webster Dictionary)

Apocalypse – A complicated word. A word with varied meanings. It is a word associated with ultimate, violent, catastrophic destruction. It is also a word hidden deep in our collective psyches, placed there by two-thousand years of exposure. It is the name of the last book of the Christian Bible. One of the oldest and most revered Bibles is the Latin Vulgate "Biblia Sacra Vulgata." The final text in this Bible is Apocalypsis Iohannis – The Apocalypsis of John – The Revelation of John – The book we call "Revelation.

In this context, the word "Apocalypse", translated as "Revelation", means something extraordinary was revealed to

John. The first few lines of the book tells us this was the Revelation of Jesus, which God gave to John.

It may surprise you to know there were many apocalypses written. At lease one, The Apocalypse of Peter, almost made it in to our Bible, and is actually cited in one list of books in the Bible.

The Apocalypse of Peter is listed in the canon of the Muratorian fragment, a 2nd-century list of approved books in Christianity and one of the earliest surviving proto-canons. While the Apocalypse of Peter influenced other Christian works in the 2nd, 3rd, and 4th centuries, it eventually became considered inauthentic and declined in use. It was replaced by the Apocalypse of Paul, a popular 4th-century work heavily influenced by the Apocalypse of Peter that provides its own updated vision of heaven and hell. The Apocalypse of Peter is an early example of the same genre of the famous Divine Comedy of Dante, wherein someone takes a tour of the realms of the afterlife and is shown heaven and hell, and the conditions of the people inhabiting these realms.

In this work, we have attempted to gather the most interesting and influential Apocalypses in the hope these books may Reveal to the reader something hitherto unknown. We hope you enjoy the Revelations.

(Parts of the information and history of these books were supplied by "Early Christian Writings" at http://www.earlychristianwritings.com/)

Twelve Books on the Apocalypse

Information on the Apocalypse of Peter

It should first be stated that in the early church, as the long and somewhat divisive period of canon acceptance was being navigated, the Apocalypse of Peter was listed in a certain canon.

Clement of Alexandria (c. 150 – 215 CE) regarded the Apocalypse of Peter as Holy Scriptures (cf. Euseb. HE VI 14.1)

The Muratorian Canon is the oldest known list of New Testament books from as early as AD 170. It lists the Apocalypse of Peter. The comment in the document lists it as a book received yet about which there was disagreement as to its use for common reading. It is noted that some authorities would not have it read in church. At line 69 The document states: "the Apocalypses also of John and Peter only do we receive, which (latter) some among us would not have read in church."

Clement of Alexandria (fl. c.200 a.d.) in his Hypotoposes, according to the testimony of Eusebius, H. E., vi., 14, gave "abridged accounts of all the canonical Scriptures, not even omitting those that are disputed. Mentioned are The Book of Jude and the other general epistles. Also the Epistle of Barnabas and that called the Revelation of Peter." Also Clement, in his Eclogæ Prophetiæ, chapters 41, 48 and 49, gives three quotations from the Revelation of Peter, mentioning it twice by name.

In the Catalogus Claromontanus, an Eastern list of Holy Scriptures, c. 250, lists at the end the Revelation of Peter (v. Westcott, Canon, p.555).

Methodius, bishop of Olympus in Lycia (died c. 311) in the beginning of the fourth century, in his Symposium, ii., 6, quotes Peter, stating: "wherefore we have also learned from divinely inspired Scriptures that untimely births even if they are the offspring of adultery are delivered to care-taking angels." He may be quoting Clement of Alexandria, who in turn quotes the Apocalypse of Peter.

Eusebius (c.339 a.d.), in his Ecclesiastical History, iii., 25, mentions the Revelation of Peter as spurious books.

Sozomen (middle of fifth century), H. E., vii., 19, says: "For instance, the so-called Apocalypse of Peter which was esteemed as entirely spurious by the ancients, we have discovered to be read in certain churches of Palestine up to the present day, once a year, on the day of preparation, during which the people most religiously fast in commemoration of the Saviour's Passion" (i.e., on Good Friday). It is to be noted that Sozomen himself belonged to Palestine.

In the list of the Sixty Books which is assigned to the fifth or sixth century the Revelation of Peter is mentioned among the Apocrypha (v. Westcott, Canon, p.551).

Robinson and James state: Up till lately these facts represented all that was positively known of the Revelation of Peter. From them we gather that it must have been written before the middle of the second century (so as to be known at Rome and included in the Muratorian Canon), that it had a wide circulation, that it was for some time very popular, so that it would appear to have run a considerable chance of achieving a place in the canon, but that it was ultimately rejected and in the long run dropped out of knowledge altogether. But even previously to the discovery at Akhmîm, the general character of the book had been inferred from the scanty fragments preserved in ancient writers and from the common elements contained in other and later apocalyptic writings which seemed to require some such book as the Revelation of Peter as their ultimate source.

(Cf. Robinson, Texts and Studies, i., 2, p.37-43, and Robinson and James, The Gospel according to Peter and the Revelation of Peter, 1892.)

From the above references we see a once esteemed book, a book once thought of as inspired, fall slowly out of favor. From 170 CE to 250 CE the Apocalypse of Peter was considered inspired and on lists of canon books. Until 300 CE it continued to be quotes. By 399 CE it became spurious or fake. By the mid 5th century it was placed in the ranks of the Apocryphal writings. And then, it was copied less, distributed less, and became less known. It would have completely disappeared from the theological stage, if not for a single monk.

In the ninth century, a Christian monk was buried with his favorite books in a gave at Akhmim, Egypt. When the grave was opened it was discovered that portions of several books were placed alongside him. The books had aged, crumbled, and fragmented. These fragments included portions of 1 Enoch, the Gospel of Peter, and the Revelation or Apocalypse of Peter, written in Greek.

The word for Revelation in Greek is Apokalypsis meaning to uncover or reveal. It is where we get the word, Apocalypse. Thus, you may hear the Apocalypse of Peter called the Revelation of Peter. The Revelation of John can be called the Apocalypse of John (although the book states it is the revelation [singular] of Jesus Christ).

The monk's burial trove proved to be a time capsule of great importance. The Apocalypse of Peter was known to have existed, since references to it are in some of the writing of the early church fathers and historians, but it had vanish from existence. The church ceased using it, so it was no longer being copied or propagated, and thus was lost to history. It had vanished, leaving very faint traces.

We do not know what compelled the monk to value this book so highly as to be buried with it. Maybe it was his love for ancient and forgotten texts. Maybe he wished to have a guide into the afterlife and felt this book was an authentic description of the bliss or torment to come. We will never know. All we know is we now have a large fragment of a once forgotten text.

When the grave of the monk was discovered in the 1880s, his treasured book shocked the scholarly world. The Apocalypse of

Peter, also called, The Revelation of Peter, was back, and it was powerful.

The text exists in two incomplete versions. There is a Greek and an Ethiopic version. These two versions diverge considerably.

J. K. Elliott, The Apocryphal New Testament (Oxford: Clarendon Press, 1993) writes:

> The loss of the Revelation of Peter for so many centuries is startling, when we recall how very popular it had once been in Christian churches around the Mediterranean world, and especially in Egypt and Palestine. For centuries, the two Revelations of Peter and John had both been debatable candidates for inclusion in the New Testament canon and in church liturgies. In the early Christian centuries, the Revelation of Peter was widely cited, and it influenced many other popular texts, including the Acts of Perpetua, the Sibylline Oracles and the Apocalypse of Paul (Visio Pauli). Particularly important in terms of its impact was the Sibylline material, as the second Sibylline gives a lengthy summary of the Revelation of Peter in Greek verse. These Oracles continued to be highly popular throughout the Christian Middle Ages.

As one will see while reading this work, it's motif is used in Dante's Divine Comedy (Date's Inferno). This same type of layered or storied structure of heaven or hell is also seen in The Book of Enoch (1 Enoch), as well as the wildly non-canon books of 2 Enoch and 3 Enoch.

H. Weinel believed the approximately the year of 135 was the likely period of origin.

Müller writes (New Testament Apocrphya, vol. 2, p. 625): "The significance of the Apocalypse of Peter as an important witness of the Petrine literature is not to be underestimated. Peter is the decisive witness of the resurrection event. Hence he is also deemed worthy of further revelations, which he hands on (in revelation documents) with authority. Revelatio and traditio, receiving and handing on, the chain of transmitters, are the central ideas of this understanding of revelation (Berger). Peter's disciple Clement (2 Clem. 5) plays the decisive role here, as witnessed by the Ethiopic version of the Apocalypse, which belongs in the framework of the Clement literature in which Peter hands on the secret revelation to Clement (on Peter as a recipient of revelation cf. Berger, 379ff.). As compared with the Canon, the eschatological functions of Peter are new (Berger, 325). In its description of heaven and hell the Apocalypse draws on the abundance of ideas from the East which has also left its deposit in the writings of late Jewish Apocalyptic and the mystery religions. The motif of the river of fire, which is one of the pregnant eschatological ideas among the Egyptian Christians, certainly goes back to ancient Egypt. In view of the abundance of traditions in Egypt and the prestige of the Petrine tradition there (veneration of Peter's disciple Mark), an origin in Egypt is probable. The Apocalypse of Peter brings together divergent traditions, for which it has not yet been possible to discover any uniform source."

The Apocalypse of Peter (also called the Revelation of Peter) gives us insight into the human imagination. In this book, Heaven is described in beautiful detail, but the passages regarding heaven are short and fleeting. Hell is also described in this work, and the description of various tortures and torments fill page upon page. Beyond the facts that we will have perfect hair and perfect skin and we will live in peace and harmony where the weather and scenery are beautiful there is not much to say about heaven or a state of bliss. It seems almost boring. Hell, however, fills our imaginations, pages and books. This may speak to our nature, whether it is macabre of fearful, hell appeals to our imagination more than heaven, at lease it does in this text. If one were to combine all fragments and texts of this book, we would see a list of torments worthy of any slasher movie.

Blasphemers are hanged by their tongues.

Those who impede others from obtaining justice are placed in a pit of fire.

Women who adorn themselves for the purpose of adultery are hung by their hair over a pool of bubbling mire or mud.

The men who had adulterous relationships are hung by their genitals.

Murderers and their allies are tormented by venomous creatures and worms that never rest.

Women who aborted their children are in a pit of blood and excrement up their throats. The children they aborted shoot sparks and fire that penetrate the eyes of the mothers.

Mothers who committed infanticide or whose children died after being aborted in a premature birth ooze breast milk, which congeals and runs down. The milk produces flesh-eating creatures that bite and torment both parents.

Dead and aborted children are delivered to a care-taking angel to raise and teach them.

Those who betray, torment or kill righteous people have their bodies set on fire and thrown into a dark pit where their entrails are eaten by a worm that never sleeps.

Those who slander and doubt God's righteousness gnaw their tongues as they have hot irons plunged into their eyes.

Those who betrayed the saints and caused the death of martyrs have their lips cut off, and fire burns their entrails.

Rich people who neglected the poor are clothed in rags and pierced by a sharp swords and sparks of fire.

Loan sharks and those who charge high interest rates in order to exact or extort profit are placed in a lake of filth and blood.

Gay men who take on the sexual role of a woman, and lesbians who take on the role of a man in their relationships fall from the precipice of a high cliff, only to be forced back up the hill to repeat the fall for eternity.

Those who carve idols are beaten with fiery whips (Ethiopic fragment) or they beat each other with fire rods (Akhmim fragment).

Those who forsook God's Commandments and heeded demons burn in flames.

Those who do not honor their parents fall into a river of fire.

Women who had premarital sex have their flesh torn to pieces.

Disobedient slaves gnaw their tongues eternally.

Sorcerers are hung on a wheel of fire which turns to roast them over flames.

The list of torments in hell seem to go on and on. Peter has much to say about hell and gives a myriad of reasons to live right and stay out of hell.

Now, we delve in to a book that was once in contention to be canon. A book, which some stated should have replaced our book of Revelation, and others thought should have accompanied it into our Holy Bible.

The Apocalypse of Peter

1 . . . . many of them will be false prophets, and will teach different ways and doctrines of hell: but these will become sons of damnation. 3. And then God will come to my faithful ones who hunger and thirst and are afflicted and purify their souls in this life; and he will judge the sons of lawlessness.

4. And furthermore the Lord said: Let us go into the mountain: Let us pray.. And going with him, we, the twelve disciples, begged that he would show us one of our brethren, the righteous who are gone forth out of the world, in order that we might see of what manner of form they are, and having taken courage, might also encourage the men who hear us.

6. And as we prayed, suddenly there appeared two men standing before the Lord towards the East, on whom we were not able to look; 7, for there came forth from their countenance a ray as of the sun, and their raiment was shining, such as eye of man never saw; for no mouth is able to express or heart to conceive the glory with which they were endued, and the beauty of their appearance. 8. And as we looked upon them, we were astounded; for their bodies were whiter than any snow and redder than any rose; 9, and the red thereof was mingled with the white, and I am utterly unable to express their beauty; 10, for their hair was curly and bright and beautiful both on their face and shoulders, as it were a wreath woven of spikenard and various colored flowers, or like a rainbow in the sky, such was their likeness.

11. Seeing therefore their beauty we were astounded by them, since they appeared suddenly. 12. And I approached the Lord and said: Who are these? 13. He saith to me: These are your brethren the righteous, whose forms you desired to see. 14. And I said to him: And where are all the righteous ones and what is this epoch of time in which they exist and have this glory?

15. And the Lord showed me a very great country outside of this world, exceedingly bright with light, and the air there was lighted with the rays of the sun, and the earth itself blooming with flowers that never wilted and the place was full of spices and plants that were beautiful, flowering and bearing blessed fruit, and never spoiled. 16. And great was the perfume that it flowed aloft from this place, even to us. 17. And the dwellers in that place were clothed in the raiment of shining angels and their raiment was like to their country; and angels hovered about them there. 18. And the glory of those who dwell there was equal, and with one voice they sang praises. First to the Lord God, and then rejoicing in that place. 19. The Lord saith to us: This is the place of your high-priests, the righteous men.

20. And over against that place I saw another place. That one of squalid conditions, and it was the place of punishment; and those who were punished there and the punishing angels had raiment that was dark like the air of the place.

21. And there were certain ones there hanging by the tongue: and these were the blasphemers of the way of righteousness; and under them lay fire, burning and punishing them. 22. And there was a huge lake, full of flaming mud, in which were certain men that pervert righteousness, and tormenting angels caused them to suffer.

23. And there were also others, women, hanged by their hair over that bubbling mud: and these were they who adorned themselves for adultery; and the men who had intercourse with them in the defilement of adultery, were hanging by the feet and their heads in that mud. And I said: I did not believe that I should come into this place.

24. And I saw the murderers and those who conspired with them, cast into a certain narrow place, full of evil snakes, and they were attacked by those beasts, and they turned and twisted back and forth in that punishment; and worms, were like clouds of darkness, and they afflicted them. And the souls of the murdered stood and looked upon the punishment of those murderers and said: O God, thy judgment is just.

25. And near that place I saw another narrow place into which the gore (blood which was shed in violence) and the excrement of those who were being punished ran down and became like a lake: and there sat women having the blood that was shed due to their violence (gore) up to their necks, and over against them sat many children who were born to them out of due time, crying; and there came forth from them (the children) sparks of fire and struck the women in the eyes: and these who conceived and caused abortion were the accursed.

Other sources add: The milk of the women running down from their breasts and congealing created small flesh eating beasts: and these run up upon them and devour them.

The children who are born out of due time (premature due to the mother's intentional act) shall be of the better part: and these are delivered over to a care-taking angel that they may attain a share of knowledge and gain the better abode after suffering what they would have suffered if they had been in the body: but the others (aborted and delivered dead) shall merely obtain salvation as injured beings to whom mercy is shown, and remain without punishment, receiving this as a reward.

Other sources state: Infants that have been exposed (to this atrocity) are delivered to a care-taking angel, by whom they are educated and so grow up, and they will be as the faithful as a person of a hundred years old are here.

Other sources state: Those of the untimely births are delivered to care-taking angels, even if they are the offspring of adultery.

26. And other men and women were burning up to the middle and were cast into a dark place and were beaten by evil spirits, and their entrails were eaten by worms which never rest: and these were they who persecuted the righteous and delivered them up (for punishment).

27. And near those there were more women and men, these were gnawing their own lips because they were being punished and receiving a red-hot iron in their eyes: and these were they who blasphemed and slandered the way of righteousness.

28. And over against these again other men and women gnawing their tongues and having flaming fire in their mouths: and these were the false witnesses.

29. And in a certain other place there were pebbles sharper than swords or any red-hot sparks of flame, and women and men in tattered and filthy clothes rolled about on them in punishment: and

these were the rich who trusted in their riches and had no pity for orphans and widows, and despised the commandment of God.

30. And in another great lake, full of pitch and blood and mire bubbling up, there stood men and women up to their knees: and these were the lenders of money who charged high interest and those who take interest on interest.

31. And other men and women were being hurled down from a high cliff and reached the bottom, and again were compelled by those who were placed in authority over them to climb up on the cliff again, and from there they were hurled down again, and had no rest from this punishment: and these were those (men) who defiled their bodies by acting as women (do with men); and those women who lay with another woman as if she were a man.

32. And alongside of that cliff there was a place full of a large fire, and there stood men who with their own hands had made for themselves carved images (idols) instead of God. And alongside these were other men and women who had rods and they were striking each other and never ceasing from such punishment.

33. And others again near them, women and men, burning and turning themselves and roasting: and these were they that left (departed) the way of God

Another source adds: The earth shall present all men before God at the day of judgment, being itself also to be judged, with the heaven also which encompasses it.

Information on Apocalypse of Abraham

Martin McNamara writes: "In it God narrates to Abraham the fall of man and the idolatry of Abraham's own descendants. Thus their infidelity will bring about the judgment. The end is said to be near. The pagan nations are soon to be punished or destroyed. The trumpet will sound and God's elect one (the Messiah) will come to gather together his own people and burn his enemies with fire." (*Intertestamental Literature*, p. 84)

James Charlesworth writes: "Extant only in Old Slavonic manuscripts, the Apocalypse of Abraham was edited best by N. Tikhonravov (*Pamiatniki otrechennoi russkoi literatury*, St. Petersburg, 1863. Vol. 1, pp. 32-53) and translated into English by G. H. Box, assisted by J. I. Landsman (*The Apocalypse of Abraham*, London: S.P.C.K.; New York: Macmillan, 1919). This interesting composition, which has not received the attention it deserves, probably dates from A.D. 80-100 and was written in a Semitic language. It is an haggadic midrash upon Genesis 15:9-17, beginning with a humorous account of Abraham's conversion from idolatry, chapters 1-8, and concluding with the apocalypse itself, 9-32. One of the most intriguing features is the 'Christian' interpolation in chapter 29, which is appreciably different from the Christianity of the New Testament." (*The Pseudepigrapha and Modern Research*, pp. 68-69)

Here is the text (and notes) of an ancient work which was known in the early church, was much valued literature, was originally written in Hebrew, then translated into Greek, and found its way into many diverse cultures. Of more recent years it has been found in Coptic and Slavonic translations, and it is to these that we now have to turn, for they are the earliest -available manuscripts. The Slavonic manuscript, the oldest known, has the title of "Codex Sylvester", which belongs to the Library of the Printing Dept. of the Holy Synod in Moscow. Sylvester was a prominent priest in the reign of Ivan the Terrible, and who made a collection of early Christian books. The manuscript dates from the first half of the 14th Century, and was written on parchment, with two columns on each page, 216 leaves in all, with the Apocalypse occupying leaves 164-182. The other leaves being descriptions of the lives of other saints.

There were two portions to this Apocalypse. The first portion was clearly not part of the original, but was added to it at an early date presumably because the material of both parts concerned the Patriarch Abraham. In this presentation, we shall omit the first portion, which gave an account of Abraham's early life with his father Terah, and how he overcame the idolatry that surrounded him.

The Apocalypse proper is the account of what happened to Abraham at the time recorded in Genesis 15, when the Lord requested him to offer a sacrifice, and when he was subsequently shown visions of the future of his people. However, no one suggests that it was written in the days of Abraham. In fact it is one of a number of works that have been given the title of Pseudepigrapha. This Greek word means pseud- (false) + epi-(upon) + grapha- (writing,) in other words it was a writing that purported to have come from the pen of someone else, and usually someone important, so as to give the writing a form of importance and authority which might have been denied to the actual author. Modern scholars have thus invented this word to describe a process that was quite common in ancient days, both in Israel and in the early church.

But the scholars have not necessarily ascertained the real PURPOSE behind the writings. Although certain glosses, additions, and omissions have to some extent spoiled the original productions, there is no doubt about the fact that such writings were highly valued, and the very fact that they are even today available to us is in itself a most remarkable fact of preservation. But the fact that they are hardly ever read, and amongst Christians almost completely unknown, must surely be due to the manner in which the church views its own origins. There is a vast library of ancient literature just waiting to be printed and made available to earnest seeking enquirers, literature that deserves to be read, and which grants the careful reader an insight into the understanding of both Testaments of the Bible. An example of this is "The Testaments of the Twelve Patriarchs" which is so uplifting in it's reading that it led Bishop Grosseteste of Lincoln (Bishop from 1235 to his death in 1253) to say that they were of equal inspiration to the Scriptures.

However, to return to the present writing, The Apocalypse of Abraham was one of a number of writings that were similarly referred back to the ancient worthies, the patriarchal men of faith, of the Old Testament. What was the real principle behind such writings? It is our present belief that holy men of God, who may have spent nearly all their lives hidden away from the idolatrous practices that surrounded them, gave themselves to prayer and fasting, and as a result were visited by the Lord and by angelic messengers with prophetic and visionary material which naturally they greatly desired to make available to a wider body of people, rather than just keep it to themselves. However, the great difficulty lay in its acceptance. If they merely recorded it in the fashion of the O.T. prophets, they would find themselves grossly abused by their own nationals. But we do not think that they would have flinched from this as such. They were men of faith and courage.

One other factor was dominant in their minds, and it could be very similar to that which obtains today, in other words, the spiritual authorities of the day would have made mincemeat of all that they published, saying that the Scriptures were complete, and no further inspired writings could be entertained as authentic. The result was that they used admissible cunning, whilst being (as our Lord said) as harmless as doves! They interwove their revelations into accounts that appeared to derive from much earlier times, and published them anonymously. The Apostle Jude in the N.T quoted one such writing, known as the First Book of Enoch. Quotations from other 'pseudepigraphal' writings can be found throughout the N.T., especially from the Testaments of the Twelve Patriarchs.

For this reason, the present authors have invented a new name for this type of literature, a name that accords with the revelation and intentions of the authors. We shall use the term **Retroprophetic Material**, because we are quite certain that God has given visions and understandings of the PAST, just as much as He has given visions of the FUTURE. We ourselves have had occasion to be thus exercised by the Lord over the last twenty years, and because of this it has made it all that much easier for us to appreciate how it could have come about in centuries gone by.

As to the text and content of the Apocalypse before us; the 'heavenly informant' of the writing is an angel of name Jaoel, who must have been of very high rank, though not found mentioned by name very much elsewhere. He could have been the same being as say Raphael or Gabriel, but we have no way of knowing. The name Jaoel consists of two parts, Jah and El both names of God in the O.T. Abraham is taken up in the spirit to the uppermost (seventh) heaven and shown mighty and wonderful things, but all the time there is the clear testimony of the duality of the universe, the 'right handed' principle and the 'left handed' principle. The Lord Himself used this principle when speaking of the 'sheep and the goats' in Matt.25. There is God and Satan, who in this writing assumes the name of Azazel, a name that appears a great deal in the Books of Enoch, and is used in the O.T. in the account of the Day of Atonement, where one goat is slain in the Tabernacle, whilst the other is set free, and the Hebrew original here says it is 'for Azazel.'

Although it is neither the time nor the place for further exposition of this intriguing entry in the O.T., no doubt those who read these notes will start a process of investigation of their own, which we believe will lead to some very enlightening conclusions. Not only God and Satan, but the polarisation appears with the People of God and the People of Azazel, of righteousness and idolatry, and so on. These are not Gnostic principles, as some churchmen have inferred, not 'Dualism', but strict spiritual principles to be found throughout the Scriptures. In fact we believe it would be right to say that the Bible is the greatest Book in the world as a POLARISING INFLUENCE, and we are living in a day and age when forces of darkness have striven to MIX everything together, so that no man can any longer see black from white, evil from good, till the Lord says about this wretched luke-warmness, "I will spew you out of my mouth." We trust that this presentation of a valuable little gem from the past will serve its purpose to add to the great Biblical tradition of separating wheat from chaff, sheep from goats, good from evil, and God from Satan, for God has made it clear that HIS EYES ARE TOO HOLY TO LOOK UPON INIQUITY.

Apocalypse of Abraham

1. Then a voice came to me speaking twice, "Abraham! Abraham!" and I said, "Here I am!" And He said, "Behold it is I, fear not for I am with you, for I AM before the ages, even the Mighty God who created the first light of the world. I am your shield and your helper."

2. "Go, take me a young heifer of three years, and a she-goat of three years, and a ram of three years, a turtledove and a pigeon, and bring me a pure sacrifice. And in this sacrifice I will lay before you the ages to come, and make known to you what is reserved, and you shall see great things that you have not hitherto seen:

3. because you have loved to search me out, and I have named you 'my friend.' (The text here in fact says 'my lover.') But abstain from every form of food that comes forth out of the fire, and from the drinking of wine, and from anointing yourself with oil, for forty days, and then set forth for me the sacrifice which I have commanded you, in a place which I will show you on a high mountain, and there I will show you the ages which have been created and established by my word, and I will make known to you what shall come to pass in them on those who have done evil and righteousness in the generations of men."

4. And it came to pass when I heard the voice of Him who spoke such words to me, and I looked here and there, I found no breath in me, and my spirit was frightened, and my soul seemed as departed from me, for I fell down as a stone, as a dead man upon the earth, and had no more strength to stand. And while I was thus lying with my face towards the earth, I heard the voice of the Holy One speaking, "Go, Jaoel, and by means of my ineffable Name raise up yonder man and strengthen him , so that he recovers from his trembling.

5. And the angel whom He had sent came to me in the likeness of a man and grasped me by my right hand and set me up upon my feet and said to me, "Stand up Abraham, 0 friend of God who loves you; let not the trembling of man seize you! For lo! I have been sent to

you to strengthen you and bless you in the name of God, who loves you, the Creator of the celestial and the terrestrial. Be fearless and hasten to Him. I am called Jaoel by Him who moves those who exist with me on the seventh expanse over the heavens, a power in virtue of the ineffable Name that is dwelling in me. I am the one who has been given to restrain, according to His commandment, the threatening attacks of the Living Ones of the Cherubim against one another, and to teach those who carry Him, the song of the seventh hour of the night of man. (These 'attacks' may be seen as the rivalry of praise in heaven, a thing that God occasionally has to restrain, but which should not be thought to be in any way a 'fallen' action.

6. I am ordered to restrain the Leviathan, for every single attack and menace of every single reptile are subject unto me. I am he who has been commissioned to loosen Hades, and destroy him who stares at the dead. (This 'staring' is an attitude of Satan, whereby he paralyses and victimises the dead.) I have been sent to bless you now, and the land which the Eternal One, whom you have invoked, has prepared for you, and for your sake I have wended my way upon earth.

7. Stand up, Abraham! Go without fear; be right glad and rejoice, and I am with you! For age-lasting honour has been prepared for you by the Eternal One. Go, fulfil the sacrifices commanded. For lo! I have been appointed to be with you, and with the generations that will spring from you, and with me Michael blesses you forever. Be of good cheer and go!" (This reference to Michael seems to destroy the scholars' contention that Jaoel might be Michael under another name.)

8. And I rose up and saw him who had grasped me by the right hand and set me upon my feet, and the appearance of his body was like sapphire, and the look of his countenance like chrysolite, and the hair of his head like snow, and the turban on his head like the appearance of the rainbow, and the clothing of his garments like purple, and a golden sceptre was in his right hand,

9. And he said to me, "Abraham!" And I said, "Here I am, your servant." And he said, "Let not my appearance frighten you, nor my speech, that your soul be not troubled. Come with me, and I will be

with you, visible, until the sacrifice, but after the sacrifice always invisible. Be of good cheer, and come!"

10. And we went, the two of us together for forty days and nights, and I ate no bread and drank no water, because my food and my drink was to see the angel who was with me, and to hear his speech. And we came to the Mount of God, Mount Horeb, and I said to the angel, "Singer of the Eternal One! I have no sacrifice with me, nor am I aware of the place of an altar on the mountain; how can I bring a sacrifice?" And he said to me, "Look around you." And when I looked around, there following us were all the prescribed animals, the young heifer, the she goat, the ram, the turtledove and the pigeon.

11. And the angel said to me, "Abraham!" And I said, "Here am I." And he said, "Slaughter all these animals, and divide them into halves, the one against the other, but do not sever the birds. And give these to the men (i.e. angels) whom I will show you, standing by you, for these are the altar upon the Mountain, to offer a sacrifice to the Eternal but the turtle dove and the pigeon give to me, for I will ascend upon the wings of the bird, so that you may be able to see in heaven, and upon earth, and in the sea, and in the abyss, and in the under-world, and in the Garden of Eden, and in its rivers, and in the fullness of the whole world and its circle - you shall gaze into them all."

12. And I did everything according to the command of the angel, and gave the angels who had come to us, the divided animals, but the angel Jaoel took the birds. And I waited until the evening sacrifice. And there flew an unclean bird down upon the carcases, and I drove it away. And the unclean bird spoke to me and said, "Abraham, what are you doing upon these holy heights, where no man eats or drinks, nor is there upon them the food of man, but these heavenly beings consume everything with fire, and will burn you up. Forsake the man who is with you and flee, for if you ascend into the heights they will make an end of "

13. And it came to pass, when I saw the bird speak, I said to the angel, "What is this, my lord?" And he said, "This is ungodliness; this is Azazel." And he said to it, "Disgrace upon you, Azazel! For

Abraham's lot is in heaven, but yours is upon the earth. Because you have chosen and loved this for the dwelling place of your uncleanness therefore the Eternal Mighty Lord made you to be a dweller upon the earth, and through you every evil spirit of lies, and through you wrath and trials for the generations of ungodly men; for God, the Eternal Mighty One, has not permitted that the bodies of the righteous should be in your hand, in order that thereby the life of the righteous and the destruction of the unclean may be assured. Hear this my friend, and be gone with shame from me. For it has not been given to you to play the tempter in regard to all the righteous. Depart from this man! You cannot lead him astray. He is an enemy to you, and to those who follow you and love what you desire. For, behold, the vesture which in heaven was formerly yours has been set aside for him, and the mortality which was his has been transferred to you."

14. And the angel said to me, "Know that from henceforth the Eternal One has chosen you. Be of good courage and use this authority so far as I bid you, against him who slanders the truth. Should I not be able to put him to shame that has scattered over the earth the secrets of heaven, and has rebelled against the Mighty One? Say to him, 'Become the burning coal of the furnace of the earth! Go, Azazel, into the inaccessible parts of the earth, for your heritage is to be over those who are with you, the ones brought forth with the stars and clouds, and with the men whose portion you are, even those who exist on account of your being. Justification shall be your enemy. Now depart from me by your perdition!

15. And I uttered the words that the angel taught me. And then the angel said to me, "Answer him not! For God has given him power over those who answer him." And the angel spoke to me again saying, "However much he speak to you, answer him not, in order that he may have no free access to you, because the Eternal One has given him 'weight and will' in this respect." And I did that which was commanded me by the angel, and no matter how much he spoke to me, I answered him nothing whatsoever.

16. And it came to pass when the sun went down, behold there was the smoke as of a furnace. And the angels who had the portions of

the sacrifice ascended from the top of the smoking furnace. And the angel took me with his right hand and set me upon the right wing of the pigeon, and set himself on the left wing of the turtle dove, neither of which birds had been slaughtered, and he bore me to the borders of the flaming fire, and we ascended upon many winds to the heavens which were above the firmament. And I saw in the air on the heights to which we ascended, a strong light impossible to describe, and within the light a fiercely burning fire of people, many people, of male appearance, all constantly changing in aspect and form, running and being transformed, and worshipping and crying with a sound of words that I could not recognise.

17. And I said to the angel, "Why have you now brought me up here, because my eyes cannot now see distinctly, and I am growing weak, and my spirit is departing from me?" And he said to me, "Remain close by me and do not fear, for the One whom you cannot see is now coming towards us with a great voice of holiness, even the Eternal One who loves you. But you yourself cannot see Him. But you must not allow your spirit to grow faint on account of the choirs of those who cry out, for I am with you to strengthen you."

18. And while he was thus speaking fire came all about us, and there was a voice within the fire like the sound of many waters, like the sound of the sea in violent motion. And I desired to fall down there and worship, and I saw that the angel who was with me bowed his head and worshipped, but the surface of the high place where I seemed to be standing changed its inclination constantly, rolling as the great waves on the surface of the sea.

19. And the angel said, "Worship, Abraham, and utter the song which I shall now teach you. Utter it without ceasing, that is, without pause, in one continuous strain from beginning to end. And the song which he taught me to sing had words appropriate to that sphere in which we then stood, for each sphere in heaven has its own song of praise, and only those who dwell there know how to utter it, and those upon earth cannot know or utter it except they be taught by the messengers of heaven. And the words of that song were of this import and signification -

'Eternal, Mighty, Holy El, God only-supreme'

You who are the Self-originated, the Beginningless One, Incorruptible,

Spotless, Uncreated, Immaculate, Immortal, Self-complete, Self-illuminating,

Without father, without mother, unbegotten,

Exalted, Fiery One! Lover of men, Benevolent One, Bountiful One,

Jealous over me, and very compassionate, Eli, My God,

Eternal, Jehovah Zebaioth, Very Glorious El, El, El, El, Jah El!

You are the One whom my soul has loved!

Eternal Protector, Shining like Fire, Whose voice is like the thunder, Whose look is like the lightning,

You are the All-seeing One, Who receives the prayers of all such as honour You,

And turn away the requests of those who embarrass You with their provocations

Who dissolves the confusions of the world,

which arise from the ungodly and the righteous mixed up in the confusion of the corruptible age,

And renewing the age of the righteous,

Shine 0 Lord, shine as a light, even as that light with which you clothed Yourself on the first day of Creation,

Shine as the Light of the Morning on Your creatures

And let it be Day upon Earth,

For in these heavenly dwelling places there is no need of any other light

> Than the unspeakable splendour from the light of Your Countenance,
>
> O answer my prayer, O be well-pleased with it,
>
> O accept my sacrifice which You have prepared for me to offer,
>
> Accept me favourably, and show me, teach me, all that You have promised!'

20. And while I was still reciting the song, the mouth of the fire that was on the surface rose up on high. And I heard a voice like the roaring of the sea, nor did it cease on account of the rich abundance of the fire. And as the fire raised itself up, ascending into the heights, I saw under the fire a throne of fire, and round about it the watchfulness of many eyes, even the all-seeing ones reciting their song, and under the throne four fiery Living Ones singing, and their appearance was one, and each one had four faces. And such was the appearance of their countenance, that each one had the face of a lion, a man, an ox and an eagle, and because of their four heads upon their bodies, they had sixteen faces, and each one had three pairs of wings, from their shoulders, from their sides, and from their loins. And with the wings from the shoulders they covered their faces, and with the wings from their loins they covered their feet, while the two middle wings were spread out for flying straight forward.

21. And it came to pass that when they had ended their singing they looked at one another and threatened one another. (Another mention of this 'praise-rivalry', which may seem strange to us, as indeed the Cherubim are altogether very strange and wonderful beings, and which we must accept as part of the vision as it was seen.)

22. And it came to pass that when the angel who was with me saw that they were threatening each other, he left me and went running to them and turned the countenance of each one away from the countenance immediately facing him, in order that they might not

look upon each other. And he began to teach them the song of peace that has its origin in the Eternal One.

23. And as I stood alone and looked, I saw behind the Living Ones a chariot with fiery wheels, each wheel full of eyes round about, (In Hebrew, the Living Ones are Chayyim, whose other names are Cherubim, and Seraphim, depending upon which function they are fulfilling at any time, and the wheels are called Ophanim.) and over the wheels was the throne which I had seen, and which was covered with fire, and the fire encircled it round about, and behold, an indescribable fire contained a mighty fiery host, and I heard its holy voice like the voice of a man.

24. And a voice came to me out of the midst of the fire, saying, "Abraham! Abraham!" and I answered saying "Here am I!" And he said, "Consider the expanses which are under the firmament on which you are now placed (i.e. the 7th heavenly sphere) and see how on no single expanse is there any other than the One whom you have sought, even the One who loves you!"

25. And while he was yet speaking, the expanses opened, and there below me were the heavens, and I saw upon the seventh firmament upon which I stood a fire widely extended, and the light which is the treasury of life, and the dew with which God will awaken the dead, and the spirits of the departed righteous, and the spirits of those souls who have yet to be born, and judgment and righteousness, peace and blessing, and an innumerable company of angels, and the Living Ones, and the Power of the Invisible Glory that sat above the Living Ones.

26. And I looked downwards from the mountain on which I stood to the sixth firmament, and there I saw a multitude of angels of pure spirit, without bodies, whose duty was to carry out the commands of the fiery angels who were upon the seventh firmament, as I was standing suspended over them. And behold, upon this sixth firmament there were no other powers of any form, save only the angels of pure spirit.

27. And He commanded that the sixth firmament should be removed from my sight, and I saw there on the fifth firmament the

powers of the stars that carry out the commands laid upon them, and the elements of the earth obeyed them.

28. And the Eternal Mighty One said to me, "Abraham! Abraham!" And I said, "Here am I!" And He said to me, "Consider from above the stars which are beneath you, and number them for me, and make known to me their number." And I said, "How can I? For I am but a man of the dust of the earth." And He said to me, "As the number of the stars and their power, so will I make your seed a nation and a people set apart for me as my own inheritance, as distinct from that of Azazel. And yet I include Azazel in my house."

29. And I said, "0 Eternal Mighty One! Let your servant speak before You, and let not your anger be kindled against your chosen one! For lo! before I came up hither, Azazel inveighed against me. How then, while he is not now before you, can you constitute yourself with him?"

30. And He said to me, "Look now beneath your feet at the firmaments and understand the creation represented and foreshadowed in this expanse, the creatures who exist upon it, and the ages prepared for it."

31. And I saw beneath the surface of my feet, even beneath the sixth heaven and what was therein, and then the earth and its fruits, and what moved upon it and its animate beings, and the power of its men, and the ungodliness of some of its souls and the righteous deeds of other souls, and I saw the lower regions and the perdition therein, the abyss and its torments. And I saw the sea and its islands, its monsters and its fishes, and Leviathan and his dominion, his camping-ground and his caves, and the world that lay above him, his movements and the destructions of the world on his account. And I saw there the streams and the rivers, and the rising of their waters, and their windings in their courses. And I saw there the Garden of Eden and its fruits, the source of the river that issues from it, the trees and their blossoms, and the ones who behaved righteously. And I saw therein their foods and their blessedness. And I saw there a great multitude, men and women and children, half of them on the right side of the vision, and half of them on the left side of the vision.

32. And I said, "0 Eternal, Mighty One! What is this vision and picture of the creatures?" And He said to me, "This is my will for those who exist in the divine world-counsel, for thus it seemed well-pleasing in my sight, and so afterwards I gave commandment to them through my word. And so it came to pass that whatever I had determined to be, was already planned beforehand in this picture-vision before you, and it has stood before me before it was created, as you have seen." (Notice the clear explanation of the predestination of the righteous, and God's action towards them based upon what He knows of their actions. Here is the teaching of Paul in Romans 8, 'predestination and foreknowledge'.)

33. And I said, "0 Lord, Mighty and Eternal! Who are the people in this picture on this side and that?" And He said to me, "Those who are on the left side are all those, born before your day and afterwards, some destined for judgment and restoration, and others for vengeance and cutting off at the end of the age. But those on the right side of the picture, they are the people who have been set apart for me, and whom I have ordained to be born of your line and called my people, even some of those who derive from Azazel.

34. Now look again in the picture, and see who it is who seduced Eve, and what is the fruit of the Tree, and you will know what is to be, and how it shall be with your seed among the people at the end of the days of the age, and all that you cannot understand I will make known to you for you are well-pleasing in my sight, and I will tell you of those things which are kept in my heart.

35. And I looked into the picture, and my eyes ran to the side of the Garden of Eden, and I saw there a man of imposing height and mighty in stature, incomparable in aspect, and he was embracing a woman, who likewise approximated to the aspect of his size and stature. And they were standing under a tree of the Garden of Eden, and the fruit of this tree was like a bunch of grapes of the vine. And standing behind the tree was one who had the aspect of a Serpent (Hebrew Nachash = shining, bright eyes) having hands and feet like those of a man, and wings on its shoulders, six pairs of wings, so that there were six wings on the right and six on the left. And as I

continued looking, I saw the man and the woman eating the fruit from the tree.

36. And I said, "Who are these who are embracing, and who is the one between them who is behind the tree, and what is the fruit that they are eating?" And He said, "This is the council of the world, this one is Adam, and this one, who is their desire upon the earth, is Eve. But he who is between them represents ungodliness and their beginnings on the way to perdition, even Azazel."

37. And I said, "O Eternal Mighty One! Why have you given such as him the power to destroy the generations of men in their works upon the earth?" And He said to me, "Those who will to do evil (and how much I hate it in those who do it) over them I gave him power, even to be beloved of them."

38. And I answered and said, "O Eternal Mighty One! Wherefore is it your will that evil should be desired in the hearts of men, since you are indeed enangered over that which you see? It is your will, and you are angry with him who is doing what is unprofitable in your counsel?"

39. And He said to me, "I am angered by mankind on your account, and on account of those who shall be of your family hereafter, for as you can see in the picture, the burden of destiny is placed upon them, and I shall tell you what shall be, and how much shall be in the last days. Look now at everything in the picture." (The purport of these remarks is to show the interaction between those who are of the 'seed' and those who persecute the seed. And Paul understood the seed to mean those who, by faith, are of their father Abraham. God is therefore angry with those who maltreat His own faithful children.)

40. And I looked and saw what was before me in creation; I saw Adam and Eve with him, and I saw the cunning adversary, and Cain who acted lawlessly through the promptings of the adversary, and I saw the slaughtered Abel, and the destruction brought about and caused upon him through the lawless one. And I saw Impurity and those who lust after it, (Items here given capital letters indicate the names of unclean spirits, as was the custom in such writings)

and its pollution and their jealousies, and the fire of their corruption in the lowest parts of the earth.

41. And I saw Theft, and those who hasten after it, and the arrangement of their retribution, at the judgment of the Great Assize. And I saw there naked men with their foreheads against each other, and their disgrace, and the passions which they had for each other, and their retribution. And I saw Desire, and in her hand the head of every kind of lawlessness, and her scorn and contempt and waste assigned to perdition.

42. And I saw there the likeness of the idol of jealousy, carved in woodwork such as my father was wont to make, and its body was of glittering bronze that covered the wood. And before it I saw a man who was worshipping the idol, and in front of him there was an altar, and upon the altar a boy slain in the presence of the idol.

43. And I said to Him, "What is this idol and this altar, and who is he who is sacrificed? And what is this great building which I see, beautiful in art and design, even with a beauty like that which lies beneath Your throne?"

44. And He said, "Hear Abraham, for that which you see is the Temple, a copy of that which is in the heavens, glorious in its aspect and beauty, even as I shall give it to the sons of men to ordain a priesthood for my glorious name, and in which the prayers of man shall be uttered, and sacrifices offered as I ordain to your people, even those who shall arise out of your generation. But the idol that you saw is the image of jealousy, (i.e. the idol which causes the jealousy of God, and His anger to arise because of it) set up by some of those who shall come forth from your own loins in later days. And the man who sacrifices in murder is he who pollutes my Temple and such are witnesses to the final judgment, and their lot has been set from the beginning of creation."

45. And I said, 0 Eternal Mighty One! Why have you established that it should be so, and then proclaimed the knowledge thereof?" And He said to me, "Hear Abraham, and understand what I say to you, and answer my question. Why did your father Terah not listen

to your voice, and why did he not cease from his idolatrous practices, together with his whole house?"

46. And I said, "O Eternal One! It was entirely because he did not choose to listen to my voice, and likewise I did not choose to listen to his counsel." And He said to me, "The will of your father is within him, and your own will is within you, and so also the counsel of my own will is within me, and is ready for the coming days, even before you have any knowledge of them or can see with your eyes what is the future of them. Now look again into the picture, and see how it will be with your seed."

47. And I looked and saw, and behold the picture swayed and from it emerged, on the left side an ungodly people and they pillaged those who were on the right side, men, women, and children, and some they murdered, and others they kept as slaves. And I saw them run towards them through four 'entrances' (a word which does not mean actual gates, but contains the idea of four 'descents' or 'generations' as given to Abraham concerning the trials of his seed for the four generations till they came out of Egypt, but which in this context is seen to prefigure a much greater vision, that of which Daniel saw in later days, with four great world powers who would oppress the people of God.) and they burned the Temple with fire, and the holy things that were therein were all plundered.

48. And I said, "O Eternal One! Behold, the people who shall spring from me, and whom you have accepted, are plundered by these ungodly men, and some are killed, whilst others they hold captives as slaves, and the Temple they have burned with fire, and the beautiful things therein they have robbed and destroyed. If this to be, why have you so torn my heart?"

49. And He said to me, "What you have seen shall happen on account of your seed, even those who anger me by reason of the idol statue which you saw, and on account of the human sacrifice in the picture, through their evil zeal and schemes in the Temple, and as you saw it, so shall it be."

50. And I said, "O Eternal, Mighty One! May these works of evil wrought in ungodliness now pass by, and rather show me those

who fulfilled the commandments, even the works of righteousness. For of a truth you can do this."

51. And He said to me, "The days of the righteous are seen in type by the lives of those righteous rulers who shall arise, and whom I have created to rule at the times appointed, but know this, that out of them shall arise others who care only for their own interests, even of the type that I have already shown you.

52. And I answered and said, "0 Mighty One! Hallowed be your power! Be favourable to my petition and show me, because for this reason you have brought me up here, whether what I saw shall happen to them for a long time?"

53. And He showed me a multitude of His people and said to me, "On their account, through four 'entrances' (i.e. descents, as in 47 above) as you saw, I shall be provoked by them, and in these (four descents) shall my retribution for their deeds be accomplished. But in the fourth descent of one hundred years, even one hour of the age, the same is a hundred years, there shall be misfortune among the nations, but also for one hour there shall be mercy and honour among those nations.

54. And I said, "0 Eternal One! How long are the hours of the age?" And He said, "Twelve hours have I ordained for this present age of ungodliness to rule among the nations and within your seed, and until the end of the times it shall be even as you saw. And now reckon and understand and look again into the picture.

55. And I looked and saw a Man going out from the left side of the nations (clearly the Messiah is here intended) and there went out men and women and children, from the side of nations, many hosts, and worshipped Him. And while I still looked, there came many from the right side, and some of these insulted Him, and some of them even struck Him, but others however worshipped Him. And as I watched, I saw Azazel approach Him and he kissed Him on the face and then stood behind Him.

56. And I said, "0 Eternal One! Who is the Man insulted and beaten, who is worshipped by the nations and kissed by Azazel?" And He

answered and said, "Hear Abraham! The Man you saw insulted and beaten and yet worshipped by many, He is the 'Relief' granted by the nations to the people who proceed from you, in the last days, in the twelfth hour of the age of ungodliness. But in the twelfth hour of my final age will I set up this Man from your generation, whom you saw issue from among my people, and all who follow will become like this Man, and such as are called by me will join the others, even those who will to change within themselves. (A neat definition of repentance!) And as for those who emerge from the left side of the picture, the meaning is this - there shall be many from the nations who shall set their hopes upon Him, but as for those whom you saw from your seed on the right of the picture who insulted Him and struck Him, many shall be offended in Him, but some shall worship Him. And He shall test those of your seed who have worshipped Him in the twelfth hour at the end, with a view to shortening the age of ungodliness.

57. Before the age of the righteous begins to grow, my judgment shall come upon the lawless peoples through the people of your seed who have been separated unto me. And in those days I will bring upon all creatures of the earth ten plagues, through misfortune and disease and the sighing of their grief. And this shall be brought upon the generations of men on account of the provocation and the corruption of mankind, whereby they provoke me. And then shall righteous men of your seed survive in the number which is kept secret by me, and will hasten the coming of the glory of My Name to that place prepared beforehand for them, which you saw devastated in the picture. (This presumably means Jerusalem, and like many other pictures, it has echelons of progressive meaning, starting, as always, with the physical, and ending with the spiritual. In this manner, the physical Jerusalem of the Bible days is replaced in the Book of Revelation by the great spiritual city that descends from God.) And they shall live and be established by sacrifices of righteousness (There is no need to imply blood sacrifice in this expression. It is used in the Psalms 4:5, 51:19, and like many other texts, may be spiritualised in the days in which we now live.) in the age of the righteous, and they shall rejoice in me continually, and receive those who return to me in repentance, for great shall be the inner torment of those who have despitefully

used them in this world, as they observe the honour placed upon my own in the day of glory.

58. See, Abraham, what you have seen and hear what you have heard, and take knowledge of all that you have come to know. Go to your heritage, and behold, I am with you unto the age."

59. But while He was still speaking to me, I found myself once again upon the earth, and I said, "0 Eternal One! I am no longer in the glory that is on high, and there is one matter that my soul longed to know and understand which has not been revealed to me.

60. And He said to me, "What your heart desired I will tell you, because you have sought to see the ten plagues which I have prepared for the godless nations, and which have been pre-determined at the passing over of the twelfth hour of the age of the earth. Hear therefore what I divulge, and so shall it come to pass. The first is the distressing pain of sickness; the second, conflagration of many cities; the third, the destruction and pestilence of animals; the fourth, hunger of the whole world and its people; the fifth, by destruction among its rulers, by earthquake and the sword; the sixth, the multiplication of hail and snow; the seventh, wild bests will be their grave; the eighth, hunger and pestilence will alternate with destruction; the ninth, punishment by the sword and flight in distress; the tenth, thunder and voices and destructive earthquake.

61. And then I will sound the trumpet out of the air, and will send my Elect One, having in Him all my power in one measure, and He shall summon my despised people from all nations, and I will send fire upon those who have insulted them and who have ruled over them in this age. And I will give those who have covered me with mockery to the scorn of the coming age, and I have prepared them to be food for the fires of Hades, and perpetual flight through the air in the underworld, for they shall see the righteousness of the Creator, and those whom He now honours, and they shall he ashamed, for I had hoped that they would come to me in repentance, rather than loving strange gods, but they forsook the Mighty Lord, and went the way that they willed to go.

62. Hear therefore, Abraham, and see, for behold, in the seventh generation from you shall they leave the land of their slavery, after they have been ill-treated as it were for an hour of the age of ungodliness, and the nation whom they shall serve I will judge." (These seven generations may thus be enumerated: Abraham, Isaac, Jacob, Levi, Kohath, Amram, and Moses.)

- - - - - - - -oOo- - - - - - - -

RESURRECTION AND JUDGMENT IN ISAIAH 25 & 26.

The following translation of Isaiah 25:6-12 & 26 is designed to bring out hidden highlights.

6. And in this 'Mountain (i.e. Zion) shall the Lord of Hosts make a feast of rich food for all people, a feast of wines on the lees, and fat things full of marrow, of wines well refined

7. And on this Mountain He will destroy the Vail that enshrouds all peoples, the pall that is thrown over all nations.

8. He will swallow up death in Victory, and the Lord God will wipe away the tears from every face, and remove the reproach of His people from the whole earth. The Lord has spoken it.

9. And it shall be said in that day, -'Behold! This is-our God! We have waited for Him and He has delivered us! He is our-Lord! We have waited for Him, and now we shall be glad and rejoice in His deliverance!'

10. For it is on this Mountain that the hands of the Lord shall rest. But Moab (a symbol of God's enemies. A play on words in the Hebrew) shall be trampled beneath Him as straw is trampled in the manure.

11. He (i.e. Moab) will spread out his hands as swimmers spread their hands, but his pride will sink with every stroke he takes.

12. And He (the Lord) will throw down your high fortified walls and lay them low. (This is Babylon, the spiritual city of the fallen angels) He will bring them down to the earth, to the very dust.

1. In that day (the day of resurrection, when death is swallowed up) shall this song be sung in the land of Judah (in which Jerusalem dwells) 'We have a strong city where salvation is appointed of God for its walls and ramparts.

2 Open up those gates! Give entrance to the righteous nation, the nation that keeps trust and fidelity!' (These are all the righteous by faith, entering Jerusalem in resurrection)

3. Perfect peace is ordained for those who keep their thoughts steadfast upon the Lord, even as they trust Him.

4. Trust in the Lord continually, for the Lord Jehovah is the rock of ages.

5. He brings down, yea, he humbles those who dwell on high;

6. He lays low the lofty city. He brings it down, even to the earth, and settles it in the dust, where feet may trample it down, even the feet of the oppressed and lowly ones.

7. The path of the just man is (now at last,) level, indeed the Upright One has Himself made smooth the way of the righteous.

8. Yes, O Lord, we have waited long for you, as we have walked in the path of your judgments. Our hearts' desire has been for the sanctification of your name, and in your remembrance.

9. With all my heart have I longed for you through the night seasons, yea, with my spirit I will eagerly search for you as the dawn begins to break, for when your judgments are in the earth the inhabitants of the world will learn righteousness.

10. (It is a solemn fact that) if God's gracious favour be shown to lawless men, they do not learn righteousness; even in an honest and upright land they will go on doing evil and disregard the majesty of the Lord.

11. O Lord, when your hand is lifted up on high they do not even see it! Let them see; let them be ashamed and (instead) envy the people (of the Lord.) Yes Lord, the fires will devour your enemies.

12. O Lord, you will bestow prosperity on us, and in very truth our ways and our works will be ordained and empowered by your hand.

13. O Lord our God, other lords beside you have domineered us, but it is your name and yours alone that we honour.

14. But now they are dead, they live no more, these Rephaim. (i.e. offspring of fallen angels) You have punished them and brought them to ruin, and made all memory of them to perish.

15. You have enlarged the nation O Lord, you have enlarged the nation! You have gained great glory for yourself, and extended all the borders of the land.

16. Lord, they came to you in their distress, and when you disciplined them, they could scarcely whisper a prayer.

17. As a woman with child and about to give birth, writhes and cries out in her birth-pangs, so were we in your presence O Lord.

18. We were with child, we writhed in pain, but we merely brought forth wind. We have not brought forth deliverance to the earth; none of your people have been born to inhabit the world.

19. (The Lord answers) But your dead shall live! Together with My dead body they shall arise! Awake and sing, all you who dwell in the dust of the earth!

20. For your dew is like the dew on the herbs. But the earth shall cast away the Rephaim. Come my people, enter your rooms and shut the doors behind you, and hide yourselves for a little while until the indignation has passed by.

21. Behold the Lord is coming out of His dwelling place to punish the people of the earth for their sins. The earth will then disclose the blood that has been shed upon it, and will conceal its slain no more.

Information on the Coptic Apocalypse of Elijah

Wilhelm Schneemelcher makes these comments (New Testament Apocrypha, vol. 2, p. 693):

Since 1885 the text of an Apoc. El. has gradually become known through some Coptic manuscripts. Since the publication of the Chester Beatty Papyrus 2018 this work is now accessible almost complete (cf. Schrage, op. cit. 198ff). The Coptic (Sahidic and Achmimic) versions go back to a Greek original text, of which we possess a papyrus fragment with six lines; but with this nothing much can be done. The papyri were written in the 4th or 5th century.

The Coptic Apoc. El. presents admonitions, predictions of the terrors of the endtime, a description of the Antichrist and his annihilation, etc.; it ends with the creation of a new heaven and a new earth and the thousand-year reign of Christ. Many elements of the older Apocalyptic are lacking, but on the other hand ancient conceptual material is abundantly used. The work is a typical example of later apocalypses: a Christian description of the endtime (to some extent with contemporary references) has been created on a Jewish foundation.

The dating of the Coptic Apoc. El. is difficult. There is much to be said for the view that the Jewish basic document originated in the second half of the 3rd century, and was taken over and reworked by Christians at the beginning of the 4th century (cf. Schrage, op. cit. 220ff.).

Concerning the external attestation for this text, Schneemelcher writes, "An Apocalypse of Elijah (Apoc. El.) is rejected in the Catalogue of the Sixty Books and probably also in the Stichometry of Nicephorus (cf. vol. 1, pp. 41f.). An apocryphon of Elijah is frequently mentioned in early Church literature, mostly in connection with the saying in 1 Cor. 2:9, of which Origen already affirms that it comes from an apocryphon of Elijah (cf. Schrage, op. cit. 195). Now on the one hand this saying is evidently a logion which frequently crops up (cf. Gos. Thom. log. 17; on this see H.-Ch. Puech in NTApo I, 217). On the other hand this logion does not occur in the extant Elijah apocrypha." (New Testament Apocrpyha, vol. 2, p. 692)

This text has "nothing to do with" an apocryphal Letter of Titus which quotes words of Elias the prophet from an unclear source "in which the punishments of Hell are described" (New Testament Apocrypha, vol. 2, p. 692). There is also mention of "an Elijah apocyphon 'On the Antichrist'" in "a Greek fragment," but this does not have "any connection with the extant Elijah texts" (New Testament Apocrypha, vol. 2, p. 692). The Coptic Apocalypse of Elijah must be also distinguished from the Hebrew Apocalypse of Elijah, "a Jewish writing from the 3rd century A.D.; there are no connections with the Coptic Apoc. El." (New Testament Apocrypha, vol. 2, p. 692)

The Apocalypse of Elijah

I   1. The word of YHWH came to me saying, "Son of man, say to his people, 'why do you add sin to your sins and anger the Lord God who created you ?'" 2. Don't love the world or the things which are in the world, for the boasting of the world and its destruction belong to the devil.

3. Remember that the Lord of glory, Who created everything, had mercy upon you so that He might save us from the captivity of this age. 4. For many times the devil desired not to let the sun rise above the earth and not to let the earth yield fruit, since he desires to consume men like a fire which rages in stubble, and he desires to swallow them like water. 5. Therefore, on account of this, the God of glory had mercy upon us, and He sent His Son to the world so that He might save us from the captivity. 6. He did not inform an angel or an archangel or any principality when He was about to come to us, but ?He changed Himself to be like a man when He was about to come to us so that He might save use [from flesh]. 7. Therefore become sons to Him since He is a father to you.

8. Remember that He has prepared thrones and crowns for you in heaven, saying, "Everyone who will obey Me will receive thrones and crowns among those who are Mine." 9. The Lord said, "I will write My name upon their forehead and I will seal their right hand, and they will not hunger or thirst. 10. Neither will the son of lawlessness prevail over them, nor will the thrones hinder them, but they will walk with the angels up to My city." 11. Now as for the sinners, they will be shamed and they will not pass by the thrones, but the thrones of death will seize them and rule over them because the angels will not agree with them. 12. They have alienated themselves from His dwellings.

13.Hear, O wise men of the land, concerning the deceivers who will multiply in the last times so that they will set down for themselves doctrines which do not belong to God, setting aside the Law of God, those who have made their belly their God, saying, "The fast does not exist, nor did God create it," making themselves strangers to the covenant of God and robbing themselves of the glorious promises. 14.Now these are not ever correctly established in the firm faith. Therefore don't let those people lead you astray.

15. Remember that from the time when He created the heavens, the Lord created the fast for a benefit to men on account of the passions and desires which fight against you so that the evil will not inflame you. 16."But it is a pure fast which I have created," said the Lord. 17.The one who fasts continually will not sin although jealousy and strife are within him. 18.Let the pure one fast, but whenever the one who fasts is not pure he has angered the Lord and also the angels. 19.And he has grieved his soul, gathering up wrath for himself for the day of wrath.

20. But a pure fast is what I created, with a pure heart and pure hands. 21.It releases sin. It heals diseases. It casts out demons. 22.It is effective up to the throne of God for an ointment and for a release from sin by means of a pure prayer.

23.Who among you , if he is honored in his craft, will go forth to the field without a tool in his hand? Or who will go forth to the battle to fight without a breastplate on? 24.If he is found, will he not be killed because he despised the service of the king? 25.Likewise no one is able to enter the holy place if he is double minded. 26.The one who is double minded in his prayer is darkness to himself. And even the angels do not trust him. 27.Therefore be single-minded in the Lord at all times so that you might know every moment.

II

1.Furthermore, concerning the kings of Assyria and the dissolution of the heaven and the earth and the things beneath the earth.

2."now therefore <those who are Mine> will not be overcome" says the Lord, "nor will they fear in the battle." 3.When they see [a king] who rises in the north, [who will be called] "the king of [Assyria" and] "the king of injustice," [he will increase] his battles and his disturbances against Egypt. 4.The land will groan together because your children will be seized. 5.Many will desire death in those days, but death will flee from them.

6.And a king who will be called "the king of peace" will rise up in the west. 7.He will run upon the sea like a roaring lion. 8.He will kill the king of injustice, and he will take vengeance on Egypt with battles and much bloodshed.

9.It will come to pass in those days that he will command a p[eace] and a [vain] gift in Egypt. 10.[He will give] peace to these who are holy, [saying], "The name of [God] is one." 11.[He will] give honors to the s[aints and] an exalting to the places of the saints. 12.He will give vain gifts to the house of God. 13.He will wander around in the cities of Egypt with guile, without their knowing. 14.He will take count of the holy places. He will weigh the idols of the heathen. He will take count of their wealth. He will establish priests for them. 15.He will command that the wise men and the great ones of the people be seized, and they will be brought to the metropolis which is by the sea, saying, "There is but one language." 16.But when you hear, "Peace and joy exist," I will...

17.Now I will tell you his signs so that you might know him. 18.For he has two sons: one on his right and one on his left. 19.The one on his right will receive a demonic face, (and) he will fight against the name of God. 20.Now four kings will descend from that king. 21.In his thirtieth year he will come up to Memphis, (and) he will build a temple in Memphis. 22.On that day his own son will rise up against him and kill him. 23.The whole land will be disturbed.

24.On that day he will issue an order over the whole land so that the priests of the land and all of the saints will be seized, saying, "You will repay doubly every gift and all of the good things which my father gave to you." 25.He will shut up the holy places. He will take their houses. He will take their sons prisoner. 26.He will order and sacrifices and abominations and bitter evils will be done in the land. 27.He will appear before the sun and the moon. 28.On that day the priests of the land will tear their clothes.

29.Woe to you , O rulers of Egypt, in those days because your day has passed. 30.The violence (being done to) the poor will turn against you, and your children will be seized as plunder. 31.In those days the cities of Egypt will groan for the voice of the one who sells and the one who buys will not be heard. The markets of the cities of Egypt will become dusty. 32.Those who are in Egypt will weep together. They will desire death, (but) death will flee and leave them.

33.In those days, they will run up to the rocks and leap off, saying, "Fall upon us." And still they will not die. 34.A double affliction will multiply upon the whole land.

35.In those days, the king will command, and all the nursing women will be seized and brought to him bound. They will suckle serpents. And their blood will be drawn from their breasts, and it will be applied as poison to the arrows. 36.On account of their distress of the cities, he will command again, and all the young lads from twelve years and under will be seized and presented in order to teach them to shoot arrows. 37.The midwife who is upon the earth will grieve. The woman who has given birth will lift her eyes to heaven, saying, "Why did I sit upon the birthstool, to bring forth a son to the earth?" 38.The barren woman and the virgin will rejoice, saying, "It is our time to rejoice, because we have no child upon the earth, but our children are in heaven."

39.In those days, three kings will arise among the Persians, and they will take captive the Jews who are in Egypt. They will bring them to Jerusalem, and the will inhabit it and dwell there.

40.Then when you hear that there is security in Jerusalem, tear you garments, O priests of the land, because the son of perdition will soon come.

41.In those days, the lawless one will appear in the holy places ---

42.In (those) days the kings of the Persians will hasten and they will stand to fight with the kings of Assyria. Four kings will fight with three. 43.They will spend three years in that place until they carry off the wealth of the temple which is in that place.

44.In those days, blood will flow from Kos to Memphis. The river of Egypt will become blood, and they will not be able to drink from it for three days.

45.Woe to Egypt and those who are in it.

46. In those days, a king will arise in the city which is called "the city of the sun," and the whole land will be disturbed. <He will> flee to Memphis (with the Persians).

47. In the sixth year, the Persian kings will plot an ambush in Memphis. They will kill the Assyrian king. 48. The Persians will take vengeance on the land, and they will command to kill all the heathen and the lawless ones. They will command to build the temples of the saints. 49. They will give double gifts to the house of God. They will say, "The name of God is one." 50. The whole land will hail the Persians.

51. Even the remnant, who did not die under the afflictions, will say, "The Lord has sent us a righteous king so that the land will not become a desert" 52. He will command that no royal matter be presented for three years and six months. The land will be full of good in an abundant well-being.

53. Those who are alive will go to those who are dead, saying, "Rise up and be with us in this rest."

III

1. In the fourth year of that king, the son of lawlessness will appear, saying, "I am the Christ," although he is not. Don't believe him!

2. When the Christ comes, He will come in the manner of a covey of doves with the crown of doves surrounding Him. He will walk upon the heaven's vaults with the sign of the cross leading Him.

3. The whole world will behold Him like the sun which shines from the eastern horizon to the western.

4. This is how He will come, with all his angels surrounding Him.

5. But the son of lawlessness will begin to stand again in the holy places.

6. He will say to the sun, "Fall," and it will fall.

He will say, "Shine," and it will do it.

He will say, "Darken," and it will do it.

7. He will say to the moon, "Become bloody," and it will do it.

8. He will go forth with them from the sky.

He will walk upon the sea and the rivers as upon dry land.

9. He will cause the lame to walk.

He will cause the deaf to hear.

He will cause the dumb to speak.

He will cause the blind to see.

10. The lepers he will cleanse.

The ill he will heal.

The demons he will cast out.

11. He will multiply his signs and his wonders in the presence of everyone.

12. He will do the works which the Christ did, except for raising the dead alone.

13. In this you will know that he is the son of lawlessness, because he is unable to give life.

14. For behold I will tell you his signs so that you might know him.

15. He is a ...of a skinny-legged young lad, having a tuft of gray hair at the front of his bald head. His eyebrows will reach to his ears. There is a leprous bare spot on the front of his hands.

16. He will transform himself in the presence of those who see him. He will become a young child. He will become old.

17. He will transform himself in every sign. But the signs of his head will not be able to change.

18. Therin you will know that he is the son of lawlessness.

IV

1. The virgin, whose name is Tabitha, will hear that the shameless one has revealed himself in the holy places. And she will put on her garment of fine linen.

2. And she will pursue him up to Judea, scolding him up to Jerusalem, saying, "O shameless one, O son of lawlessness, O you who have been hostile to all the saints.

3. Then the shameless one will be angry at the virgin. He will pursue her up to the regions of the sunset. He will suck her blood in the evening.

4. And he will cast her upon the temple, and she will become a healing for the people.

5. She will rise up at dawn. And she will live and scold him, saying, "o shameless one, you have no power against my soul or my body, because I live in the Lord always.

6. And also my blood which you have cast upon the temple has become a healing for the people."

7. Then when Elijah and Enoch hear that the shameless one has revealed himself in the holy place, they will come down and fight with him saying,

8. Are you indeed not ashamed? When you attach yourself to the saints, because you are always estranged.

9. you have been hostile to those who belong to heaven. you have acted against those belonging to the earth.

10. You have been hostile to the thrones. you have acted against the angels. you are always a stranger.

11. you have fallen from heaven like the morning stars. you were changed, and your tribe became dark for you.

12. But you are not ashamed, when you stand firmly against God you are a devil.

13. The shameless one will hear and he will be angry, and he will fight with them in the market place of the great city. And he will spend seven days fighting with them.

14. And they will spend three and one half days in the market place dead, while all the people see them

15. But on the fourth day they will rise up and they will scold him saying. "O shameless one, O son of lawlessness. Are you indeed not ashamed of yourself since you are leading astray the people of God for whom you did not suffer? Do you not know that we live in the Lord?"

16. As the words were spoken, they prevailed over him, saying, "Furthermore, we will lay down before the flesh for the spirit, and we will kill you since you are unable to speak on that day because we are always strong in the Lord. But you are always hostile to God.

17. The shameless one will hear, and he will be angry and fight them.

18. And the whole city will surround them.

19. On that day they will shout up to heaven as they shine while all the people and all the world see them.

20. The son of lawlessness will not prevail over them. He will be angry at the land, and he will seek to sin against the people.

21. He will pursue all of the saints. They and the priests of the land will be brought back bound.

22. He will kill them and destroy them...them. And their eyes will be removed with iron spikes.

23. He will remove their skin from their heads. He will remove their nails one by one. He will command that vinegar and lime be put in their nose.

24. Now those who are unable to bear up under the tortures of that king will take gold and flee over the fords to the desert places. They will lie down as one who sleeps.

25. The Lord will receive their spirits and their souls to Himself.

26. Their flesh will petrify. No wild animals will eat them until the last day of the great judgment.

27. And they will rise up and find a place of rest. but they will not be in the kingdom of the Christ as those who have endured because the Lord said, "I will grant to them that they sit on my right hand."

28. They will receive favor over others, and they will triumph over the son of lawlessness. And they will witness the dissolution of heaven and earth.

29. They will receive the thrones of glory and the crowns.

30. The sixty righteous ones who are prepared for this hour will hear.

31. And they will gird on the breastplate of YHWH, and they will run to Jerusalem and fight with the shameless one, saying, "All powers which the prophets have done from the beginning you have done. But you were unable to raise the dead because you have no power to give life. Therein we have known that you are the son of lawlessness."

32. He will hear, and he will be angry and command to kindle altars

33. And the righteous ones will be bound. They will be lifted up and burned.

V

1. And on that day the heart of many will harden and they will flee from him, saying, "This is not the Christ. The Christ does not kill the righteous. He does not pursue men so that he might seek them, but He persuades them with signs and wonders."

2. On that day the Christ will pity those who are His own. And He will send from heaven his sixty-four thousand angels, each of whom has six wings.

3. The sound will move heaven and earth when they give praise and glorify.

4. Now those upon whose forehead the name of Christ is written and upon whose hand is the seal both the small and the great, will be taken up upon their wings and lifted up before his wrath.

5. Then Gabriel and Uriel will become a pillar of light leading them into the holy land.

6. It will be granted to them to eat from the tree of life. They will wear white garments...and angels will watch over them. They will not thirst, nor will the son of lawlessness be able to prevail over them.

7. And on that day the earth will be disturbed, and the sun will darken, and peace will be removed from the earth.

8. The birds will fall on the earth, dead.

9. The earth will be dry. The waters of the sea will dry up.

10. The sinners will groan upon the earth saying, "What have you done to us, O son of lawlessness, saying I am the Christ, when you are the devil?

11. You are unable to save yourself so that you might save us. You produced signs in our presence until you alienated us from the Christ who created us. Woe to us because we listened to you.

12. Lo now we will die in a famine. Where indeed is now the trace of a righteous one and we will worship him, or where indeed is the one who will teach us and we will appeal to him.

13. Now indeed we will be wrathfully destroyed because we disobeyed YHWH.

14. We went to the deep places of the sea, and we did not find water. We dug in the rivers and papyrus reeds, and we did not find water."

15. Then on that day, the shameless one will speak, saying, "Woe to me because my time has passed by for me while I was saying that my time would not pass by for me.

16. My years became months and my days have passed away as dust passes away. Now therefore I will perish together with you.

17. Now therefore run forth to the desert. Seize the robbers and kill them.

18. Bring up the saints. For because of them, the earth yields fruit. for because of them the sun shines upon the earth. For because of them the dew will come upon the earth."

19. The sinners will weep saying, "You made us hostile to YHWH. If you are able, rise up and pursue them."

20. Then he will take his fiery wings and fly out after the saints. He will fight with them again.

21. The angels will hear and come down. They will fight with him a battle of many swords.

22. It will come to pass on that day that the Lord will hear and command the heaven and the earth with great wrath. And they will send for fire.

23. And the fire will prevail over the earth seventy-two cubits. It will consume the sinners and the devils like stubble.

24. A true judgment will occur.

25. On that day, the mountains and the earth will utter speech. The byways will speak with one another, saying, "Have you heard today the voice of a man who walks who has not come to the judgment of the Son of YHWH."

26. The sins of each one will stand against him in the place where they were committed, whether those of the day or of the night.

27. Those who belong to the righteous and ... will see the sinners and those who persecuted them and those who handed them over to death in their torments.

28. Then the sinners [in torment] will see the place of the righteous.

29. And thus grace will occur. In those days, that which the righteous will ask for many times will be given to them.

30. On that day, YHWH will judge the heaven and the earth. He will judge those who transgressed in heaven, and those who did so on earth.

31. He will judge the shepherds of the people. He will ask about the flock of sheep, and they will be given to Him, without any deadly guile existing in them.

32. After these things, Elijah and Enoch will come down. They will lay down the flesh of the world, and they will receive their spiritual flesh. They will pursue the son of lawlessness and kill him since he is not able to speak.

33. On that day, he will dissolve in their presence like ice which was dissolved by a fire. He will perish like a serpent which has no breath in it.

34. They will say to him, "Your time has passed by for you. Now therefore you wand those who believe you will perish."

35. They will be cast into the bottom of the abyss and it will be closed for them.

36. On that day, the Christ, the King and all His saints will come forth from heaven.

37. He will burn the earth. He will spend a thousand years upon it.

38. Because the sinners prevailed over it, He will create a new heaven and a new earth. No deadly devil will exist in them.

39. He will rule with His saints, ascending and descending, while they are always with the angels and they are with the Christ for a thousand years.

Information on the Apocalypse of Paul

Hugo Duensing, as revised by Aurelio de Santos Otero, writes concerning the citations of this text (*New Testament Apocrypha*, vol. 2., pp. 712-713):

> In his *Nomocanon* (VII 9) Barhebraeus introduces a quotation from Origen according to which the Apocalypse of Paul, with other apocalypses and also other early Christian writings enumerated there, was accepted by the Church. If this quotation is not altered, with Zahn, to read Peter instead of Paul, and so is accepted as genuine as it stands, then one might also assume acquaintance at least with the material of our apocalypse in his *Homil. in Psalmos* (ed. Lommatzsch XII. 233), where he gives a description of the destiny of souls after death which is closely related with chs. 13ff. of the Apocalypse of Paul. That he cannot in any case have had our recension before him follows not only on grounds of content but also from Sozomen (*Hist. eccl.* VII 19, ed. Bidez-Hansen, GCS 50, 1960, 331) who says of the Apocalypse of Paul that none of the ancients knew it; rather it was allegedly found under the emperor of the time, by which he alludes to the story of its discovery which it contains, but after inquiry from an ancient presbyter in Tarsus it turned out to be a fraud. If Origen knew a document of the same title, it could not have beenthe apocalypse in the form in which we now have it. We find a more reliable witness to its existence in Augustine (*In Ioh. tract.* 98.8, ed. R. Willems, CChrSL 36, 1954, 581), who says that some have concocted an Apocalypse of Paul which the true church does not accept. And when in the Enchiridion (112-113, CChrSL 46, 109f.) he discusses the idea of the relaxation of the lot of the damned souls on the day of the Lord, he will have drawn that from our document; for at almost the same time (around 402) Prudentius produces this conception in his Cathemerinon (V. 125ff., ed. J. Bergman, CSEl 61, 1926, 30). In the Decretum Gelasianum the Apocalypse

of Paul appears among the apocryphal books which are not accepted (ed. v. Dobschütz, TU 38.4, 1912, 12). Later testimonies only evidence continued knowledge of this apocryphon and the eventual extension of its influence.

The internal evidence may be taken to suggest a late fourth century date (*New Testament Apocrypha*, vol. 2, p. 713):

> in 2 Cor. 12 Paul tells of being caught up into Paradise and this gave someone who was familiar with the apocalyptic tradition the opportunity of putting in Paul's mouth what he himself knew or thought about the next world. He gets over the difficulty that Paul had described what he heard as unutterable by distinguishing between some things which Paul could not tell and others which he was permitted to relate (cf. ch. 21). The introductory report of the discovery of these important revelations serves to explain how it happened that they were not made public earlier, possibly even in the time of Paul himself. If this account comes form the (first) author himself the date of the work is fixed as the end of the 4th or beginning of the 5th century. In any case the recension which we have must date from that period.

So might the allusions made to other texts in the Apocalypse of Paul (*New Testament Apocrypha*, vol. 2, p. 715):

> It is clear that he knew the contents of the Apocalypse of Peter; this is seen above all in the description of the places of punishment and especially in that for those guilty of abortion; this conclusion would be quite incontrovertible if the Coptic has preserved the original ending, in which after his heavenly journey Paul returns to the circle of the apostles gathered on the Mount of Olives. The author would then understandably have altered his source only in so far as he replaces Clement, as in the Apocalypse of Peter, by Paul's disciples Mark and Timothy as those who wrote down what Paul saw. Other borrowings are Lake Acherusia (cf. supra), the

encounter with the Patriarchs, the fiery stream, the angel Tartaruchus or Temeluchus. The ferrying over Lake Acherusia occurs also in the Apocalypse of Zephaniah (G. Steindorff, TU 17.3a, 1899); in it we have also the recording angel with the manuscript (chirographon - agreeing in the Greek expression!) and the encounter with all the righteous in the heavenly world, in particular with the Patriarchs, Enoch, Elijah and David. There is a striking contact with the Apocalypse of Elijah (TU 17.3a) at the very beginning in ch. 3, where with very little variation the sentence is repeated 'The word of the Lord came to me thus: 'O son of man, say to this people, "why do you heap sin on sin and anger God the Lord, who made you?".'" (Steindorff, 155; Schrage, 231) If the additional material at the end of the Coptic is original, then the author copied from the Apocalypse of Zephaniah, where it says, "Be strong that you may conquer and be mighty that you may overcome the accuser and come up out of the underworld." (Steindorff, 170; cf. ibid. p. 55, ch. 12, lines 12ff. of the Apocalypse of Elijah, and p.1 153: "Be triumphant and strong, for you are strong and are overcoming the accuser and coming up out of the underworld and the abyss." Cf. also the last four lines on the same page.) Casey (pp. 22ff.) draws attention to an agreement with Slavonic Enoch, chs. 8-9 (Morfil-Charles, pp. 7-9), in the description of Paradise; James (P. 552 n. 1) likewise draws attention to a contact with the Testament of Job. It is impossible to say from where the author may have drawn his fantastic representation of the colossal fruitfulness of eternity (ch. 22), which corresponds with the description of Papias (in Irenaeus, V 33. 3f.). All these borrowings render a later date probable.

This text has no connection to the Coptic Apocalypse of Paul discovered at Nag Hammadi.

Apocalypse of Paul

From "The Apocryphal New Testament" M.R. James-Translation and Notes Oxford: Clarendon Press, 1924

Introduction

Epiphanius tells us that the Caianites or Cainites had forged a book full of unspeakable matter in the name of Paul, which was also used by those who are called Gnostics, which they call the Anabaticon of Paul, Basing it on the words of the apostle -that he was taken up into the third heaven. This has left no trace (Heresy, 38. 2).

St. Augustine laughs at the folly of some who had forged an Apocalypse of Paul, full of fables, and pretending to contain the unutterable things which the apostle had heard. This is, I doubt not, our book. (Aug. on John, Tract 98.) Sozomen, in his Ecclesiastical History (vii. 19), says: The book now circulated as the Apocalypse of Paul the apostle, which none of the ancients ever saw, is commended by most monks; but some contend that this book was found in the reign we write of (of Theodosius). For they say that by a Divine manifestation there was found underground at Tarsus of Cilicia, in Paul's house a marble chest, and that in it was this book. However, when I inquired about this, a Cilician, a priest of the church of Tarsus, told me it was a lie. He was a man whose grey hairs showed him to be of considerable age and he said that no such thing had happened in their city, and that he wondered whether the tale (or, the book) had not been made up by heretics.

Sozomen's story is that which appears in our book; and we need not doubt that this Apocalypse made its appearance in the last years of the fourth century.

It is condemned in the Gelasian Decree, and is mentioned with disapproval by various late church writers.

Though not an early book, it is made up very largely of early matter; and it had an immense vogue, especially in the West. Greek copies of it are rare, and the texts they contain are disfigured by many omissions. Of the Eastern versions -Syriac, Coptic, Ethiopic- the Syriac is the best. But possibly the full Latin version is superior to all other authorities. There are several abridged Latin texts, and from these were made the many versions which were current in almost every European language.

In an early canto of the Inferno (ii. 28) Dante mentions the visit of the 'Chosen Vessel' to Hell -an undoubted allusion to the Apocalypse. And both in the Divine Comedy and in the hundreds of earlier medieval visions of the next world the influence of this book is perceptible, sometimes faintly, often very plainly indeed.

The reader will soon see for himself that Paul is a direct descendant of Peter, especially in his description of Hell-torments. He will also see that the book is very badly put together; and that whole episodes, e.g. visit to Paradise, are repeated. This means that the author is combining different sources in a very unintelligent way.

In the Greek, Latin, and Syriac the book is incomplete: it ends abruptly in a speech of Elijah. The Coptic version -only recently published- has a long continuation; part of this is, I think, original but it tails off into matter which cannot be. This conclusion has even a third visit to Paradise! I give some particulars of it later.

The plan of the book is briefly this:

1, 2. Discovery of the revelation.

3-6. Appeal of creation to God against man

7-10. The report of the angels to God about men.

11-18. Deaths and judgements of the righteous and the wicked.

19-30. First vision of Paradise.

31-44. Hell. Paul obtains rest on Sunday for the lost.

45-51. Second vision of Paradise.

The full Latin version is the basis of my translation: the Greek, Syriac, and Coptic are used where the Latin is corrupt.

Here beginneth the Vision of Saint Paul the Apostle.

But I will come to visions and revelations of the Lord. I knew a man in Christ fourteen years ago, whether in the body I know not or whether out of the body I know not -God knoweth- that such an one was caught up unto the third heaven: and I knew such a man, whether in the body or out of the body I know not -God knoweth- that he was caught up into paradise and heard secret words which it is not lawful for men to utter. For such an one will I boast, but for myself I will boast nothing, save of mine infirmities.

1 At what time was it made manifest In the consulate of Theodosius Augustus the younger and Cynegius, a certain honourable man then dwelling at Tarsus, in the house which had been the house of Saint Paul, an angel appeared unto him by night and gave him a revelation, saying that he should break up the foundation of the house and publish that which he found; but he thought this to be a lying vision. 2 But a third time the angel came, and scourged him and compelled him to break up the foundation. And he dug, and found a box of marble inscribed upon the sides: therein was the revelation of Saint Paul, and his shoes wherein he walked when he taught the word of God. But he feared to open that box, and brought it to the judge; and the judge took it, sealed as it was with lead, and sent it to the emperor Theodosius fearing that it might be somewhat strange; and the emperor when he received it, opened it and found the revelation of Saint Paul. A copy thereof he sent to Jerusalem and the original he kept with him. (Gr. reverses this: he kept the copy and sent away the original. It adds: And there was written therein as followeth.)

3 Now while I was in the body, wherein I was caught up unto the third heaven, the word of the Lord came unto me, saying: Speak unto this people: How long will ye transgress, and add sin upon sin, and tempt the Lord that made you Saying that ye are Abraham's children but doing the works of Satan (so Gr.; Lat. Ye are the sons of God, doing the work of the devil), walking in the confidence of God, boasting in your name only, but being poor because of the

matter of sin. Remember therefore and know that the whole creation is subject unto God, but mankind only sinneth. It hath dominion over the whole creation, and sinneth more than the whole of nature. 4 For oftentimes hath the sun, the great light, appealed unto the Lord, saying: O Lord God Almighty, I look forth upon the ungodliness and unrighteousness of men. Suffer me, and I will do unto them according to my power, that they may know that thou art God alone. And there came a voice unto it, saying: All these things do I know, for mine eye seeth and mine ear heareth, but my long-suffering beareth with them until they turn and repent. But if they return not unto me, I will judge them all. 5 And sometimes the moon and the stars have appealed unto the Lord, saying: O Lord God Almighty, unto us hast thou given rule over the night; how long shall we look upon the ungodliness and fornications and murders which the children of men commit suffer us to do unto them according unto our powers, that they may know that thou art God alone. And there came a voice unto them, saying: I know all these things, and mine eye looketh upon them and mine ear heareth, but my long-suffering beareth with them until they turn and repent. But if they return not unto me, I will judge them. 6 Oftentimes also the sea hath cried out, saying: O Lord God Almighty, men have polluted thine holy name in me: suffer me and I will arise and cover every wood and tree and all the world, till I blot out all the children of men from before thy face, that they may know that thou art God alone. And again a voice came, saying: I know all, for mine eye seeth all things, and mine ear heareth, but my long-suffering beareth with them until they turn and repent. But if they return not I will judge them.

Sometimes also the waters have appealed against the children of men, saying: O Lord God Almighty, the children of men have all defiled thine holy name. And there came a voice, saying: I know all things before they come to pass, for mine eye seeth and mine ear heareth all things: but my long-suffering beareth with them until they turn. And if not, I will judge. Often also hath the earth cried out unto the Lord against the children of men, saying: O Lord God Almighty, I suffer hurt more than all thy creation, bearing the fornications, adulteries, murders, thefts forswearings, sorceries, and witchcrafts of men, and all the evils that they do, so that the father riseth up against the son, and the son against the father, the stranger against the stranger, every one to defile his neighbour's wife. The father goeth up upon his son's bed, and the son likewise goeth up upon the couch of his father; and with all these evils have they that offer a sacrifice unto thy name polluted thine holy place. Therefore do I suffer hurt more than the whole creation, and I would not yield mine excellence and my fruits unto the children of men. Suffer me and I will destroy the excellence of my fruits. And there came a voice and said: I know all things, and there is none that can hide himself from his sin. And their ungodliness do I know, but my holiness suffereth them until they turn and repent. But if they return not unto me, I will judge them. 7 Behold then ye children of men. The creature is subject unto God, but mankind alone sinneth.

Therefore, ye children of men, bless ye the Lord God without ceasing at all hours and on all days; but especially when the sun setteth. For in that hour do all the angels go unto the Lord to worship him and to present the deeds of men which every man doeth from morning until evening, whether they be good or evil. And there is an angel that goeth forth rejoicing from the man in whom he dwelleth.

When therefore the sun is set, at the first hour of the night, in the same hour goeth the angel of every people and of every man and woman, which protect and keep them, because man is the image of God: and likewise at the hour of morning, which is the twelfth hour of the night, do all the angels of men and women go to meet God and present all the work which every man hath wrought, whether good or evil. And every day and night do the angels present unto God the account of all the deeds of mankind. Unto you, therefore, I say, O children of men, bless ye the Lord God without ceasing all the days of your life.

8 At the hour appointed, therefore, all the angels, every one rejoicing, come forth before God together to meet him and worship him at the hour that is set; and lo, suddenly at the set time there was a meeting, and the angels came to worship in the presence of God, and the spirit came forth to meet them, and there was a voice, saying: Thence could ye, our angels, bringing burdens of news 9

They answered and said: We are come from them that have renounced the world for thy holy name's sake, wandering as strangers and in the caves of the rocks, and weeping every hour that they dwell on the earth and hungering and thirsting for thy name's sake; with their loins girt, holding in their hands the incense of their heart, and praying and blessing at every hour, suffering anguish and subduing themselves, weeping and lamenting more than all that dwell on the earth. And we that are their angels do mourn with them, whither therefore it pleaseth thee, command us to go and minister lest they do otherwise, but the poor more than all that dwell on the earth. (The sense required as shown by Gr. is that the angels ask that these good men may continue in goodness.) And the voice of God came unto them, saying: Know ye that from henceforth my grace shall be established with you, and mine help which is my dear]y beloved Son, shall be with them, ruling them at all times; and he shall minister unto them and never forsake them, for their place is his habitation. 10 When, then, these angels departed, lo, there came other angels to worship in the presence of the majesty, to meet therewith, and they were weeping. And the spirit of God went forth to meet them, and the voice of God came, saying: Whence are ye come, our angels bearing burdens, ministers of the news of the world They answered and said in the presence of God: We are come from them which have called upon thy name, and the snares of the world have made them wretched, devising many excuses at all times, and not making so much as one pure prayer out of their whole heart all the time of their life. Wherefore then must we be with men that are sinners And the voice of God came unto them: Ye must minister unto them until they turn and repent; but if they return not unto me, I will judge them.

Know therefore, O children of men, that whatsoever is wrought by you, the angels tell it unto God, whether it be good or evil.

11 [Syr. Again, after these things, I saw one of the spiritual ones coming unto me, and he caught me up in the spirit, and carried me to the third heaven.]

And the angel answered and said unto me: Follow me, and I will show thee the place of the righteous where they are taken when they are dead. And there after will I take thee to the bottomless pit and show thee the souls of the sinners, into what manner of place they are taken when they are dead.

And I went after the angel, and he took me into heaven, and I looked upon the firmament, and saw there the powers; and there was forgetfulness which deceiveth and draweth unto itself the hearts of men, and the spirit of slander and the spirit of fornication and the spirit of wrath and the spirit of insolence and there were the princes of wickedness. These things saw I beneath the firmament of the heaven.

And again I looked and saw angels without mercy, having no pity, whose countenances were full of fury, and their teeth sticking forth out of their mouth: their eyes shone like the morning star of the cast, and out of the hairs of their head and out of their mouth went forth sparks of fire. And I asked the angel, saying: Who are these, Lord And the angel answered and said unto me: These are they which are appointed unto the souls of sinners in the hour of necessity, even of them that have not believed that they had the Lord for their helper and have not trusted in him.

[Apocalypse of Zephaniah (Steindorff's 'anonymous Apocalypse;): I went with the angel of the Lord and looked before me and saw a place through which passed thousand thousands and myriads of myriads of angels, whose faces were as of panthers, and their teeth stuck forth out of their mouth, and their eyes were bloodshot, and their hair loose like woman's hair, and burning scourges were in their hands. (I feared and asked: Who are these The angel answered:) These are the ministers of the whole creation, which come unto the souls of the ungodly and take them and lay them down here: they fly three days with them in the air before they take them and cast them into their everlasting torment.]

12 And I looked into the height and beheld other angels whose faces shone like the sun, and their loins were girt with golden girdles, holding palms in their hands, and the sign of God, clad in raiment whereon was written the name of the Son of God, full of all gentleness and mercy. And I asked the angel and said: Who are these, Lord, that are of so great beauty and compassion And the

angel answered and said unto me: These are the angels of righteousness that are sent to bring the souls of the righteous in the hour of necessity, even them that have believed that they had the Lord for their helper. And I said unto him: Do the righteous and the sinners of necessity meet [witnesses] when they are dead And the angel answered and said unto me: The way whereby all pass unto God is one: but the righteous having an holy helper with them are not troubled when they go to appear in the presence of God.

13 And I said unto the angel: I would see the souls of the righteous and of the sinners as they depart out of the world. And the angel answered and said unto me: Look down upon the earth. And I looked down from heaven upon the earth and beheld the whole world, and it was as nothing in my sight; and I saw the children of men as though they were nought, and failing utterly; and I marvelled, and said unto the angel: Is this the greatness of men And the angel answered and said unto me: This it is, and these are they that do hurt from morning until evening. And I looked, and saw a great cloud of fire spread over the whole world, and said unto the angel: What is this, Lord And he said to me: This is the unrighteousness that is mingled by the princes of sinners (Gr. mingled with the destruction of sinners; Syr. mingled with the prayers of the sons of men).

14 And I when I heard that sighed and wept, and said unto the angel: I would wait for the souls of the righteous and of the sinners, and see in what fashion they depart out of the body. And the angel answered and said unto me: Look again upon the earth. And I looked and saw the whole world: and men were as nought, and failing utterly; and I looked and saw a certain man about to die; and the angel said to me: He whom thou seest is righteous. And again I looked and saw all his works that he had done for the name of God, and all his desires which he remembered and which he remembered not, all of them stood before his face in the hour of necessity. And I saw that the righteous man had grown in righteousness, and found rest and confidence: and before he departed out of the world there stood by him holy angels, and also evil ones: and I saw them all; but the evil ones found no abode in him, but the holy ones had power over his soul and ruled it until it went out of the body. And they

stirred up the soul, saying: O soul, take knowledge of thy body whence thou art come out; for thou must needs return into the same body at the day of resurrection, to receive that which is promised unto all the righteous. They received therefore the soul out of the body, and straightway kissed it as one daily known of them, saying unto it: Be of good courage, for thou hast done the will of God while thou abodest on the earth. And there came to meet it the angel that watched it day by day, and he said unto it: Be of good courage, O soul: for I rejoice in thee because thou bast done the will of God on the earth; for I told unto God all thy works, how they stood. Likewise also the spirit came forth to meet it and said: O soul, fear not, neither be troubled, until thou come unto a place which thou never knewest; but I will be thine helper, for I have found in thee a place of refreshment in the time when I dwelt in thee, when I was (thou wast) on the earth. And the spirit [thereof] strengthened it, and the angel thereof took it up and carried it into the heaven. And the angel said (Syr. And there went out to meet it wicked powers, those that are under heaven. And there reached it the spirit of error, and said): Whither runnest thou, O soul, and presumest to enter heaven stay and let us see if there be aught of ours in thee. And lo! we have found nothing in thee. I behold also the help of God, and thine angel; and the spirit rejoiceth with thee because thou didst the will of God upon earth. (Syr. has more here. There is a conflict between the good and evil angels. The spirit of error first laments. Then the spirit of the tempter and of fornication meet it and it escapes, and they lament. All the principalities and evil spirits come to meet it and find nothing, and gnash their teeth. The guardian angel bids them go back, 'Ye tempted this soul and it would not listen to you.' And the voice of many angels is heard rejoicing over the soul. Probably this is original matter.) And they brought it until it did worship in the presence of God. And when they (it) had ceased, forthwith Michael and all the host of the angels fell and worshipped the footstool of his feet and his gates, and said together unto the soul: This is the God of all, which made thee in his image and likeness. And the angel returned and declared, saying: Lord, remember his works; for this is the soul whereof I did report the works unto thee, Lord, doing according to thy judgement. And likewise the spirit said: I am the spirit of quickening that breathed upon it; for I had refreshment in it in the time when I dwelt therein, doing according to thy judgement. And the voice of God came, saying: Like as this soul hath not grieved me neither will I grieve it, for like as it hath had mercy, I also will have mercy. Let it be delivered therefore unto Michael the angel of the covenant, and let him lead it into the paradise of rejoicing that it become fellow-heir with all the saints. And thereafter I heard the voices of thousands of thousands of angels and archangels and the cherubim and the four-and-twenty elders uttering hymns and glorifying the Lord and crying: Righteous art thou, O Lord, and just are thy judgements, and there is no respect of persons with thee, but thou rewardest every man according to thy judgement. And the angel answered and said unto me: Hast thou believed and known that whatsoever every one of you hath done, he beholdeth it at the hour of his necessity And I said: Yea, Lord.

15 And he said unto me: Look down again upon the earth and wait for the soul of a wicked man going forth of the body, one that hath provoked the Lord day and night, saying: I know nought else in this world, I will eat and drink and enjoy the things that are in the world. For who is he that hath gone down into hell and come up and told us that there is a judgement there And again I looked and saw all the despising of the sinner, and all that he did, and they stood together before him in the hour of necessity: and it came to pass in that hour when he was led out of his body to the judgement, that he (MS. I) said: It were better for me (MS. him) that I (he) had not been born. And after that the holy angels and the evil and the soul of the sinner came together, and the holy angels found no place in it. But the evil angels threatened (had power over) it, and when they brought it forth out of the body, the angels admonished it thrice, saying: O wretched soul, look upon thy flesh whence thou art come out; for thou must needs return into thy flesh at the day of resurrection to receive the due reward for thy sins and for thy wickedness; 16 And when they had brought it forth, the accustomed (i.e. guardian) angel went before it and said unto it: O miserable soul, I am the angel that clave unto thee and day by day reported unto the Lord thine evil deeds, whatsoever thou wroughtest by night or day; and if it had been in my power I would not have ministered unto thee even one day; but of this I could do nothing, for God is merciful and a just judge, and he commanded us not to

cease ministering unto your soul till ye should repent: but thou hast lost the time of repentance. I indeed am become a stranger unto thee and thou to me. Let us go then unto the just judge: I will not leave thee until I know that from this day I am become a stranger unto thee. (Here Copt. inserts a quite similar speech of the spirit to the soul, which may be original.) And the spirit confounded it, and the angel troubled it. When therefore they were come unto the principalities, and it would now go to enter into heaven, one burden (labour, suffering) was laid upon it after another: error and forgetfulness and whispering met it, and the spirit of fornication and the rest of the powers, and said unto it: Whither goest thou, wretched soul and darest to run forward into heaven Stay, that we may see whether we have property of ours in thee, for we see not with thee an holy helper. (Syr. adds: And the angel answered and said: Know ye that it is a soul of the Lord, and he will not cast it aside, neither will I surrender the image of God into the hand of the wicked one. The Lord supported me all the days of the life of the soul, and he can support and help me: and I will not cast it off until it go up before the throne of God on high. When he shall see it, he hath power over it, and will send it whither he pleases.) And after that I heard voices in the height of the heavens, saying: Present this miserable soul unto God, that it may know that there is a God, whom it hath despised. When therefore it was entered into the heaven, all the angels, even thousands of thousands, saw it, and all cried out with one voice saying: Woe unto thee, miserable soul, for thy works which thou didest upon the earth, what answer wilt thou make unto God when thou drawest near to worship him The angel which was with it answered and said: Weep with me, my dearly beloved, for I have found no rest in this soul. And the angels answered him and said: Let this soul be taken away out of our midst, for since it came in, the stench of it is passed upon us the angels. And thereafter it was presented, to worship in the presence of God, and the angel showed it the Lord God that made it after his own image and likeness. And its angel ran before it, saying: O Lord God Almighty, I am the angel of this soul, whose works I presented unto thee day and night, not doing according to thy judgement. And likewise the spirit said: I am the spirit which dwelt in it ever since it was made, and I know it in itself, and it followed not my will: judge it, Lord, according to thy judgement. And the voice of

God came unto it and said: Where is thy fruit that thou hast yielded, worthy of those good things which thou hast received did I put a distance even of a day between thee and the righteous did I not make the sun to rise upon thee even as upon the righteous And it was silent, having nothing to answer; and again the voice came, saying: Just is the judgement of God, and there is no respect of persons with God, for whosoever hath done his mercy he will have mercy on him, and whoso hath not had mercy, neither shall God have mercy on him. Let him therefore be delivered unto the angel Tartaruchus (Gr. Temeluchus) that is set over the torments, and let him cast him into the outer darkness where is weeping and gnashing of teeth, and let him be there until the great day of judgement. And after that I heard the voice of the angels and archangels saying: Righteous art thou, O Lord, and just is thy judgement.

17 And again I beheld, and lo, a soul which was brought by two angels, weeping and saying: Have mercy on me, thou righteous God, O God the judge; for to-day it is seven days since I went forth out of my body, and I was delivered unto these two angels, and they have brought me unto those places which I had never seen. And God the righteous judge said unto it: What hast thou done for thou hast never wrought mercy; therefore wast thou delivered unto such angels, which have no mercy, and because thou hast not done right, therefore neither have they dealt pitifully with thee in the hour of thy necessity. Confess therefore thy sins which thou hast committed when thou wert in the world. And it answered and said: Lord, I have not sinned. And the righteous Lord God was wroth with indignation when it said: I have not sinned, for it lied. And God said: Thinkest thou that thou art yet in the world If every one of you there when he sinneth, hideth and concealeth his sin from his neighbour, yet here no thing is hidden, for when the souls come to worship before the throne both the good works and the sins of every one are made manifest. And when the soul heard that, it held its peace, having no answer. And I heard the Lord God, the righteous judge, saying again: Come, thou angel of this soul, and stand in the midst. And the angel of the sinful soul came, having a writing in his hands, and said: These, Lord, that are in mine hands, are all the sins of this soul from its youth up unto this day, even

from ten years from its birth: and if thou bid me, Lord, I can tell the acts thereof since it began to be fifteen years old. [Apocalypse of Zephaniah: I looked and saw that a writing (the same word, chirographum) was in his hand: he began to open it, and when he had spread it out I read it in mine own language, and I found all my sins that I had committed, recorded by him, even those which I had committed from my childhood up unto this day.] And the Lord God the righteous judge said: I say unto thee, O angel, I desire not of thee the account since it began to be fifteen years old; but declare its sins of five years before that it died and came hither. And again God the righteous judge said: For by myself I swear, and by mine holy angels and by my power, that if it had repented five years before it died, even for the walk (conversation) of one year, there should be forgetfulness of all the evil which it committed before and it should have pardon and remission of sins: but now let it perish. And the angel of the sinful soul answered and said: Command, Lord, that (such and such an) angel to bring forth those (such and such) souls. 18 And in that same hour the souls were brought forth into the midst, and the soul of the sinner knew them. And the Lord said unto the soul of the sinner: I say unto thee, O soul, confess thy deeds which thou didst upon these souls whom thou seest, when they were in the world. And it answered and said: Lord, it is not yet a full year since I slew this one and shed its blood upon the earth, and with another I committed fornication; and not that only, but I did it much harm by taking away its substance. And the Lord God the righteous judge said: Knewest thou not that he that doth violence to another, if he that suffered violence die first, he is kept in this place until he that hurt him dieth, and then do both of them appear before the judge and now hath every one received according as he did. And I heard a voice saying: Let that soul be delivered into the hands of Tartaruchus, and he must be taken down into hell. Let him take him into the lower prison and let him be cast into torments and be left there until the great day of judgement. And again I heard thousands of thousands of angels singing an hymn unto the Lord and saying: Righteous art thou, O Lord, and just are thy judgements.

19 The angel answered and said unto me: Hast thou perceived all these things And I said: Yea, Lord. And he said unto me: Follow me

again, and I will take thee and show thee the places of the righteous. And I followed the angel and he took me up unto the third heaven and set me before the door of a gate; and I looked on it and saw, and the gate was of gold, and there were two pillars of gold full of golden letters; and the angel turned again to me and said: Blessed art thou if thou enterest in by these gates, for it is not permitted to any to enter save only to those that have kept goodness and pureness of their bodies in all things. And I asked the angel and said: Lord, tell me for what cause are these letters set upon these tables The angel answered and said unto me: These are the names of the righteous that minister unto God with their whole heart, which dwell on the earth. And again I said: Lord, then are their names also their countenance and the likeness of them that serve God is in heaven, and they are known unto the angels: for they know them that with their whole heart serve God before they depart out of the world.

20 And when I had entered within the gate of paradise there came to meet me an old man whose face shone like the sun, and he embraced me and said: Hail, Paul, dearly beloved of God And he kissed me with a joyful countenance, but he wept, and I said unto him: Father (Lat. Brother), why weepest thou And again sighing and weeping he said: Because we are vexed by men, and they grieve us sore; for many are the good things which the Lord hath prepared, and great are his promises, but many receive them not. And I asked the angel and said: Who is this, Lord And he said unto me: This is Enoch the scribe of righteousness.

And I entered within that place and straightway I saw Elias I and he came and saluted me with gladness and joy. And when he had seen me, he turned himself away and wept and said unto me: Paul, mayest thou receive the reward of thy labour which thou hast done among mankind. As for me, I have seen great and manifold good things which God hath prepared for all the righteous, and great are the promises of God, but the more part receive them not; yea hardly through much toil doth one and another enter into these places.

21 And the angel answered and said unto me: What things soever I now show thee here, and whatsoever thou hearest, reveal them not

unto any upon earth. And he led me and showed me: and I heard there words which it is not lawful for a man to utter; and again he said: Yet again follow me and I will show thee that which thou must relate and tell openly.

And he brought me down from the third heaven, and led me into the second heaven, and again he led me to the firmament, and from the firmament he led me unto the gates of heaven. And the beginning of the foundation thereof was upon the river that watereth all the earth. And I asked the angel and said: Lord, what is this river of water and he said unto me: This is the Ocean. And suddenly I came out of heaven, and perceived that it is the light of the heaven that shineth upon all the earth (or, all that land). And there the earth (or, land) was seven times brighter than silver. And I said: Lord, what is this place and he said unto me: This is the land of promise. Hast thou not yet heard that which is written: Blessed are the meek, for they shall inherit the earth The souls therefore of the righteous when they are gone forth of the body are sent for the time into this place. And I said unto the angel: Shall then this land be made manifest after (lat. before) a time The angel answered and said unto me: When Christ whom thou preachest cometh to reign, then by the decree of God the first earth shall be dissolved, and then shall this land of promise be shown and it shall be like dew or a cloud; and then shall the Lord Jesus Christ the eternal king be manifested and shall come with all his saints to dwell therein; and he shall reign over them a thousand years, and they shall eat of the good things which now I will show thee.

22 And I looked round about that land and saw a river flowing with milk and honey. And there were at the brink of the river trees planted, full of fruits: now every tree bare twelve fruits in the year, and they had various and divers fruits: and I saw the fashion (creation) of that place and all the work of God, and there I saw palm-trees of twenty cubits and others of ten cubits: and that land was seven times brighter than silver. And the trees were full of fruits from the root even to the upper branches. (Lat. is confused here. Copt. has: From the root of each tree up to its heart there were ten thousand branches with tens of thousands of clusters, [and there were ten thousand clusters on each branch,] and there were ten

thousand dates in each cluster. And thus was it also with the vines. Every vine had ten thousand branches, and each branch had upon it ten thousand bunches of grapes, and every bunch had on it ten thousand grapes. And there were other trees there, myriads of myriads of them, and their fruit was in the same proportion.) And I said unto the angel: Wherefore doth every tree bring forth thousands of fruits The angel answered and said unto me: Because the Lord God of his bounty giveth his gifts in abundance unto the worthy; for they also of their own will afflicted themselves when they were in the world, doing all things for his holy name's sake.

And again I said unto the angel: Lord, are these the only promises which the most holy Lord God promiseth and he answered and said unto me: No; for there are greater by seven times than these. But I say unto thee, that when the righteous are gone forth out of the body and shall see the promises and the good things which God hath prepared for them, yet again they shall sigh and cry, saying: Wherefore did we utter a word out of our mouth to provoke our neighbour even for a day And I asked again and said: Be these the only promises of God And the angel answered and said unto me: These which now thou seest are for them that are married and keep the purity of their marriage, being continent. But unto the virgins, and unto them that hunger and thirst after righteousness and afflict themselves for the name of the Lord, God will give things sevenfold greater than these, which now I will show thee.

And after that he took me out of that place where I saw these things, and lo, a river, and the waters of it were white exceedingly, more than milk, and I said unto the angel: What is this and he said to me: This is the lake Acherusa where is the city of Christ: but not every man is suffered to enter into that city: for this is the way that leadeth unto God, and if any be a fornicator or ungodly, and turn and repent and bear fruits meet for repentance, first when he cometh out of the body he is brought and worshippeth God, and then by the commandment of the Lord he is delivered unto Michael the angel, and he washeth him in the lake Acherusa and so bringeth him in to the city of Christ with them that have done no sin. And I marvelled and blessed the Lord God for all the things which I saw.

23 And the angel answered and said unto me: Follow me and I will bring thee into the city of Christ. And he stood by (upon) the lake Acherusa, and set me in a golden ship, and angels as it were three thousand sang an hymn before me until I came even unto the city of Christ. And they that dwelt in the city of Christ rejoiced greatly over me as I came unto them, and I entered in and saw the city of Christ. And it was all of gold, and twelve walls compassed it about, and there were twelve towers within (a tower on each wall, Copt.; 12,000 towers, Syr.), and every wall had a furlong between them (i.e. the walls were a furlong apart, so Syr., Copt. the circumference of each was 100 furlongs) round about; and I said unto the angel: Lord, how much is one furlong The angel answered and said unto me: It is as much as there is betwixt the Lord God and the men that are on the earth, for the great city of Christ is alone. And there were twelve gates in the circuit of the city, of great beauty, and four rivers that compassed it about. There was a river of honey, and a river of milk, and a river of wine, and a river of oil. And I said unto the angel: What are these rivers that compass this city about And he saith to me: These are the four rivers which flow abundantly for them that are in this land of promise, whereof the names are these: the river of honey is called Phison, and the river of milk Euphrates, and the river of oil Geon, and the river of wine Tigris. Whereas therefore when the righteous were in the world they used not their power over these things, but hungered and afflicted themselves for the Lord God's sake, therefore when they enter into this city, the Lord will give them these things without number () and without all measure.

24 And I when I entered in by the gate saw before the doors of the city trees great and high, having no fruits, but leaves only. And I saw a few men scattered about in the midst of the trees, and they mourned sore when they saw any man enter into the city. And those trees did penance for them, humbling themselves and bowing down, and again raising themselves up.

And I beheld it and wept with them, and I asked the angel and said: Lord, who are these that are not permitted to enter into the city of Christ And he said unto me: These are they that did earnestly renounce the world day and night with fasting, but had an heart proud above other men, glorifying and praising themselves, and doing nought for their neighbours. For some they greeted friendly, but unto others they said not even 'Hail', and unto whom they would they opened, and if they did any small thing for their neighbour they were puffed up. And I said: What then, Lord their pride hath prevented them from entering into the city of Christ And the angel answered and said unto me: The root of all evils is pride. Are they better than the Son of God who came unto the Jews in great humility And I asked him and said: Wherefore is it then that the trees humble themselves and are again raised up And the angel answered and said unto me: All the time that these spent upon earth (Of old time they were on the earth, Copt.) serving God (they served God): But because of the shame and reproaches of men they were ashamed (did blush) for a time and humbled themselves, but they were not grieved, neither did repent, to cease from this pride that was in them (and one day they bowed themselves because of the disgrace of man, for they cannot endure the pride that is in him, Copt.). This is the cause why the trees humble themselves and again are raised up. And I asked and said: For what cause are they let in unto the gates of the city The angel answered and said unto me: Because of the great goodness of God, and because this is the entry of all his saints which do enter into this city. Therefore are they left in this place, that when Christ the eternal king entereth in with his saints, when he cometh in, all the righteous shall entreat for them, and then shall they enter into the city with them: yet none of them is able to have confidence such as they have that have humbled themselves, serving the Lord God all their life long.

25 But I went forward and the angel led me and brought me unto the river of honey, and I saw there Esaias and Jeremias and Ezekiel and Amos and Micheas and Zacharias, even the prophets lesser and greater, and they greeted me in the city. I said unto the angel: What is this path and he said unto me: This is the path of the prophets: every one that hath grieved his soul and not done his own will for God's sake, when he is departed out of the world and hath been brought unto the Lord God and worshipped him, then by the commandment of God he is delivered unto Michael, and he bringeth him into the city unto this place of the prophets, and they

greet him as their friend and neighbour because he hath performed the will of God.

26 Again he led me where was the river of milk, and I saw in that place all the children whom the king Herod slew for the name of Christ, and they greeted me, and the angel said unto me: All they that keep chastity in cleanness, when they are gone out of the body, after they worship the Lord God, are delivered unto Michael and brought unto the children: and they greet them saying: They are our brothers and friends and members: among them shall they inherit the promises of God.

27 Again he took me and brought me to the north side of the city, and led me to where was the river of wine, and I saw there Abraham, Isaac, and Jacob, Lot and Job and other saints, and they greeted me. [Apocalypse of Zephaniah: (The angel) ran unto all the righteous that are there, Abraham, Isaac, Jacob, Enoch, Elias, and David. He conversed with them as a friend with a friend, who talk together.] And I asked and said: What is this place, Lord The angel answered and said unto me: All they that are entertainers of strangers, when they are departed out of the world first worship the Lord God, and then are delivered unto Michael and brought by this path into the city, and all the righteous greet him as a son and brother, and say unto him: Because thou hast kept kindliness and the entertainment of strangers, come thou and have an inheritance in the city of our Lord God. Every one of the righteous shall receive the good things of God in the city according to his deeds.

28 And again he took me to the river of oil on the east side of the city. And I saw there men rejoicing and singing psalms, and said: Who are these, Lord and the angel said unto me: These are they that have devoted themselves unto God with their whole heart, and had in them no pride. For all that rejoice in the Lord God and sing praises to the Lord with their whole heart are brought here into this city.

29 And he took me into the midst of the city, by the twelve walls (to the twelfth wall, Copt.). Now there was in that place an higher wall; and I asked and said: Is there in the city of Christ a wall more excellent in honour than this place And the angel answered and

said unto me: The second is better than the first, and likewise the third than the second; for one excelleth the other even unto the twelfth wall. And I said: Wherefore Lord, doth one excel another in glory show me. And the angel answered and said unto me: All they that have in them even a little slandering or envy or pride, somewhat is taken away from his glory, even if he be in the city of Christ. Look thou behind thee.

And I turned myself and saw golden thrones set at the several gates, and upon them men having golden crowns and jewels: and I looked and saw within among the twelve men, thrones set in another order (row, fashion), which appeared of much glory so that no man is able to declare the praise of them. And I asked the angel and said: Lord, who is upon the throne And the angel answered and said unto me: These are the thrones of them that had goodness and understanding of heart and yet made themselves foolish for the Lord God's sake, knowing neither the Scriptures nor many psalms, but keeping in mind one chapter of the precepts of God they performed it with great diligence, and had a right intent before the Lord God; and for these great wonder shall take hold upon all the saints before the Lord God, who shall speak one with another, saying: Stay and behold the unlearned that know nothing [more], how they have earned such and so fair raiment and so great glory because of their innocency.

And I saw in the midst of the city an altar exceeding high. And there was one standing by the altar whose visage shone like the sun, and he held in his hands a psaltery and an harp and sang praises, saying: Alleluia. And his voice filled all the city. And when all that were upon the towers and the gates heard him, they answered: Alleluia, so that the foundations of the city were shaken. And I asked the angel and said: Who is this, Lord, that is of so great might And the angel said unto me: This is David. This is the city of Jerusalem; and when Christ the king of eternity shall come in the fullness (confidence, freedom) of his kingdom, he shall again go before him to sing praises, and all the righteous together shall sing praises, answering: Alleluia. And I said: Lord, how is it that David only above the rest of the saints maketh (made) the beginning of singing praises And the angel answered and said unto me: When (or, because) Christ the Son of God sitteth on the right hand of his Father, this David shall sing praises before him in the seventh heaven: and as it is done in the heavens, so likewise is it below: for without David it is not lawful to offer a sacrifice unto God: but it must needs be that David sing praises at the hour of the offering of the body and blood of Christ: as it is performed in heaven, so also is it upon earth. 30 And I said unto the angel: Lord, what is Alleluia And the angel answered and said unto me: Thou dost examine and inquire of all things. And he said unto me: Alleluia is spoken in the Hebrew, that is the speech of God and of the angels: now the interpretation of Alleluia is this: tecel . cat . marith . macha (Gr.thebel marematha). And I said: Lord, what is tecel cat marith macha And the angel answered and said unto me: This is tecel cat marith macha: Let us bless him all together. I asked the angel and said: Lord, do all they that say Alleluia bless God And the angel answered and said unto me: So it is: and again, if any sing Alleluia, and they that are present sing not with him, they commit sin in that they sing not with him. And I said: Lord, doth a man likewise sin if he be doting or very aged The angel answered and said unto me: Not so: but he that is able, and singeth not with him, know ye that such a one is a despiser of the word, for it would be proud and unworthy that he should not bless the Lord God his creator.

31 And when he had ceased speaking unto me, he led me out without the city through the midst of the trees and back from the place of the land of good things (or, men) and set me at the river of milk and honey: and after that he led me unto the ocean that beareth the foundations of the heaven.

The angel answered and said unto me: Perceivest thou that thou goest hence And I said: Yea, Lord. And he said unto me: Come, follow me, and I will show thee the souls of the ungodly and the sinners, that thou mayest know what manner of place they have. And I went with the angel and he took me by the way of the sunsetting, and I saw the beginning of the heaven founded upon a great river of water, and I asked: What is this river of water And he said unto me: This is the ocean which compasseth the whole earth about. And when I was come beyond (to the outside of) the ocean, I looked and there was no light in that place, but darkness and sorrow and sadness: and I sighed.

And I saw there a river of fire burning with heat, and in it was a multitude of men and women sunk up to the knees, and other men up to the navel; others also up to the lips and others up to the hair: and I asked the angel and said: Lord, who are these in the river of fire And the angel answered and said unto me: They are neither hot nor cold,: for they were not found either in the number of the righteous or in the number of the wicked, for they passed the time of their life upon the earth, spending some days in prayer, but other days in sins and fornications, until their death. And I asked and said: Who are these, Lord, that are sunk up to their knees in the fire He answered and said unto me: These are they which when they are come out of the church occupy themselves in disputing with idle (alien) talk. But these that are sunk up to the navel are they who, when they have received the body and blood of Christ, go and commit fornication, and did not cease from their sins until they died; and they that are sunk up to their lips are they that slandered one another when they gathered in the church of God; but they that are sunk up to the eyebrows are they that beckon one to another, and privily devise evil against their neighbours.

32 And I saw on the north side a place of sundry and diverse torments, full of men and women, and a river of fire flowed down upon them. And I beheld and saw pits exceeding deep, and in them many souls together, and the depth of that place was as it were three thousand cubits; and I saw them groaning and weeping and saying: Have mercy on us, Lord. And no man had mercy on them. And I asked the angel and said: Who are these, Lord And the angel answered and said unto me: These are they that trusted not in the Lord that they could have him for their helper. And I inquired and said: Lord, if these souls continue thus, thirty or forty generations being cast one upon another, if (unless) they be cast down yet deeper, I trow the pits would not contain them. And he said to me; The abyss hath no measure: for beneath it there followeth also that which is beneath: and so it is that if a strong man took a stone and cast it into an exceeding deep well and after many hours (long time) it reacheth the earth, so also is the abyss. For when the souls are cast

therein, hardly after five hundred years do they come at the bottom. 33 And I when I heard it, mourned and lamented for the race of men. The angel answered and said unto me: Wherefore mournest thou art thou more merciful than God for inasmuch as God is good and knoweth that there are torments, he beareth patiently with mankind, leaving every one to do his own will for the time that he dwelleth on the earth.

34 Yet again I looked upon the river of fire, and I saw there a man caught by the throat (Copt. an old man who was being dragged along, and they immersed him up to the knees. And the angel Aftemeloukhos came with a great fork of fire, &c. Syr. similar. Some sentences are lost in Lat.) by angels, keepers of hell (Tartaruchi), having in their hands an iron of three hooks wherewith they pierced the entrails of that old man. And I asked the angel and said: Lord, who is this old man upon whom such torments are inflicted And the angel answered and said unto me: He whom thou seest was a priest who fulfilled not well his ministry, for when he was eating and drinking and whoring he offered the sacrifice unto the Lord at his holy altar.

35 And I saw not far off another old man whom four evil angels brought, running quickly, and they sank him up to his knees in the river of fire, and smote him with stones and wounded his face like a tempest, and suffered him not to say: Have mercy on me. And I asked the angel and he said unto me: He whom thou seest was a bishop, and he fulfilled not well his bishopric: for he received indeed a great name, but entered not into (walked not in) the holiness of him that gave him that name all his life; for he gave not righteous judgement, and had not compassion on widows and orphans: but now it is recompensed unto him according to his iniquity and his doings.

36 And I saw another man in the river of fire sunk up to the knees: and his hands were stretched out and bloody, and worms issued out of his mouth and his nostrils, and he was groaning and lamenting and crying out, and said: Have mercy on me for I suffer hurt more than the rest that are in this torment. And I asked: Who is this, Lord And he said unto me: This whom thou seest was a

deacon, who devoured the offerings and committed fornication and did not right in the sight of God: therefore without ceasing he payeth the penalty. And I looked and saw beside him another man whom they brought with haste and cast him into the river of fire, and he was there up to the knees; and the angel that was over the torments came, having a great razor, red-hot, and therewith he cut the lips of that man and the tongue likewise. And I sighed and wept and asked: Who is this man, Lord And he said unto me: This that thou seest was a reader and read unto the people: but he kept not the commandments of God: now also he payeth his own penalty.

37 And I saw another multitude of pits in the same place, and in the midst thereof a river filled with a multitude of men and women, and worms devoured them. But I wept and sighed and asked the angel: Lord, who are these And he said unto me: These are they that extorted usury on usury and trusted in their riches, not having hope in God, that he was their helper.

And after that I looked and saw a very strait place, and there was as it were a wall, and round about it fire. And I saw within it men and women gnawing their tongues, and asked: Who are these, Lord And he said unto me: These are they that mocked at the word of God in the church, not attending thereto, but as it were making nought of God and of his angels: therefore now likewise do they pay the due penalty.

38 And I looked in and saw another pool (lat. old man!) beneath in the pit, and the appearance of it was like blood: and I asked and said: Lord, what is this place And he said unto me: Into this pit do all the torments flow. And I saw men and women sunk up to the lips, and asked: Who are these, Lord And he said unto me: These are the sorcerers which gave unto men and women magical enchantments, and they found no rest (i.e. did not cease) until they died.

And again I saw men and women of a very black countenance in a pit of fire, and I sighed and wept and asked: Who are these, Lord And he said unto me: These are whoremongers and adulterers who, having wives of their own, committed adultery, and likewise the women after the same sort committed adultery, having their own husbands: therefore do they pay the penalty without ceasing.

39 And I saw there girls clad in black raiment, and four fearful angels holding in their hands red-hot chains, and they put them upon their necks (heads) and led them away into darkness. And again I wept and asked the angel: Who are these, Lord And he said unto me: These are they which being virgins defiled their virginity, and their parents knew it not: wherefore without ceasing they pay the due penalty.

And again I beheld there men and women with their hands and feet cut off and naked, in a place of ice and snow, and worms devoured them. And when I saw it I wept and asked: Who are these, Lord and he said unto me: These are they that injured the fatherless and widows and the poor, and trusted not in the Lord: wherefore without ceasing they pay the due penalty.

And I looked and saw others hanging over a channel of water, and their tongues were exceeding dry, and many fruits were set in their sight, and they were not suffered to take of them. And I asked: Who are these, Lord And he said unto me: These are they that brake the fast before the time appointed: therefore without ceasing do they pay this penalty.

And I saw other men and women hanged by their eyebrows and their hair, and a river of fire drew them, and I said: Who are these, Lord And he said unto me: These are they that gave themselves not unto their own husbands and wives, but unto adulterers, and therefore without ceasing they pay the due penalty. (For this Copt. has: men and women hung head downwards torches burning before their faces, serpents girt about them devouring them. These are the women that beautified themselves with paints and unguents and went to church to ensnare men. Syr. and Gr. omit.)

And I saw other men and women covered with dust, and their appearance was as blood, and they were in a pit of pitch and brimstone and borne down in a river of fire. And I asked: Who are these, Lord And he said unto me: These are they that committed the wickedness of Sodom and Gomorrah, men with men, wherefore they pay the penalty without ceasing. (Copt., Syr., Gr. omit this paragraph.)

40 And I looked and saw men and women clad in white (bright) apparel, and their eyes were blind, and they were set in a pit, and I asked: Who are these, Lord And he said unto me: These are they of the heathen that gave alms and knew not the Lord God; wherefore without ceasing they pay the due penalty.

And I looked and saw other men and women upon a spit of fire, and beasts tearing them, and they were not suffered to say: Lord, have mercy on us. And I saw the angel of the torments (Aftemeloukhos, Copt.) laying most fierce torments upon them and saying: Acknowledge the Son of God. For it was told you before, but when the scriptures of God were read unto you, ye paid no heed: wherefore the judgement of God is just, for your evil doings have taken hold upon you, and brought you into these torments. But I sighed and wept, and I inquired and said : Who are these men and women that are strangled in the fire and pay the penalty And he answered me: These are the women which defiled the creation of God when they brought forth children from the womb, and these are the men that lay with them. But their children appealed unto the Lord God and unto the angels that are over the torments, saying: Avenge us of our parents: for they have defiled the creation of God. Having the name of God, but not observing his commandments, they gave us for food unto dogs and to be trampled on by swine, and others they cast into the river (Copt. adds: and did not permit us to grow up into righteous men and to serve God). But those children were delivered unto the angels of Tartarus (Gr. unto an angel) that they should bring them into a spacious place of mercy: but their fathers and mothers were haled (strangled) into everlasting torment.

And thereafter I saw men and women clad in rags full of pitch and brimstone of fire, and there were dragons twined about their necks and shoulders and feet, and angels having horns of fire constrained them and smote them and closed up their nostrils, saying unto them: Wherefore knew ye not the time wherein it was right for you to repent and serve God, and ye did not And I asked: Who are these, Lord And he said unto me: These are they that seemed to renounce the world (lat. God), wearing our garb, but the snares of the world made them to be miserable: they showed no charity and had no pity upon the widows and fatherless: the stranger and pilgrim they did not take in, neither offered one oblation nor had pity on their neighbour: and their prayer went not up even one day pure unto the Lord God; but the many snares of the world held them back, and they were not able to do right in the sight of God. And the angels carried (lat. surrounded) them about into the place of torments: and they that were in torments saw them and said unto them: We indeed when we lived in the world neglected God, and ye did so likewise. And we when we were in the world knew that we were sinners, but of you it was said: These are righteous and servants of God: now we know that ye were only called by the name of the Lord. Wherefore also they pay the due penalty.

And I sighed and wept and said: Woe unto men! woe unto the sinners! to what end were they born And the angel answered and said unto me: Wherefore weepest thou Art thou more merciful than the Lord God which is blessed for ever, who hath established the judgement and left every man of his own will to choose good or evil and to do as pleaseth him Yet again I wept very sore, and he said unto me: Weepest thou, when as yet thou hast not seen the greater torments Follow me, and thou shalt see sevenfold greater than these.

41 And he took me from the north side (to the west, Syr.) and set me over a well, and I found it sealed with seven seals. And the angel that was with me answered and said unto the angel of that place: Open the mouth of the well, that Paul the dearly beloved of God may behold; for power hath been given unto him to see all the torments of hell. And the angel said unto me: Stand afar off, that thou mayest be able to endure the stench of this place. When therefore the well was opened, straightway there arose out of it a stench hard and evil exceedingly, which surpassed all the torments: and I looked into the well and saw masses (lumps) of fire burning on every side, and anguish, and there was straitness in the mouth of the pit so as to take but one man in. And the angel answered and said unto me: If any be cast into the well of the abyss, and it be

sealed over him, there shall never be remembrance made of him in the presence of the Father and the Son and the Holy Ghost or of the holy angels. And I said: Who are they, Lord, that are cast into this well And he said unto me: They are whosoever confesseth not that Christ is come in the flesh and that the Virgin Mary bare him and whosoever saith of the bread and the cup of blessing of the Eucharist that it is not the body and blood of Christ.

The Syriac has: Those who do not confess Jesus Christ, nor His resurrection, nor His humanity, but consider Him as all mortal, and who say that the sacrament of the body of our Lord is bread.

The word θεοτόκος in the text was the occasion of the three years' struggle between Nestorius and Cyril of Alexandria, which ended by the condemnation of the former by the Council of Ephesus, A.D. 431.

The view of the Eucharist in the text is not inconsistent with an early date, though it must be remembered that the idea of a substantial presence became the orthodox doctrine only after the Second Council of Nicæa in A.D. 787.

42 And I looked from the north unto the west and saw there the worm that sleepeth not, and in that place was gnashing of teeth. And the worms were of the measure of one cubit, and on them were two heads; and I saw there men and women in cold and gnashing of teeth. And I asked and said: Lord, who are they that are in this place And he said unto me: These are they which say that Christ rose not from the dead, and that this flesh riseth not again. And I inquired and said: Lord, is there no fire nor heat in this place And he said unto me: In this place is nothing else but cold and snow. And again he said to me: Even if the sun (seven suns, Copt.) rose upon them, they would not be warmed, because of the excessive cold of this place, and the snow. And when I heard this I spread forth mine hands and wept and sighed, and again I said: It were better for us if we had not been born, all we that are sinners. 43 But when they that were in that place saw me weeping, with the angel, they also cried out and wept, saying: Lord God, have mercy upon us.

And after that I beheld the heaven open and Michael the archangel coming down out of heaven, and with him all the host of the angels; and they came even unto them that were set in torment. And they when they saw them wept again and cried out and said: Have mercy upon us, thou Michael, archangel, have mercy upon us and upon the race of men, for it is by thy prayers that the earth standeth. We have now seen the judgement and have known the Son of God. It was not possible for us to pray for this before we came into this place: for we heard that there was a judgement, before we departed out of the world, but the snares and the life of the world suffered us not to repent. And Michael answered and said: Hearken when Michael speaketh: I am he that stands in the presence of God alway. As the Lord liveth, before whose face I stand, I cease not for one day nor one night to pray continually for the race of men; and I indeed pray for them that are upon earth: but they cease not from committing wickednesses and fornication. And they bring not forth aught of good while they are upon earth; and ye have wasted in vanity the time wherein ye ought to have repented. But I have prayed alway, and now do I entreat that God would send dew and that rain may be sent upon the earth, and still pray I until the earth yield her fruits: and I say that if any man doeth but a little good I will strive for him and protect him until he escape the judgement of torment. Where then be your prayers Where be your repentances ye have lost the time despicably. Yet now weep ye, and I will weep with you, and the angels that are with me, together with the dearly beloved Paul, if peradventure the merciful God will have pity and grant you refreshment. And they when they heard these words cried out and wept sore, and all said with one voice: Have mercy upon us, O Son of God. And I, Paul, sighed and said: O Lord God, have mercy upon thy creature, have mercy on the children of men, have mercy upon thine image.

44 I beheld and saw the heaven shake like unto a tree that is moved by the wind: and suddenly they cast themselves down upon their faces before the throne: and I saw the four-and- twenty elders and the four beasts worshipping God: and I saw the altar and the veil and the throne, and all of them were rejoicing, and the smoke of a sweet odour rose up beside the altar of the throne of God; and I heard a voice saying: For what cause do ye entreat me, our angels,

and our ministers And they cried out, saying: We entreat thee, beholding thy great goodness unto mankind. And thereafter I saw the Son of God coming down out of heaven, and on his head was a crown. And when they that were in torments saw him they all cried out with one voice, saying: Have mercy upon us, O exalted Son of God (or, Son of God Most High): thou art he that hast granted refreshment unto all that are in heaven and earth; have mercy upon us likewise: for since we beheld thee we have been refreshed. And there went forth a voice from the Son of God throughout all the torments, saying: What good works have ye done that ye should ask of me refreshment My blood was shed for you, and not even so did ye repent: for your sake I bare a crown of thorns on mine head, for you I received buffets upon my cheeks, and not even so did ye repent. I asked for water when I hanged upon the cross, and they gave me vinegar mingled with gall: with a spear did they open my right side: for my name's sake have they slain my servants the prophets, and the righteous: and for ail these things did I give you a place of repentance, and ye would not. Yet now because of Michael the archangel of my covenant and the angels that are with him, and because of Paul my dearly beloved whom I would not grieve. and because of your brethren that are in the world and do offer oblations, and because of your sons, for in them are my commandments,l and yet more because of mine own goodness: on that day whereon I rose from the dead I grant unto all you that are in torment refreshment for a day and a night for ever. And all they cried out and said: We bless thee, O Son of God, for that thou hast granted us rest for a day and a night: for better unto us is the refreshment of one day than the whole time of our life wherein we were upon earth: and if we had known clearly that this place was appointed for them that sin, we should have done none other work whatsoever, neither traded nor done any wickedness. For what profit was our pride in the world (Copt. What profit was it to us to be born into the world) For this our pride is taken captive, which came up out of our mouth against our neighbour (Copt. our life is like the breath of our mouth): and this pain and our sore anguish and tears and the worms which are under us, these are worse unto us than the torments which we suffer. (This is hardly sense, but Copt. agrees; should it not have been ' these are worse than not to have been born ') And as they thus spake, the angels of torment and the evil angels were wroth with them and said: How long have ye wept and sighed for ye have had no mercy. For this is the judgement of God on him that hath not had mercy. Yet have ye received this great grace, even refreshment for the night and day of the Lord's day, because of Paul the dearly beloved of God who hath come down unto you.

45 And after these things the angel said unto me: Hast thou seen all these things And I said: Yea, Lord. And he said unto me: Follow me, and I will bring thee into Paradise, that the righteous which are there may see thee: for, behold, they hope to see thee, and are ready to come and meet thee with joy and exultation. And I followed after the angel in the swiftness of the Holy Ghost, and he set me in Paradise and said unto me: This is Paradise, wherein Adam and his wife erred. And I entered into Paradise and saw the head of the waters, and the angel beckoned unto me and said to me: Behold, saith he, these waters: for this is the river Phison that compasseth about all the land of Evila. and this other is Geon that goeth about all the land of Egypt and Ethiopia, and this other is Tigris that is over against the Assyrians, and this other is Euphrates that watereth the land of Mesopotamia. And I entered in further and saw a tree planted, out of whose roots flowed waters, and out of it was the beginning of the four rivers, and the Spirit of God rested upon that tree, and when the spirit breathed the waters flowed forth: and I said: Lord, is this tree that which maketh the waters to flow And he said unto me: Because in the beginning, before the heaven and the earth were made to appear, and all things were invisible, the Spirit of God moved (was borne) upon the waters; but since by the commandment of God the heaven and the earth appeared the spirit hath rested upon this tree; wherefore when the spirit breatheth, the waters flow out from the tree. And he took hold on mine hand and led me unto the tree of the knowledge of good and evil, and said: This is the tree whereby death entered into the world, and Adam taking of it from his wife did eat, and death entered into the world. And he showed me another tree in the midst of Paradise, and saith unto me: This is the tree of life.

46 And as I yet looked upon the tree, I saw a virgin coming from afar off, and two hundred angels before her singing hymns: and I

inquired and said: Lord, who is this that cometh in such glory and he said unto me: This is Mary the virgin, the mother of the Lord. And she came near and saluted me, and said: Hail, Paul, dearly beloved of God and angels and men. For all the saints have besought my son Jesus who is my Lord, that thou shouldest come here in the body that they might see thee before thou didst depart out of the world. And the Lord said to them: Wait and be ye patient: yet a little while, and ye shall see him, and he shall be with you for ever. And again they all with one accord said unto him: Grieve us not, for we desire to see him while he is in the flesh, for by him hath thy name been greatly glorified in the world, and we have seen that he hath excelled (done away with) all the works whether of the lesser or the greater. For we inquire of them that come hither, saying: Who is he that guided you in the world and they have told us: There is one in the world whose name is Paul; he declareth Christ, preaching him, and we believe that by the power and sweetness of his speech many have entered into the kingdom. Behold, all the righteous are behind me, coming to meet thee. But I say unto thee, Paul, that for this cause I come first to meet them that have performed the will of my son and my Lord Jesus Christ, even I come first to meet them and leave them not as strangers until they meet with him in peace.

47 While she was yet speaking I saw three men coming from afar, very beautiful, after the appearance of Christ, and their forms were shining, and their angels; and I asked: Who are these, Lord And he answered: These are the fathers of the people, Abraham, Isaac, and Jacob. And they came near and greeted me, and said: Hail, Paul, dearly beloved of God and men: blessed is he that endureth violence for the Lord's sake. And Abraham answered me and said: This is my son Isaac, and Jacob my best beloved, and we knew the Lord and followed him. Blessed are all they that have believed thy word that they may inherit the kingdom of God by labour and self-sacrifice (renunciation) and sanctification and humility and charity and meekness and right faith in the Lord: and we also had devotion unto the Lord whom thou preachest, covenanting that we will come unto every soul of them that believe in him, and minister unto him as fathers minister unto their sons.

Twelve Books on the Apocalypse

While they yet spake I saw twelve men coming from afar with honour, and I asked: Who are these, Lord And he said: These are the patriarchs. And they came and saluted me and said: Hail, Paul, dearly beloved of God and men. The Lord hath not grieved us, that we might see thee yet being in the body, before thou departedst out of the world. And every one of them signified his name unto me in order, from Ruben unto Benjamin; and Joseph said unto me: I am he that was sold; and I say unto thee, Paul, that for all that my brethren did unto me, in nothing did I deal evilly with them, not in all the labour which they laid upon me, nor did I hurt them in any thing (Copt. kept no evil thought against them) from morning until evening. Blessed is he that is hurt for the Lord's sake and hath endured, for the Lord will recompense him manifold more when he departeth out of the world.

48 While he yet spake I saw another coming from afar, beautiful, and his angels singing hymns, and I asked: Who is this, Lord, that is fair of countenance And he said unto me: Dost thou not know him And I said: No, Lord. And he said to me: This is Moses the lawgiver, unto whom God gave the law. And when he was nigh me, straightway he wept, and after that he greeted me; and I said unto him: Why weepest thou for I have heard that thou excellest all men in meekness. And he answered, saying: I weep for them whom I planted with much labour, for they have borne no fruit, neither doth any of them do well. And I have seen all the sheep whom I fed that they are scattered and become as having no shepherd, and that all the labours which I have endured for the children of Israel are come to nought, and however great wonders I did in their midst [and] they understood not: and I marvel how the strangers and uncircumcised and idolaters are converted and entered into the promises of God, but Israel hath not entered in: and now I say unto thee, O brother Paul, that in that hour when the people hanged up Jesus whom thou preachest, God the Father of all, which gave me the law, and Michael and all the angels and archangels, and Abraham and Isaac and Jacob and all the righteous wept over the Son of God that was hanged on the cross. And in that hour all the saints waited upon me, looking on me and saying: Behold, Moses, what they of thy people have done unto the Son of God. Therefore

blessed art thou O Paul, and blessed is the generation and people that hath believed thy word.

49 While he yet spake there came other twelve and saw me and said: Art thou Paul that is glorified in heaven and upon earth And I answered and said: Who are ye The first answered and said: I am Esaias whose head Manasses cut with a saw of wood. And the second said likewise: I am Jeremias who was stoned by the children of Israel, and slain. And the third said: I am Ezechiel whom the children of Israel dragged by the feet over the stones in the mountain until they scattered my brains abroad: and all of us endured these labours, desiring to save the children of Israel: and I say unto thee that after the toils which they laid upon me I would cast myself down upon my face before the Lord, praying for them and bowing my knees unto the second hour of the Lord's day, even until Michael came and raised me up from the earth. Blessed art thou, Paul, and blessed is the people that hath believed through thee.

And as they passed by, I saw another, fair of countenance and asked: Who is this, Lord [And when he saw me he was glad] and he said unto me: This is Lot, which was found righteous in Sodom. And he came near and greeted me and said: Blessed art thou, Paul, and blessed is the generation unto whom thou hast ministered. And I answered and said unto him: Art thou Lot, that wast found righteous in Sodom And he said: I entertained angels in mine house as strangers, and when they of the city would have done them violence I offered them my two daughters, virgins, that had never known man, and gave them to them, saying: Use them as ye will, only do no ill unto these men, for therefore have they entered under the roof of mine house. Therefore ought we to have confidence, and know that whatsoever any man hath done, God recompenseth him manifold more when he cometh (they come) unto him. Blessed art thou Paul, and blessed is the generation which hath believed thy word.

When therefore he had ceased speaking unto me, I saw another coming from afar off, very beautiful in the face, and smiling, and his angels singing hymns, and I said unto the angel that was with me:

Hath, then, every one of the righteous an angel for his fellow And he saith to me: Every one of the saints hath his own, that standeth by him and singeth hymns, and the one departeth not from the other. And I said: Who is this, Lord And he said: This is Job. And he drew near and greeted me and said: Brother Paul, thou hast great praise with God and men. Now I am Job, which suffered much for the season of thirty years by the issue of a plague, and in the beginning the blains that came forth of my body were as grains of wheat; but on the third day they became like an ass's foot, and the worms that fell from them were four fingers long: and thrice the devil appeared unto me and saith to me: Speak a word against the Lord, and die. But I said unto him: If thus be the will of God that I continue in the plague all the time of my life until I die, I will not rest from blessing the Lord God, and I shall receive the greater reward. For I know that the sufferings of this world are nought compared with the refreshment that is thereafter: wherefore blessed art thou, Paul, and blessed is the people which hath believed by thy means.

50 While he yet spake there came another crying out from afar off and saying: Blessed art thou, Paul, and blessed am I that have seen thee the beloved of the Lord. And I asked the angel: Who is this, Lord and he answered and said unto me: This is Noe of the days of the flood. And straightway we greeted one another, and he, rejoicing greatly, said unto me: Thou art (or, Art thou) Paul the best beloved of God. And I asked him: Who art thou And he said: I am Noe that was in the days of the flood: but I say unto thee, Paul, that I spent an hundred years making the ark, not putting off the coat (tunic) which I wore, and I shaved not the hair of mine head. Furthermore I kept continence, not coming near mine own wife, and in those hundred years the hair of mine head grew not in greatness, neither was my raiment soiled. And I besought men at that time, saying: Repent, for a flood of waters cometh upon you. But they mocked me and derided my words; and again they said unto me: This is the time of them that would play and sin as much as they will, that have leave to fornicate not a little (lat. confused; other versions omit): for God looketh not on these things, neither knoweth what is done of us men, and moreover there is no flood of waters coming upon this world. And they ceased not from their sins until God blotted out all flesh that had the breath of life in it. But

know thou that God loveth one righteous man more than all the world of the wicked. Therefore blessed art thou, O Paul, and blessed is the people that hath believed by thy means.

51 And I turned myself and saw other righteous ones coming from afar off, and I asked the angel: Who are these, Lord and he answered me: These are Elias and Eliseus. And they greeted me, and I said unto them: Who are ye And one of them answered and said: I am Elias the prophet of God. I am Elias that prayed, and because of my word the heaven rained not for three years and six months, because of the iniquities of men. Righteous and true is God, who doeth the will of his servants; for oftentimes the angels besought the Lord for rain, and he said: Be patient until my servant Elias pray and entreat for this, and I will send rain upon the earth.

[Here the Greek, latin, and Syriac texts end, save that the Syriac adds thus much:

And he gave not, until I called upon him again; then he gave unto them. But blessed art thou, O Paul, that thy generation and those thou teachest are the sons of the kingdom. And know thou, O Paul, that every man who believes through thee hath a great blessing, and a blessing is reserved for him. Then he departed from me.

And the angel who was with me led me forth, and said unto me: Lo, unto thee is given this mystery and revelation: as thou pleasest, make it known unto the sons of men.

And I, Paul, returned unto myself, and I knew all that I had seen: and in life I had not rest that I might reveal this mystery, but I wrote it and deposited it under the ground and the foundations of the house of a certain faithful man with whom I used to be in Tarsus a city of Cilicia. And when I was released from this life of time, and stood before my Lord, thus said he unto me: Paul, have we shown all these things unto thee that thou shouldst deposit them under the foundations of a house Then send and disclose concerning this revelation, that men may read it and turn to the way of truth, that they also may not come to these bitter torments.

And thus was this revelation discovered....

Then follows the history of the finding, which in the other texts is prefixed to the book.]

But this conclusion can hardly be the original one. The Coptic seems in part better. After the words 'rain upon the earth', it continues:

The sufferings which each endureth for God's sake will God requite unto him twofold. Blessed art thou, Paul, and blessed are the heathen who shall believe through thee. And whilst he was speaking, Enoch (here Enoch replaces Elisha) also came and saluted me and said unto me: The man who endureth suffering for God's sake, God will not afflict when he goeth out of the world.

Then there are similar meetings with Zacharias and John Baptist, and Abel. Zacharias says:

' I am he whom they killed when I was offering up the offering unto God: and when the angels came for the offering, they carried my body up to God, and no man found my body whither it had been taken.'

Then Adam, taller than the rest, appears. And this seems a suitable finale to the procession of saints.

After this Paul is carried into the third heaven. The angel who is with him changes in appearance and bursts into flames of fire, and a voice forbids Paul to reveal what he has seen.

There is a description of a mysterious vision of an altar with seven eagles of light on the right and seven on the left. And this is followed by more descriptions of Paradise-partly resembling a vision seen by one Siophanes, in the Book of Bartholomew. Some sentences also are taken from, or at least found in, the Apocalypse of Zephaniah. The meek, the prophets, David, all figure again in this episode: last are the martyrs. The conclusion runs thus (in substance):

The angel of the Lord took me up and brought me to the Mount of Olives. I found the apostles assembled and told them all I had seen. They praised God and commanded us, that is me, Mark, and

Timothy, to write the revelation. And while they were talking, Christ appeared from the chariot of the cherubim and spoke greetings to Peter, John, and especially Paul. He promised blessings to those who should write or read the Apocalypse, and curses on those who should deride it. Peter and Paul should end their course on the fifth of Epiphi (29 June). He then bade a cloud take the apostles to the various countries allotted to them, and commanded them to preach the Gospel of the Kingdom. And a doxology follows.

I am disposed to think that nothing after the appearance of Adam in this version can be original. The rest is to a great extent, I think a pasticcio from other Coptic apocrypha. It is quite possible, of course that the original end of the Apocalypse was lost at an early date, but the supposition is probable that after the appearance of Adam a short conclusion followed in which Paul returned to earth. With so ill-proportioned and inartistic a book it is not perhaps worth while to spend much time on conjectural restoration. Yet another possibility should be pointed out. The climax of the Apocalypse is reached when the Sunday is granted as a day of rest from torment. Paul has seen Paradise and hell, and there is no more for him to do. Everything after ch. 44 is an otiose appendix.

And we do find in the Ethiopic Apocalypse of the Virgin, which copies that of Paul very literally, that the end comes at ch. 44, when the Virgin procures rest from Friday evening to Monday morning for the lost. The Greek Apocalypse -one form at least ends when she has gained for them the days of Pentecost.

It may be the case, then, that the Apocalypse of Paul as first issued ended here, and that it was reissued with the appendix about Paradise (45-end). In the shorter Latin recensions there is no trace of anything after ch. 44: but this does not furnish a conclusive argument. More to the point would be the discovery of a copy of the full text ending with 44.

Gnosticism

The next three books of Revelation or Apocalypse are Gnostic writings, thus it behooves us to explore and understand this particular religious sect before we examine the texts.

"Gnosticism: A system of religion mixed with Greek and Oriental philosophy of the 1st through 6th centuries A.D. Intermediate between Christianity and paganism, Gnosticism taught that knowledge rather than faith was the greatest good and that through knowledge alone could salvation be attained."

- Webster's Dictionary

The word Gnostic is based on the Greek word "Gnosis," which means "knowledge." The "Gnosis" is the knowledge of the ultimate, supreme God and his spirit, which is contained within us all. It is this knowledge that allows one to transcend this material world with its falsities and spiritual entrapments and ascend into heaven to be one with God.

For centuries the definition of Gnosticism has been a point of confusion and contention within the religious community. This is due in part to the ever-broadening application of the term and the fact that various sects of Gnosticism existed as the theology evolved and began to merge into what became mainstream Christianity.

Even though Gnosticism continued to evolve, it is the theology in place at the time that the Gnostic Gospels were written that should be considered and understood before attempting to render or read a translation. To do otherwise would make the translation cloudy and obtuse.

It becomes the duty of both translator and reader to understand the ideas being espoused and the terms conveying those ideas. A grasp of theology, cosmology, and relevant terms is necessary for a clear transmission of the meaning within the text in question.

With this in mind, we will briefly examine Gnostic theology, cosmology, and history. We will focus primarily on Gnostic sects existing in the first through fourth centuries A.D. since it is believed most Gnostic texts were written during that time. It was also during that time that reactions within the emerging orthodoxy began to intensify.

The downfall of many books written on the topic of religion is the attempt to somehow remove history and people from the equation. History shapes religion because it shapes the perception and direction of religious leaders. Religion also develops and evolves in an attempt to make sense of the universe as it is seen and understood at the time. Thus, to truly grasp a religious concept it is important to know the history, people, and cosmology of the time. These areas are not separate but are continually interacting. This is how the information in this book will be presented to the reader.

The roots of the Gnosticism may pre-date Christianity. Similarities exist between Gnosticism and the wisdom and mystery cults found in Egypt and Greece. Gnosticism contains the basic terms and motifs of Plato's cosmology as well as the mystical qualities of Buddhism. Plato was steeped in Greek mythology, and the Gnostic creation myth has elements owing to this. Both cosmology and mysticism within Gnosticism present an interpretation of Christ's existence and teachings, thus, Gnostics are considered a Christian sect. Gnostic followers are urged to look within themselves for the truth and the Christ spirit hidden, asleep in their souls. The battle cry can be summed up in the words of the Gnostic Gospel of Thomas, verse 3:

> *Jesus said: If those who lead you say to you: Look, the Kingdom is in the sky, then the birds of the sky would enter before you. If they say to you: It is in the sea, then the fish of the sea would enter ahead of you. But the Kingdom of God exists within you and it exists outside of you. Those who come to know (recognize) themselves will find it, and when you come to know yourselves you will become known and you will realize that you are the children of the Living Father. Yet if*

you do not come to know yourselves then you will dwell in poverty and it will be you who are that poverty.

Paganism was a religious traditional society in the Mediterranean leading up to the time of the Gnostics. Centuries after the conversion of Constantine, mystery cults worshipping various Egyptian and Greco-Roman gods continued. These cults taught that through their secret knowledge worshippers could control or escape the mortal realm. The Gnostic doctrine of inner knowledge and freedom may have part of its roots here. The concept of duality and inner guidance taught in Buddhism added to and enforced Gnostic beliefs, as we will see later.

The belief systems of Plato, Buddha, and paganism melted together, spread, and found a suitable home in the mystical side of the Christian faith as it sought to adapt and adopt certain Judeo-Christian beliefs and symbols.

Like modern Christianity, Gnosticism had various points of view that could be likened to Christian denominations of today. Complex and elaborate creation myths took root in Gnosticism, being derived from those of Plato. Later, the theology evolved, and Gnosticism began to shed some of its more unorthodox myths, leaving the central theme of inner knowledge or gnosis to propagate.

The existence of various sects of Gnosticism, differing creation stories, along with the lack of historical documentation, has left scholars in a quandary about exactly what Gnostics believed. Some have suggested that the Gnostics represented a free thinking and idealistic movement much like that of the "Hippie" movement active in the United States during the 1960's.

Just as the "Hippie" movement in the U.S. influenced political thought, some early sects of Gnostics began to exert direct influence on the Christian church and its leadership.

Although it appears that there were several sects of Gnosticism, we will attempt to discuss the more universal Gnostic beliefs along with the highlights of the major sects.

Gnostic cosmology, (which is the theory of how the universe is created, constructed, and sustained), is complex and very different from orthodox Christianity cosmology. In many ways Gnosticism may appear to be polytheistic or even pantheistic.

To understand some of the basic beliefs of Gnosticism, let us start with the common ground shared between Gnosticism and modern Christianity. Both believe the world is imperfect, corrupt, and brutal. The blame for this, according to mainstream Christianity, is placed squarely on the shoulders of man himself. With the fall of man (Adam), the world was forever changed to the undesirable and harmful place in which we live today. However, Gnostics reject this view as an incorrect interpretation of the creation myth.

According to Gnostics, the blame is not in ourselves, but in our creator. The creator of this world was himself somewhat less than perfect and in fact, deeply flawed and cruel, making mankind the child of a lesser God. It is in the book, *The Apocryphon of John*, that the Gnostic view of creation is presented to us in great detail.

Gnosticism also teaches that in the beginning a Supreme Being called The Father, The Divine All, The Origin, The Supreme God, or The Fullness, emanated the element of existence, both visible and invisible. His intent was not to create but, just as light emanates from a flame, so did creation shine forth from God. This manifested the primal element needed for creation. This was the creation of Barbelo, who is the Thought of God.

The Father's thought performed a deed and she was created from it. It is she who had appeared before him in the shining of his light. This is the first power which was before all of them and which was created from his mind. She is the Thought of the All and her light shines like his light. It is the perfect power which is the visage of the invisible. She is the pure, undefiled Spirit who is perfect. She is the first power, the glory of Barbelo, the perfect glory of the kingdom (kingdoms), the glory revealed. She glorified the pure, undefiled Spirit and it was she who praised him, because thanks to him she had come forth.

The Apocryphon of John

It could be said that Barbelo is the creative emanation and, like the Divine All, is both male and female. It is the "agreement" of Barbelo and the Divine All, representing the union of male and female, that created the Christ Spirit and all the Aeons. In some renderings the word "Aeon" is used to designate an ethereal realm or kingdom. In other versions "Aeon" indicates the ruler of the realm. One of these rulers was called Sophia or Wisdom. Her fall began a chain of events that led to the introduction of evil into the universe.

Seeing the divine flame of God, Sophia sought to know its origin. She sought to know the very nature of God. Sophia's passion ended in tragedy when she managed to capture a divine and creative spark, which she attempted to duplicate with her own creative force, without the union of a male counterpart. It was this act that produced the Archons, beings born outside the higher divine realm. In the development of the myth, explanations seem to point to the fact that Sophia carried the divine essence of creation from God within her but chose to attempt creation by using her own powers. It is unclear if this was an attempt to understand the Supreme God and his power, or an impetuous act that caused evil to enter the cosmos in the form of her creations.

The realm containing the Fullness of the Godhead and Sophia is called the pleroma or Realm of Fullness. This is the Gnostic heaven. The lesser Gods created in Sophia's failed attempt were cast outside the pleroma and away from the presence of God. In essence, she threw away and discarded her flawed creations.

"She cast it away from her, outside the place where no one of the immortals might see it, for she had created it in ignorance. And she surrounded it with a glowing cloud, and she put a throne in the middle of the cloud so that no one could see it except the Holy Spirit who is called the mother of all that has life. And she called his name Yaldaboth." Apocryphon of John

The beings Sophia created were imperfect and oblivious to the Supreme God. Her creations contained deities even less perfect than herself. They were called the Powers, the Rulers, or the Archons. Their leader was called the Demiurge, but his name was Yaldaboth **(also called Sakla, Ialdabaoth or Yaldabaoth)**. It was the flawed, imperfect, spiritually blind Demiurge, (Yaldaboth), who became the creator of the material world and all things in it. Gnostics considered Yaldaboth to be the same as Jehovah (Yahweh), who is the Jewish creator God. These beings, the Demiurge and the Archons, would later equate to Satan and his demons, or Jehovah and his angels, depending on which Gnostic sect is telling the story. Both are equally evil.

In one Gnostic creation story, the Archons created Adam but could not bring him to life. In other stories Adam was formed as a type of worm, unable to attain personhood. Thus, man began as an incomplete creation of a flawed, spiritually blind, and malevolent god. In this myth, the Archons were afraid that Adam might be more powerful than the Archons themselves. When they saw Adam was incapable of attaining the human state, their fears were put to rest, thus, they called that day the "Day of Rest."

Sophia saw Adam's horrid state and had compassion, because she knew she was the origin of the Archons and their evil. Sophia descended to help bring Adam out of his hopeless condition. It is this story that set the stage for the emergence of the sacred feminine force in Gnosticism that is not seen in orthodox Christianity. Sophia brought within herself the light and power of the Supreme God. Metaphorically, within the spiritual womb of Sophia was carried the life force of the Supreme God for Adam's salvation.

In the Gnostic text called, *The Apocryphon of John* or *The Secret Book of John*, Sophia is quoted:

> "I entered into the midst of the cage which is the prison of the body. And I spoke saying: 'He who hears, let him awake from his deep sleep.' Then Adam wept and shed tears. After he wiped away his bitter tears he asked: 'Who calls my name, and from where has this hope arose in me even while

> *I am in the chains of this prison?' And I (Sophia) answered: 'I am the one who carries the pure light; I am the thought of the undefiled spirit. Arise, remember, and follow your origin, which is I, and beware of the deep sleep.'"*

Sophia would later equate to the Holy Spirit as it awakened the comatose soul.

As the myth evolved, Sophia, after animating Adam, became Eve to assist Adam in finding the truth. She offered it to him in the form of the fruit of the tree of knowledge. To Gnostics, this was an act of deliverance.

Other stories have Sophia becoming the serpent in order to offer Adam a way to attain the truth. In either case, the apple represented the hard sought truth, which was the knowledge of good and evil, and through that knowledge Adam could become a god. Later, the serpent would become a feminine symbol of wisdom, probably owing to the connection with Sophia. Eve, being Sophia in disguise, would become the mother and sacred feminine of us all. As Gnostic theology began to coalesce, Sophia would come to be considered a force or conduit of the Holy Spirit, in part due to the fact that the Holy Spirit was also considered a feminine and creative force from the Supreme God. The Gospel of Philip echoes this theology in verse six as follows:

> *In the days when we were Hebrews we were made orphans, having only our Mother. Yet when we believed in the Messiah (and became the ones of Christ), the Mother and Father both came to us.* Gospel of Philip

As the emerging orthodox church became more and more oppressive to women, later even labeling them "occasions of sin," the Gnostics countered by raising women to equal status with men, saying Sophia was, in a sense, the handmaiden or wife of the Supreme God, making the soul of Adam her spiritual offspring.

In Gnostic cosmology the "living" world is under the control of entities called Aeons, of which Sophia is head. This means the Aeons influence or control the soul, life force, intelligence, thought, and mind. Control of the mechanical or inorganic world is given to the Archons. They rule the physical aspects of systems, regulation, limits, and order in the world. Both the ineptitude and cruelty of the Archons are reflected in the chaos and pain of the material realm.

The lesser God that created the world, Yaldaboth. began his existence in a state that was both detached and remote from the Supreme God in aspects both spiritual and physical. Since Sophia had misused her creative force, which passed from the Supreme God to her, Sophia's creation, the Demiurge, Yaldaboth, contained only part of the original creative spark of the Supreme Being. He was created with an imperfect nature caused by his distance in lineage and in spirit from the Divine All or Supreme God. It is because of his imperfections and limited abilities the lesser God is also called the "Half-Maker".

The Creator God, the Demiurge, and his helpers, the Archons took the stuff of existence produced by the Supreme God and fashioned it into this material world.

Since the Demiurge (Yaldaboth) had no memory of how he came to be alive, he did not realize he was not the true creator. The Demiurge believed he somehow came to create the material world by himself. The Supreme God allowed the Demiurge and Archons to remain deceived.

The Creator God (the Demiurge) intended the material world to be perfect and eternal, but he did not have it in himself to accomplish the feat. What comes forth from a being cannot be greater than the highest part of him, can it? The world was created flawed and transitory, and we are part of it. Can we escape? The Demiurge was imperfect and evil. So was the world he created. If it was the Demiurge who created man and man is called upon to escape the Demiurge and find union with the Supreme God, is this not demanding that man becomes greater than his creator? Spiritually this seems impossible, but as many children become greater than their parents, man is expected to become greater than his maker, the Demiurge. This starts with the one fact that the Demiurge denies: the existence and supremacy of the Supreme God.

Man was created with a dual nature as the product of the material world of the Demiurge with his imperfect essence, combined with the spark of God that emanated from the Supreme God through Sophia. A version of the creation story has Sophia instructing the Demiurge to breath into Adam that spiritual power he had taken from Sophia during his creation. It was the spiritual power from Sophia that brought life to Adam.

It is this divine spark in man that calls to its source, the Supreme God, and which causes a "divine discontent," that nagging feeling that keeps us questioning if this is all there is. This spark and the feeling it gives us keeps us searching for the truth.

The Creator God sought to keep man ignorant of his defective state by keeping him enslaved to the material world. By doing so, he continued to receive man's worship and servitude. He did not wish man to recognize or gain knowledge of the true Supreme God. Since he did not know or acknowledge the Supreme God, he views any attempt to worship anything else as spiritual treason.

The opposition of forces set forth in the spiritual battle over the continued enslavement of man and man's spiritual freedom set up the duality of good and evil in Gnostic theology. There was a glaring difference between the orthodox Christian viewpoint and the Gnostic viewpoint. According to Gnostics, the creator of the material world was an evil entity and the Supreme God, who was his source, was the good entity. Christians quote John 1:1 "In the beginning was the Word, and the Word was with God, and the Word was God."

According to Gnostics, only through the realization of man's true state or through death can he escape captivity in the material realm. This means the idea of salvation does not deal with original sin or blood payment. Instead, it focuses on the idea of awakening to the fullness of the truth.

According to Gnostic theology, neither Jesus nor his death can save anyone, but the truth that he came to proclaim can allow a person to save his or her own soul. It is the truth, or realization of the lie of the material world and its God, that sets one on a course of freedom.

To escape the earthly prison and find one's way back to the pleroma (heaven) and the Supreme God, is the soteriology (salvation doctrine) and eschatology (judgment, reward, and doctrine of heaven) of Gnosticism.

The idea that personal revelation leads to salvation, may be what caused the mainline Christian church to declare Gnosticism a heresy. The church could better tolerate alternative theological views if the views did not undermine the authority of the church and its ability to control the people. Gnostic theology placed salvation in the hands of the individual through personal revelations and knowledge, excluding the need for the orthodox church and its clergy to grant salvation or absolution. This fact, along with the divergent interpretation of the creation story, which placed the creator God, Yaldaboth or Jehovah, as the enemy of mankind, was too much for the church to tolerate. Reaction was harsh. Gnosticism was declared to be a dangerous heresy.

Gnosticism may be considered polytheistic because it espoused many "levels" of Gods, beginning with an ultimate, unknowable, Supreme God and descending as he created Sophia, and Sophia created the Demiurge (Creator God); each becoming more inferior and limited.

There is a hint of pantheism in Gnostic theology due to the fact that creation is caused by a deterioration of the Godhead and the dispersion of creative essence, which eventually devolves into the creation of man.

In the end, there occurs a universal reconciliation as being after being realizes the existence of the Supreme God and renounces the material world and its inferior   creator.

Combined with its Christian influences, the cosmology of the Gnostics may have borrowed from the Greek philosopher, Plato, as well as from Buddhism. There are disturbing parallels between the creation myth set forth by Plato and some of those recorded in Gnostic writings.

Plato lived from 427 to 347 B.C. He was the son of wealthy Athenians and a student of the philosopher, Socrates, and the mathematician, Pythagoras. Plato himself was the teacher of Aristotle.

In Plato's cosmology, the Demiurge is an artist who imposed form on materials that already existed. The raw materials were in a chaotic and random state. The physical world must have had visible form which was put together much like a puzzle is constructed. This later gave way to a philosophy which stated that all things in existence could be broken down into a small subset of geometric shapes.

In the tradition of Greek mythology, Plato's cosmology began with a creation story. The story was narrated by the philosopher Timaeus of Locris, a fictional character of Plato's making. In his account, nature is initiated by a creator deity, called the "Demiurge," a name which may be the Geek word for "craftsman" or "artisan" or, according to how one divides the word, it could also be translated as "half-maker."

The Demiurge sought to create the cosmos modeled on his understanding of the supreme and original truth. In this way he created the visible universe based on invisible truths. He set in place rules of process such as birth, growth, change, death, and dissolution. This was Plato's "Realm of Becoming." It was his Genesis. Plato stated that the internal structure of the cosmos had innate intelligence and was therefore called the World Soul. The cosmic super-structure of the Demiurge was used as the framework on which to hang or fill in the details and parts of the universe. The Demiurge then appointed his underlings to fill in the details which allowed the universe to remain in a working and balanced state. All phenomena of nature resulted from an interaction and interplay of the two forces of reason and necessity.

Plato represented reason as constituting the World Soul. The material world was a necessity in which reason acted out its will in the physical realm. The duality between the will, mind, or reason of the World Soul and the material universe and its inherent flaws set in play the duality of Plato's world and is seen reflected in the beliefs of the Gnostics.

In Plato's world, the human soul was immortal, each soul was assigned to a star. Souls that were just or good were permitted to return to their stars upon their death. Unjust souls were reincarnated to try again. Escape of the soul to the freedom of the stars and out of the cycle of reincarnation was best accomplished by following the reason and goodness of the World Soul and not the physical world, which was set in place only as a necessity to manifest the patterns of the World Soul.

Although in Plato's cosmology the Demiurge was not seen as evil, in Gnostic cosmology he was considered not only to be flawed and evil, but he was also the beginning of all evil in the material universe, having created it to reflect his own malice.

Following the path of Plato's cosmology, some Gnostics left open the possibility of reincarnation if the person had not reached the truth before his death.

In the year 13 A.D. Roman annals record the visit of an Indian king named Pandya or Porus. He came to see Caesar Augustus carrying a letter of introduction in Greek. He was accompanied by a monk who burned himself alive in the city of Athens to prove his faith in Buddhism. The event was described by Nicolaus of Damascus as, not surprisingly, causing a great stir among the people. It is thought that this was the first transmission of Buddhist teaching to the masses.

In the second century A.D., Clement of Alexandria wrote about Buddha: "Among the Indians are those philosophers also who follow the precepts of Boutta (Buddha), whom they honour as a god on account of his extraordinary sanctity." (Clement of Alexandria, "The Stromata, or Miscellanies" Book I,

Chapter XV).

"Thus philosophy, a thing of the highest utility, flourished in antiquity among the barbarians, shedding its light over the nations. And afterwards it came to Greece." (Clement of Alexandria, "The Stromata, or Miscellanies").

To clarify what "philosophy" was transmitted from India to Greece, we turn to the historians Hippolytus and Epiphanius who wrote of Scythianus, a man who had visited India around 50 A.D. They report; "He brought 'the doctrine of the Two Principles.'" According to these writers, Scythianus' pupil Terebinthus called himself a Buddha. Some scholars suggest it was he that traveled to the area of Babylon and transmitted his knowledge to Mani, who later founded Manichaeism.

Adding to the possibility of Eastern influence, we have accounts of the Apostle Thomas' attempt to convert the people of Asia-Minor. If the Gnostic gospel bearing his name was truly written by Thomas, it was penned after his return from India, where he also encountered the Buddhist influences.

Ancient church historians mention that Thomas preached to the Parthians in Persia, and it is said he was buried in Edessa. Fourth century chronicles attribute the evangelization of India (Asia-Minor or Central Asia) to Thomas.

The texts of the Gospel of Thomas, which some believe predate the four gospels, has a very "Zen-like" or Eastern flavor.

Since it is widely held that the four gospels of Matthew, Mark, Luke, and John have a common reference in the basic text of Mark, it stands to reason that all follow the same general insight and language. If The Gospel of Thomas was written in his absence from the other apostles or if it was the first gospel written, one can assume it was written outside the influences common to the other gospels.

Although the codex found in Egypt is dated to the fourth century, the actual construction of the text of Thomas is placed by most Biblical scholars at about 70–150 A.D. Most agree the time of writing was in the second century A.D.

Following the transmission of the philosophy of "Two Principals," both Manichaeism and Gnosticism retained a dualistic viewpoint. The black-versus-white dualism of Gnosticism came to rest in the evil of the material world and its maker, versus the goodness of the freed soul and the Supreme God with whom it seeks union.

Oddly, the disdain for the material world and its Creator God drove Gnostic theology to far-flung extremes in attitude, beliefs, and actions. Gnostics idolize the serpent in the "Garden of Eden" story. After all, if your salvation hinges on secret knowledge the offer of becoming gods through the knowledge of good and evil sounds wonderful. So powerful was the draw of this "knowledge myth" to the Gnostics that the serpent became linked to Sophia by some sects. This can still be seen today in our medical and veterinarian symbols of serpents on poles, conveying the ancient meanings of knowledge and wisdom.

Genesis 3 (King James Version)

1 Now the serpent was more subtil than any beast of the field which the LORD God had made. And he said unto the woman, Yea, hath God said, Ye shall not eat of every tree of the garden?

2 And the woman said unto the serpent, We may eat of the fruit of the trees of the garden:

3 But of the fruit of the tree which is in the midst of the garden, God hath said, Ye shall not eat of it, neither shall ye touch it, lest ye die.

4 And the serpent said unto the woman, Ye shall not surely die:

5 For God doth know that in the day ye eat thereof, then your eyes shall be opened, and ye shall be as Gods, knowing good and evil.

It is because of their vehement struggle against the Creator God and the search for some transcendent truth, that Gnostics held the people of Sodom in high regard. The people of Sodom sought to "corrupt" the messengers sent by their enemy, the Creator God. Anything done to thwart the Demiurge and his minions was considered valiant.

Genesis 19 (King James Version)

1 And there came two angels to Sodom at even; and Lot sat in the gate of Sodom: and Lot seeing them rose up to meet them; and he bowed himself with his face toward the ground;

2 And he said, Behold now, my lords, turn in, I pray you, into your servant's house, and tarry all night, and wash your feet, and ye shall rise up early, and go on your ways. And they said, Nay; but we will abide in the street all night.

3 And he pressed upon them greatly; and they turned in unto him, and entered into his house; and he made them a feast, and did bake unleavened bread, and they did eat.

4 But before they lay down, the men of the city, even the men of Sodom, compassed the house round, both old and young, all the people from every quarter:

5 And they called unto Lot, and said unto him, Where are the men which came in to thee this night? bring them out unto us, that we may know them.

6 And Lot went out at the door unto them, and shut the door after him,

7 And said, I pray you, brethren, do not so wickedly.

8 Behold now, I have two daughters which have not known man; let me, I pray you, bring them out unto you, and do ye to them as is good in your eyes: only unto these men do nothing; for therefore came they under the shadow of my roof.

9 And they said, Stand back. And they said again, This one fellow came in to sojourn, and he will needs be a judge: now will we deal worse with thee, than with them. And they pressed sore upon the man, even Lot, and came near to break the door.

10 But the men put forth their hand, and pulled Lot into the house to them, and shut to the door.

To modern Christians, the idea of admiring the serpent, which we believe was Satan, may seem unthinkable. Supporting the idea of attacking and molesting the angels sent to Sodom to warn of the coming destruction seems appalling; but to Gnostics the real evil was the malevolent entity, the Creator God of this world. To destroy his messengers, as was the case in Sodom, would impede his mission. To obtain knowledge of good and evil, as was offered by the serpent in the garden, would set the captives free.

To awaken the inner knowledge of the true God was the battle. The material world was designed to prevent the awakening by entrapping, confusing, and distracting the spirit of man. The aim of Gnosticism was the spiritual awakening and freedom of man.

Gnostics, in the age of the early church, would preach to converts (novices) about this awakening, saying the novice must awaken the God within himself and see the trap that was the material world. Salvation came from the recognition or knowledge contained in this spiritual awakening.

Not all people are ready or willing to accept the Gnosis. Many are bound to the material world and are satisfied to be only as and where they are. These have mistaken the Creator God for the Supreme God and do not know there is anything beyond the Creator God or the material existence. These people know only the lower or earthly wisdom and not the higher wisdom above the Creator God. They are referred to as "dead."

Gnostic sects split primarily into two categories. Both branches held that those who were truly enlightened could no longer be influenced by the material world. Both divisions of Gnosticism believed that their spiritual journey could not be impeded by the material realm since the two were not only separate but in opposition. Such an attitude influenced some Gnostics toward Stoicism, choosing to abstain from the world, and others toward Epicureanism, choosing to indulge.

Major schools fell into two categories; those who rejected the material world of the Creator God, and those who rejected the laws of the Creator God. For those who rejected the world the Creator God had spawned, overcoming the material world was accomplished by partaking of as little of the world and its pleasures as possible. These followers lived very stark and ascetic lives, abstaining from meat, sex, marriage, and all things that would entice them to remain in the material realm. Other schools believed it was their duty to simply defy the Creator God and all laws that he had proclaimed. Since the Creator God had been identified as Jehovah, God of the Jews, these followers set about to break every law held dear by Christians and Jews.

As human nature is predisposed to do, many Gnostics took up the more wanton practices, believing that nothing done in their earthly bodies would affect their spiritual lives. Whether it was excesses in sex, alcohol, food, or any other assorted debaucheries, the Gnostics were safe within their faith, believing nothing spiritually bad could come of their earthly adventures.

The actions of the Gnostics are mentioned by early Church leaders. One infamous Gnostic school is actually mentioned in the Bible, as we will read later.

The world was out of balance, inferior, and corrupt. The spirit was perfect and intact. It was up to the Gnostics to tell the story, explain the error, and awaken the world to the light of truth. The Supreme God had provided a vehicle to help in their effort. He had created a teacher of light and truth.

Since the time of Sophia's mistaken creation of the Archons, there was an imbalance in the cosmos. The Supreme God began to re-establish the balance by producing Christ to teach and save man. That left only Sophia, now in a fallen and bound state, along with the Demiurge, and the Archons to upset the cosmic equation. In this theology one might loosely equate the Supreme God to the New Testament Christian God, Demiurge to Satan, the Archons to demons, the pleroma to heaven, and Sophia to the creative or regenerative force of the Holy Spirit. This holds up well except for one huge problem. If the Jews believed that Jehovah created all things, and the Gnostic believed that the Demiurge created all things, then to the Gnostic mind, the Demiurge must be Old Testament god, Jehovah, and that made Jehovah their enemy.

For those who seek that which is beyond the material world and its flawed creator, the Supreme God has sent Messengers of Light to awaken the divine spark of the Supreme God within us. This part of us will call to the True God as deep calls to deep. The greatest and most perfect Messenger of Light was the Christ. He is also referred to as The Good, Christ, Messiah, and The Word. He came to reveal the Divine Light to us in the form of knowledge.

According to the Gnostics, Christ came to show us our own divine spark and to awaken us to the illusion of the material world and its flawed maker. He came to show us the way back to the divine Fullness (The Supreme God). The path to enlightenment was the knowledge sleeping within each of us. Christ came to show us the Christ spirit living in each of us. Individual ignorance or the refusal to awaken our internal divine spark was the only original sin. Christ was the only Word spoken by God that could awaken us. Christ was also the embodiment of the Word itself. He was part of the original transmission from the Supreme God that took form on the earth to awaken the soul of man so that man might search beyond the material world.

One Gnostic view of the Incarnation was "docetic," which is an early heretical position that Jesus was never actually present in the flesh, but only appeared to be human. He was a spiritual being and his human appearance was only an illusion. Of course, the title of "heretical" can only be decided by the controlling authority of the time. In this case it was the church that was about to emerge under the rule of the emperor Constantine.

Most Gnostics held that the Christ spirit indwelt the earthly Jesus at the time of his baptism by John, at which time Jesus received the name, and thus the power, of the Lord or Supreme God.

The Christ spirit departed from Jesus' body before his death. These two viewpoints remove the idea of God sacrificing himself as an atonement for the sins of man. The idea of atonement was not necessary in Gnostic theology since it was knowledge and not sacrifice that set one free.

Since there was a distinction in Gnosticism between the man Jesus and the Light of Christ that came to reside within him, it is not contrary to Gnostic beliefs that Mary Magdalene could have been the consort and wife of Jesus. Neither would it have been blasphemous for them to have had children.

Various sects of Gnosticism stressed certain elements of their basic theology. Each had its head teachers and its special flavor of beliefs. One of the oldest types was the Syrian Gnosticism. It existed around 120 A.D. In contrast to other sects, the Syrian lacked much of the embellished mythology of Aeons, Archons, and angels.

The fight between the Supreme God and the Creator God was not eternal, though there was strong opposition to Jehovah, the Creator God. He was considered to have been the last of the seven angels who created this world out of divine material which emanated from the Supreme God. The Demiurge attempted to create man, but only created a miserable worm which the Supreme God had to save by giving it the spark of divine life. Thus, man was born.

According to this sect, Jehovah, the Creator God, must not be worshiped. The Supreme God calls us to his service and presence through Christ his Son. They pursued only the unknowable Supreme God and sought to obey the Supreme Deity by abstaining from eating meat and from marriage and sex, and by leading an ascetic life. The symbol of Christ was the serpent, who attempted to free Adam and Eve from their ignorance and entrapment to the Creator God.

Another Gnostic school was the Hellenistic or Alexandrian School. These systems absorbed the philosophy and concepts of the Greeks, and the Semitic nomenclature was replaced by Greek names. The cosmology and myth had grown out of proportion and appear to our eyes to be unwieldy. Yet, this school produced two great thinkers, Basilides and Valentinus. Though born at Antioch, in Syria, Basilides founded his school in Alexandria around the year A.D. 130, where it survived for several centuries.

Valentinus first taught at Alexandria and then in Rome. He established the largest Gnostic movement around A.D. 160. This movement was founded on an elaborate mythology and a system of sexual duality of male and female interplay, both in its deities and its savior.

Tertullian wrote that between 135 A.D. and 160 A.D. Valentinus, a prominent Gnostic, had great influence in the Christian church. Valentinus ascended in church hierarchy and became a candidate for the office of bishop of Rome, the office that quickly evolved into that of Pope. He lost the election by a narrow margin. Even though Valentinus was outspoken about his Gnostic slant on Christianity, he was a respected member of the Christian community until his death and was probably a practicing bishop in a church of lesser status than the one in Rome.

The main platform of Gnosticism was the ability to transcend the material world through the possession of privileged and directly imparted knowledge. Following this doctrine, Valentinus claimed to have been instructed by a direct disciple of one of Jesus' apostles, a man by the name of Theodas.

Valentinus is considered by many to be the father of modern Gnosticism. His vision of the faith is summarized by G.R.S. Mead in the book "Fragments of a Faith Forgotten."

"The Gnosis in his hands is trying to embrace everything, even the most dogmatic formulation of the traditions of the Master. The great popular movement and its incomprehensibilities were recognized by Valentinus as an integral part of the mighty outpouring; he labored to weave all together, external, and internal, into one piece, devoted his life to the task, and doubtless only at his death perceived that for that age he was attempting the impossible. None but the very few could ever appreciate the ideal of the man, much less understand it." (Fragments of a Faith Forgotten, p. 297)

Gnostic theology seemed to vacillate from polytheism to pantheism to dualism to monotheism, depending on the teacher and how he viewed and stressed certain areas of their creation myths. Marcion, a Gnostic teacher, espoused differences between the God of the New Testament and the God of the Old Testament, claiming they were two separate entities. According to Marcion, the New Testament God was a good true God while the Old Testament God was an evil angel. Although this may be a heresy, it pulled his school back into monotheism. The church, however, disowned him.

Syneros and Prepon, disciples of Marcion, postulated three different entities, carrying their teachings from monotheism into polytheism in one stroke. In their system the opponent of the good God was not the God of the Jews, but Eternal Matter, which was the source of all evil. Matter, in this system became a principal creative force. Although it was created imperfect, it could also create, having the innate intelligence of the "world soul."

Of all the Gnostic schools or sects the most famous is the Antinomian School. Believing that the Creator God, Jehovah, was evil, they sat out to disrupt all things connected to the Jewish God. This included his laws. It was considered their duty to break any law of morality, diet, or conduct given by the Jewish God, who they considered the evil Creator God. The leader of the sect was called Nicolaites. The sect existed in Apostolic times and is mentioned in the Bible.

Revelation 2 (King James Version)

5 Remember therefore from whence thou art fallen, and repent, and do the first works; or else I will come unto thee quickly, and will remove thy candlestick out of his place, except thou repent.

6 But this thou hast, that thou hatest the deeds of the Nicolaitanes, which I also hate.

Revelation 2 (King James Version)

14 But I have a few things against thee, because thou hast there them that hold the doctrine of Balaam, who taught Balac to cast a stumbling block before the children of Israel, to eat things sacrificed unto idols, and to commit fornication.

15 So hast thou also them that hold the doctrine of the Nicolaitanes, which thing I hate.

16 Repent; or else I will come unto thee quickly and will fight against them with the sword of my mouth.

One of the leaders of the Nocolaitanes, according to Origen, was Carpocrates, whom Tertullian called a magician and a fornicator. Carpocretes taught that one could only escape the cosmic powers by discharging one's obligations to them and disregarding their laws. The Christian church fathers, St. Justin, Irenaeus, and Eusebius wrote that the reputation of these men (the Nicolaitanes), brought infamy upon the whole race of Christians.

Although Gnostic sects varied, they had certain points in common. These commonalities included salvation through special knowledge, and the fact that the world was corrupt as it was created by an evil God.

According to Gnostic theology, nothing can come from the material world that is not flawed. Because of this, Gnostics did not believe that Christ could have been a corporeal being. Thus, there must be some separation or distinction between Jesus, as a man, and

Christ, as a spiritual being born from the Supreme, unrevealed, and eternal God.

To closer examine this theology, we turn to Valentinus, the driving force of early Gnosticism, for an explanation. Valentinus divided Jesus Christ into two very distinct parts; Jesus, the man, and Christ, the anointed spiritual messenger of God. These two forces met in the moment of Baptism when the Spirit of God came to rest on Jesus and the Christ power entered his body.

Here Gnosticism runs aground on its own theology, for if the spiritual cannot mingle with the material, then how can the Christ spirit inhabit a body? The result of the dichotomy was a schism within Gnosticism. Some held to the belief that the specter of Jesus was simply an illusion produced by Christ himself to enable him to do his work on earth. It was not real, not matter, not corporeal, and did not actually exist as a physical body would. Others came to believe that Jesus must have been a specially prepared vessel and was the perfect human body formed by the very essence of the Pleroma (heaven). It was this path of thought that allowed Jesus to continue as human, lover, and father.

Jesus, the man, became a vessel containing the Light of God, called Christ. In the Gnostic view we all could and should become Christs, carrying the Truth and Light of God. We are all potential vehicles of the same Spirit that Jesus held within him when he was awakened to the Truth.

The suffering and death of Jesus then took on much less importance in the Gnostic view, as Jesus was simply part of the corrupt world and was suffering the indignities of this world as any man would. Therefore, from their viewpoint, he could have been married and been a father without disturbing Gnostic theology in the least.

The Gnostic texts seem to divide man into parts, although at times the divisions are somewhat unclear. The divisions alluded to may include the soul, which is the will of man; the spirit, which is depicted as wind or air (pneuma) and contains the holy spark that is the spirit of God in man; and the material human form, the body.

The mind of man sits as a mediator between the soul, or will, and the spirit, which is connected to God.

Without the light of the truth, the spirit is held captive by the Demiurge, which enslaves man. This entrapment is called "sickness." It is this sickness that the Light came to heal and then to set us free. The third part of man, his material form, was considered a weight, an anchor, and a hindrance, keeping man attached to the corrupted earthly realm.

As we read the text, we must realize that Gnosticism conflicted with traditional Christianity. Overall theology can rise and fall upon small words and terms. If Jesus was not God, his death and thus his atonement meant nothing. His suffering meant nothing. Even the resurrection meant nothing, if one's view of Jesus was that he was not human to begin with, as was true with some Gnostics.

For the Gnostics, resurrection of the dead was unthinkable since flesh as well as all matter is destined to perish. According to Gnostic theology, there was no resurrection of the flesh, but only of the soul. How the soul would be resurrected was explained differently by various Gnostic groups, but all denied the resurrection of the body. To the enlightened Gnostic the actual person was the spirit who used the body as an instrument to survive in the material world but did not identify with it. This belief is echoed in the Gospel of Thomas.

29. Jesus said: If the flesh came into being because of spirit, it is a marvel, but if spirit came into being because of the body, it would be a marvel of marvels. I marvel indeed at how great wealth has taken up residence in this poverty.

Owing to the Gnostic belief of such a separation of spirit and body, it was thought that the Christ spirit within the body of Jesus departed the body before the crucifixion. Others said the body was an illusion and the crucifixion was a sham perpetrated by an eternal spirit on the men that sought to kill it. Lastly, some suggested that

Jesus deceived the soldiers into thinking he was dead. The resurrection under this circumstance became a lie which allowed Jesus to escape and live on in anonymity, hiding, living as a married man, and raising a family until his natural death.

Think of the implications to the orthodox Christian world if the spirit of God departed from Jesus as it fled and laughed as the body was crucified. This is the implication of the Gnostic interpretation of the death of Jesus when he cries out, "My power, my power, why have you left me," as the Christ spirit left his body before his death. What are the ramifications to the modern Christian if the Creator God, the Demiurge, is more evil than his creation? Can a Creation rise above its creator? Is it possible for man to find the spark within himself that calls to the Supreme God and free himself of his evil creator?

Although, in time, the creation myth and other Gnostic differences began to be swept under the rug, it was the division between Jesus and the Christ spirit that put them at odds with the emerging orthodox church. At the establishment of the doctrine of the trinity, the mainline church firmly set a divide between themselves and the Gnostics.

To this day there is a battle raging in the Christian world as believers and seekers attempt to reconcile today's Christianity to the sect of the early Christian church called, "Gnosticism."

Information on the Apocalypse of Adam

Bentley Layton writes, "The Revelation of Adam ('Apocalypse of Adam') tells the gnostic myth from the creation of Eve down to the savior's final advent and the ultimate damnation of non-gnostic Christianity. The story line seems to be based primarily on the myth rather than Genesis. An important role is played by angels whose names are known from highly developed works such as [the Egyptian Gospel and Zostrianos]; this may indicate that a sophisticated form of the myth is presupposed. Yet in [the Revelation of Adam] the tale is abbreviated to the point of obscurity; a single biblical term ('god') is used, for example, to describe both the satanic creator **(Sakla, also called Ialdabaoth, Yaldabaoth or Yaldaboth)** and the ineffable parent. No distinctive elements of non-gnostic Christianity occur in the work, leading some scholars to regard [the Revelation of Adam] as textbook evidence for the existence of non-Christian, i.e. Jewish, gnostic religion; such scholars are obliged to minimize its connection with other, more obviously Christian, versions of the gnostic myth." (The Gnostic Scriptures, p. 52)

Birger A. Pearson writes, "This final act of redemption [by the 'Illuminator of Knowledge'] is disturbed in the text by what appears to be a lengthy interpolation (77,18-83,4) in which thirteen kingdoms present different erroneous notions of who the Illuminator is. Reflected in this passage are various mythic traditions found in Greco-Roman religious lore. Only the 'generation without a king over it' knows him and the gnosis that he brings ... This interpolation disturbs a pattern of statements regarding the Illuminator that some scholars have taken as evidence of Christian influence. This pattern is rooted in biblical literature dealing with the suffering and exaltation of a righteous person (for example, Isaiah 52-53; Wisdom 1-6). ... This pattern of events dealing with the Gnostic savior correspond to the salvation history of Seth: Threatened with destruction by flood and fire, they are rescued by heavenly intervention. In the final catastrophe, a manifestation of Seth suffers with his seed, and final vindication and victory is achieved. This is intelligible without any reference to Jesus Christ or Christianity." (Ancient Gnosticism, pp. 72-73)

Madeleine Scopello writes, "The Revelation of Adam has probably been the object of redactional attention. Charles W. Hedrick sees two distinct redactional sources in the composition of the treatise; Françoise Morard, on the other hand, underscores the coherence of the text. There is no agreement among scholars about the background of this apocalypse. Is it a Jewish text that offers a polemic against mainstream Judaism? Is it a pre-Christian Gnostic text that has been influenced by Jewish apocalypticism and has adapted traditional apocalyptic themes to Gnostic thought? Is it possible to distinguish in it any Christian references, especially in the description of the third illuminator? The date of the text can be ascribed to the end of the first century or the beginning of the second; interpolations, particularly the hymnic section of stories of the origin of the illuminator, can be dated somewhat later." (The Nag Hammadi Scriptures, p. 345)

Apocalypse of Adam

Translated by George W. MacRae

The revelation which Adam taught his son Seth in the seven hundreth year, saying:

Listen to my words, my son Seth. When God had created me out of the earth, along with Eve, your mother, I went about with her in a glory which she had seen in the aeon from which we had come forth. She taught me a word of knowledge of the eternal God. And we resembled the great eternal angels, for we were higher than the god who had created us and the powers with him, whom we did not know.

Then God, the ruler of the aeons and the powers, divided us in wrath. Then we became two aeons. And the glory in our heart(s) left us, me and your mother Eve, along with the first knowledge that breathed within us. And it (glory) fled from us; it entered into [...] great [...] which had come forth, not from this aeon from which we had come forth, I and Eve your mother. But it (knowledge) entered into the seed of great aeons. For this reason I myself have called you by the name of that man who is the seed of the great generation or from whom (it comes). After those days, the eternal knowledge of the God of truth withdrew from me and your mother Eve. Since that time, we learned about dead things, like men. Then we recognized the God who had created us. For we were not strangers to his powers. And we served him in fear and slavery. And after these things, we became darkened in our heart(s). Now I slept in the thought of my heart.

And I saw three men before me whose likeness I was unable to recognize, since they were not the powers of the God who had created us. They surpassed [...] glory, and [...] men [...] saying to me,

"Arise, Adam, from the sleep of death, and hear about the aeon and the seed of that man to whom life has come, who came from you and from Eve, your wife."

When I had heard these words from the great men who were standing before me, then we sighed, I and Eve, in our heart(s). And the Lord, the God who had created us, stood before us. He said to us, "Adam, why were you (both) sighing in your hearts? Do you not know that I am the God who created you? And I breathed into you a spirit of life as a living soul." Then darkness came upon our eyes.

Then the God who created us, created a son from himself and Eve, your mother. I knew sweet desire for your mother, for [...] in the thought of my [...] I knew a sweet desire for your mother. Then the vigor of our eternal knowledge was destroyed in us, and weakness pursued us. Therefore the days of our life became few. For I knew that I had come under the authority of death.

Now then, my son Seth, I will reveal to you the things which those men whom I saw before me at first revealed to me: after I have completed the times of this generation and the years of the generation have been accomplished, then [...] slave [...]. (p.68 blank)

For rain-showers of God the almighty will be poured forth, so that he might destroy all flesh [of God the almighty, so that he might destroy all flesh] from the earth on account of the things that it seeks after, along with those from the seed of the men to whom passed the life of the knowledge which came from me and Eve, your mother. For they were strangers to him. Afterwards, great angels will come on high clouds, who will bring those men into the place where the spirit of life dwells [...] glory [...] there, [...] come from heaven to earth. Then the whole multitude of flesh will be left behind in the waters.

Then God will rest from his wrath. And he will cast his power upon the waters, and he will give power to his sons and their wives by means of the ark along with the animals, whichever he pleased, and the birds of heaven, which he called and released upon the earth. And God will say to Noah - whom the generations will call 'Deucalion' - "Behold, I have protected <you> in the ark, along with your wife and your sons and their wives and their animals and the birds of heaven, which you called and released upon the earth. Therefore I will give the earth to you - you and your sons. In kingly fashion you will rule over it - you and your sons. And no seed will come from you of the men who will not stand in my presence in another glory."

Then they will become as the cloud of the great light. Those men will come who have been cast forth from the knowledge of the great aeons and the angels. They will stand before Noah and the aeons. And God will say to Noah, "Why have you departed from what I told you? You have created another generation so that you might scorn my power." Then Noah will say, "I shall testify before your might that the generation of these men did not come from me nor from my sons. [...] knowledge.

And he will [...] those men and bring them into their proper land, and build them a holy dwelling place. And they will be called by that name and dwell there six hundred years in a knowledge of imperishability. And the angels of the great Light will dwell with them. No foul deed will dwell in their heart(s), but only the knowledge of God.

Then Noah will divide the whole earth among his sons, Ham and Japheth and Shem. He will say to them, "My sons, listen to my words. Behold, I have divided the earth among you. But serve him in fear and slavery all the days of your life. Let not your seed depart from the face of God the Almighty. [...] I and your [...] son of Noah, "My seed will be pleasing before you and before your power. Seal it by your strong hand, with fear and commandment, so that the whole seed which came forth from me may not be inclined away from you and God the Almighty, but it will serve in humility and fear of its knowledge."

Then others from the seed of Ham and Japheth will come, four hundred thousand men, and enter into another land and sojourn with those men who came forth from the great eternal knowledge. For the shadow of their power will protect those who have sojourned with them from every evil thing and every unclean desire. Then the seed of Ham and Japheth will form twelve kingdoms, and their seed also will enter into the kingdom of another people.

Then [...] will take counsel [...] who are dead, of the great aeons of imperishability. And they will go to Sakla, their God. They will go in to the powers, accusing the great men who are in their glory.

They will say to Sakla, "What is the power of these men who stood in your presence, who were taken from the seed of Ham and Japheth, who will number four hundred <thousand> men? They have been received into another aeon from which they had come forth, and they have overturned all the glory of your power and the dominion of your hand. For the seed of Noah through his sons has done all your will, and (so have) all the powers in the aeons over which your might rules, while both those men and the ones who are sojourners in their glory have not done your will. But they have turned (aside) your whole throng."

Then the god of the aeons will give them (some) of those who serve him [...]. They will come upon that land where the great men will be who have not been defiled, nor will be defiled, by any desire. For their soul did not come from a defiled hand, but it came from a great commandment of an eternal angel. Then fire and sulphur and asphalt will be cast upon those men, and fire and (blinding) mist will come over those aeons, and the eyes of the powers of the illuminators will be darkened, and the aeons will not see them in those days. And great clouds of light will descend, and other clouds of light will come down upon them from the great aeons.

Abrasax and Sablo and Gamaliel will descend and bring those men out of the fire and the wrath, and take them above the aeons and the rulers of the powers, and take them away [...] of life [...] and take them away [...] aeons [...] dwelling place of the great [...] there, with the holy angels and the aeons. The men will be like those angels, for they are not strangers to them. But they work in the imperishable seed.

Once again, for the third time, the illuminator of knowledge will pass by in great glory, in order to leave (something) of the seed of Noah and the sons of Ham and Japheth - to leave for himself fruit-bearing trees. And he will redeem their souls from the day of death. For the whole creation that came from the dead earth will be under the authority of death. But those who reflect upon the knowledge of the eternal God in their heart(s) will not perish. For they have not received spirit from this kingdom alone, but they have received (it) from a [...] eternal angel. [...] illuminator [...] will come upon [...] that is dead [...] of Seth. And he will perform signs and wonders in order to scorn the powers and their ruler.

Then the god of the powers will be disturbed, saying, "What is the power of this man who is higher than we?" Then he will arouse a great wrath against that man. And the glory will withdraw and dwell in holy houses which it has chosen for itself. And the powers will not see it with their eyes, nor will they see the illuminator either. Then they will punish the flesh of the man upon whom the holy spirit came.

Then the angels and all the generations of the powers will use the name in error, asking, "Where did it (the error) come from?" or "Where did the words of deception, which all the powers have failed to discover, come from?"

Now the first kingdom says of him that he came from [...]. A spirit [...] to heaven. He was nourished in the heavens. He received the glory of that one and the power. He came to the bosom of his mother. And thus he came to the water.

And the second kingdom says about him that he came from a great prophet. And a bird came, took the child who was born, and brought him onto a high mountain. And he was nourished by the bird of heaven. An angel came forth there. He said to him "Arise! God has given glory to you." He received glory and strength. And thus he came to the water.

The third kingdom says of him that he came from a virgin womb. He was cast out of his city, he and his mother. He was brought to a desert place. He was nourished there. He came and received glory and strength. And thus he came to the water.

The fourth kingdom says of him that he came from a virgin. [...] Solomon sought her, he and Phersalo and Sauel and his armies, which had been sent out. Solomon himself sent his army of demons to seek out the virgin. And they did not find the one whom they sought, but the virgin who was given them. It was she whom they fetched. Solomon took her. The virgin became pregnant and gave birth to the child there. She nourished him on a border of the desert.

When he had been nourished, he received glory and power from the seed from which he was begotten. And thus he came to the water.

And the fifth kingdom says of him that he came from a drop from heaven. He was thrown into the sea. The abyss received him, gave birth to him, and brought him to heaven. He received glory and power. And thus he came to the water.

And the sixth kingdom says that [...] down to the aeon which is below, in order to gather flowers. She became pregnant from the desire of the flowers. She gave birth to him in that place. The angels of the flower garden nourished him. He received glory there, and power. And thus he came to the water.

And the seventh kingdom says of him that he is a drop. It came from heaven to earth. Dragons brought him down to caves. He became a child. A spirit came upon him and brought him on high to the place where the drop had come forth. He received glory and power there. And thus he came to the water.

And the eighth kingdom says of him that a cloud came upon the earth and enveloped a rock. He came from it. The angels who were above the cloud nourished him. He received glory and power there. And thus he came to the water.

And the ninth kingdom says of him that from the nine Muses one separated away. She came to a high mountain and spent (some) time seated there, so that she desired herself alone in order to become androgynous. She fulfilled her desire and became pregnant from her desire. He was born. The angels who were over the desire nourished him. And he received glory there, and power. And thus he came to the water.

The tenth kingdom says of him that his god loved a cloud of desire. He begot him in his hand and cast upon the cloud above him (some) of the drop, and he was born. He received glory and power there. And thus he came to the water.

And the eleventh kingdom says that the father desired his own daughter. She herself became pregnant from her father. She cast [...] tomb out in the desert. The angel nourished him there. And thus he came to the water.

The twelfth kingdom says of him that he came from two illuminators. He was nourished there. He received glory and power. And thus he came to the water.

And the thirteenth kingdom says of him that every birth of their ruler is a word. And this word received a mandate there. He received glory and power. And thus he came to the water, in order that the desire of those powers might be satisfied.

But the generation without a king over it says that God chose him from all the aeons. He caused a knowledge of the undefiled one of truth to come to be in him. He said, "Out of a foreign air, from a great aeon, the great illuminator came forth. And he made the generation of those men whom he had chosen for himself shine, so that they could shine upon the whole aeon"

Then the seed, those who will receive his name upon the water and (that) of them all, will fight against the power. And a cloud of darkness will come upon them.

Then the peoples will cry out with a great voice, saying, "Blessed is the soul of those men because they have known God with a knowledge of the truth! They shall live forever, because they have not been corrupted by their desire, along with the angels, nor have they accomplished the works of the powers, but they have stood in his presence in a knowledge of God like light that has come forth from fire and blood.

"But we have done every deed of the powers senselessly. We have boasted in the transgression of all our works. We have cried against the God of truth because all his works [...] is eternal. These are against our spirits. For now we have known that our souls will die the death."

Then a voice came to them, saying "Micheu and Michar and Mnesinous, who are over the holy baptism and the living water, why were you crying out against the living God with lawless voices and tongues without law over them, and souls full of blood and foul deeds? You are full of works that are not of the truth, but your ways are full of joy and rejoicing. Having defiled the water of life, you have drawn it within the will of the powers to whom you have been given to serve them.

"And your thought is not like that of those men whom you persecute [...] desire [...]. Their fruit does not wither. But they will be known up to the great aeons, because the words they have kept, of the God of the aeons, were not committed to the book, nor were they written. But angelic (beings) will bring them, whom all the generations of men will not know. For they will be on a high mountain, upon a rock of truth. Therefore they will be named "The Words of Imperishability and Truth," for those who know the eternal God in wisdom of knowledge and teaching of angels forever, for he knows all things."

These are the revelations which Adam made known to Seth, his son, And his son taught his seed about them. This is the hidden knowledge of Adam, which he gave to Seth, which is the holy baptism of those who know the eternal knowledge through those born of the word and the imperishable illuminators, who came from the holy seed: Yesseus, Mazareus, Yessedekeus, the Living Water.

Information on the
First and Second Apocalypse of James

-Preface-

The First Apocalypse of James and the Second Apocalypse of James are Gnostic texts, which are both over 1500 years old. The scrolls or books containing these works are brittle and fragmented. Pieces of the texts are missing. At times, it is difficult to follow the message and dialog. In a few instances, it is unclear as to who is speaking and whom they are addressing. Great attention was given to add notes and render the text in such a way as to make it as clear and easy to follow as possible. Therefore, this is not a word for word translation, nor even a sentence-by-sentence translation. It is a translation that attempts to convey each of the writer's thoughts and messages in the most complete, direct and understandable form. In this manner, it was hoped the difficulties of alien and complex theology, and language could be more easily overcome. To further aid in the reader's understanding of Gnostic theology a brief overview of Gnosticism is included within the introduction of the First Apocalypse of James. The same theology will apply to both texts of James. Although the text may be broken and difficult in places, it is amazingly rich in the Gnostic beliefs of the time and thus gives us a view into a "Christianity" which is part of our history, and which influenced the modern faith.

Introduction to
The First Apocalypse of James

The First Apocalypse of James was written in the Coptic language around the second half of the third century CE. It is regarded as part of the New Testament apocrypha. The text was first discovered in the last part of the month of December in 1945. It was found among 52 other Gnostic Christian texts contained in 13 codices or scrolls. The discovery was made by two peasant Egyptian brothers as they dug for fertilizer near their home. While digging in the rich soil around the Jabal al-Ṭārif caves near present-day Hamra Dom in Upper Egypt, they found several papyri in a large earthenware vessel. The find of these codices came to be known as the Nag Hammadi library because of their proximity to the Egyptian town of Nag Hammadi, which was the nearest major settlement.

The brothers wanted to make money by selling the manuscripts, but when they brought some of the scrolls home their mother burned several of the manuscripts. One source indicates she burned them as kindling, while another source claims she was superstitious and worried that the writing might be dangerous.

News of the discovery appeared gradually as the brothers tried to sell certain scrolls. The full significance of the new find was not immediately apparent until sometime after the initial discovery. As more of the scrolls were examined it was revealed that the find included a large number of primary Gnostic Gospels, some of which had never been seen before.

In 1946, the brothers became involved in a feud, and left the manuscripts with a Coptic priest. In October of that year a codex, now called codex lll, was sold to the Coptic Museum in Old Cairo. The resident Coptologist and religious historian Jean Doresse realized the significance of the artifact and published the first reference to it in 1948.

After Egypt's political revolution in 1952, these texts were handed to the Coptic Museum in Cairo where they were declared national property.

The Apocalypse of James, found within the collection of discovered scrolls, seems to be founded on Valentinian Gnosticism, although it does seem to have element of Sethian Gnosticism also. The name, Adonaios comes up in the text. He is an offspring of Yaldaboth, the Demiurge and is one of the twelve Powers created or spawned by Yaldaboth. Adonaios is mentioned in The Second Treatise of the Great Seth.

One the great Gnostic schools was the Hellenistic or Alexandrian School. The system absorbed the philosophy and concepts of the Greeks, and the Semitic nomenclature was replaced by Greek names. The cosmology and myth had grown out of proportion and appear to our eyes to be unwieldy. Yet, this school produced two great thinkers, Basilides and Valentinus. Though born at Antioch, in Syria, Basilides founded his school in Alexandria around the year A.D. 130, where it survived for several centuries.

Epiphanius (ca. 390) wrote that he learned through word of mouth that Valentinus was born in Phrebonis in the Nile Delta, and thus was a native of Paralia in Egypt. His sources were not confirmed as reliable and the information is speculative. Valentinus received his Greek education in nearby Alexandria, an important and metropolitan center of early Christianity. There he may have heard the Christian philosopher Basilides. Valentinus was familiar with Hellenistic Middle Platonism and the culture of Hellenized Jews like the great Alexandrian Jewish allegorist and philosopher Philo.

Valentinus first taught at Alexandria and then in Rome. He established the largest Gnostic movement around A.D. 160. This movement was founded on an elaborate mythology and a system of sexual duality of male and female interplay, both in its deities and its savior.

Tertullian stated that between 135 A.D. and 160 A.D. Valentinus, a prominent Gnostic, had great influence in the Christian church. Valentinus ascended in church hierarchy and became a candidate for the office of bishop of Rome, the office that quickly evolved into that of Pope. He lost the election by a narrow margin. Even though Valentinus was outspoken about his Gnostic slant on Christianity, he was a respected member of the Christian community until his death and was probably a practicing bishop in a church of lesser status than the one in Rome.

The main platform of Gnosticism was the ability of its followers to transcend the material world through the possession of privileged and directly imparted knowledge. Following this doctrine, Valentinus claimed to have been instructed by a direct disciple of one of Jesus' apostles, a man by the name of Theodas.

Valentinus is considered by many to be the father of modern Gnosticism. His vision of the faith is summarized by G.R.S. Mead in the book "Fragments of a Faith Forgotten."

"The Gnosis in his hands is trying to embrace everything, even the most dogmatic formulation of the traditions of the Master. The great popular movement and its incomprehensibilities were recognized by Valentinus as an integral part of the mighty outpouring; he laboured to weave all together, external and internal, into one piece, devoted his life to the task, and doubtless only at his death perceived that for that age he was attempting the impossible. None but the very few could ever appreciate the ideal of the man, much less understand it. "(Fragments of a Faith Forgotten, p. 297)

The mainline or orthodox Christian church had sought to eliminate Gnosticism and destroy all Gnostic documents. There were times in early church history that Gnostics were hunted down and killed for heresy, but these texts were saved and sealed by Gnostics as they attempted to preserve some of their most holy books, and thus they came to us with some of the texts still intact.

The translation of the Nag Hammadi library was completed in the 1970's and the information contained in the cache' would turn Christianity on its head by revealing an unknown history of Christianity and a fight for control of doctrine and the faith. Among the Gnostic works are scriptures such as the Gospel of Thomas, the Gospel of Philip, the Gospel of Truth, and many others. Gnosticism is an undeniable part of the history of Christianity. By both influence and opposition, it has helped shape what we now know as the Christian faith.

The First Apocalypse of James is reasonably well preserved and fairly legible, but there are fragments missing, as the codex was brittle and pieces were broken away from the scroll. The Apocalypse of James should not be confused with the Apocryphon of James, which is a completely different text and was found in the Codex Jung. Another copy of the Apocalypse of James has recently been found in the Codex Tchacos, where it is simply titled 'James'. A Greek copy of the text, dating to the fifth century CE, was discovered in 2017 at Oxford University by Geoffrey Smith and Brent Landau, religious studies scholars at the University of Texas at Austin. It is thought this copy was used in a school environment to teach students to read and write. This is because each word in the document was broken into syllables with a dot mid-line between each syllable. This approach broke each word into smaller parts so the student could read each syllable separately and more easily construct each word.

As the title implies, the text reports to have been written by James, one of the most influential leaders of the early church. The 1st century theologian, Clement of Rome, wrote that James was called the "bishop of bishops, who ruled Jerusalem, the Holy Church of the Hebrews, and all the Churches everywhere." According to this James was over the early Christian Church, which at that time consisted mostly of Jewish converts, although Paul's influence and the coming pagan converts were on the horizon.

The Apocalypse of James is a revelation dialogue between Jesus and James, the man the Lord calls "Brother". In the manuscript, Jesus clarifies the title by explaining that James is a brother in a purely spiritual sense. Jesus identifies his place and essence by saying, "I am an alien, a son of the Father's race". This separates the "race" of the Lord from the human "race" of man and means their very substance is somehow different.

In the text, James knows of the upcoming events of the Lord's suffering and death. The knowledge, along with James' inability to change the upcoming events engenders anxiety and questions. The Lord's gives James secret knowledge in the form of teachings and explanation. This gnosis or knowledge places the Apocalypse of James in the realm of Valentinian Gnosticism.

Gilles Quispel states that for Valentinus, a Gnostic teacher of the second century, Christ is "the Paraclete from the Unknown who reveals…the discovery of the Self, which is the divine spark within you."

The heart of the human problem for the Gnostic is ignorance, sometimes called "sleep," "intoxication," or "blindness." But Jesus redeems man from such ignorance. Stephan Hoeller says that in the Valentinian system "there is no need whatsoever for guilt, for repentance from so-called sin, neither is there a need for a blind belief in vicarious salvation by way of the death of Jesus." Rather, Jesus is savior in the sense of being a "spiritual maker of wholeness" who cures us of our sickness of ignorance.

According to Valentinus, the seeker awakens through knowledge or Gnosis. This secret Gnosis provides the key that is essential for a complete understanding of Jesus' message. The Valentinus doctrine states, "The scriptures are ambiguous and the truth cannot be extracted from them by those who are ignorant of tradition." (Irenaeus Against Heresies 3:2:1). One must be spiritually mature to comprehend the full meaning of the scriptures.

1 Corinthians 2:14 New International Version (NIV)

The person without the Spirit does not accept the things that come from the Spirit of God but considers them foolishness, and cannot understand them because they are discerned only through the Spirit.

According to the Valentinian tradition, Paul and the other apostles revealed these teachings only to those who were 'spiritually mature'. This is the transmission of Gnosis from master to student.

1 Corinthians 2:4-6 New International Version (NIV)

4 My message and my preaching were not with wise and persuasive words, but with a demonstration of the Spirit's power, 5 so that your faith might not rest on human wisdom, but on God's power.

6 We do, however, speak a message of wisdom among the mature, but not the wisdom of this age or of the rulers of this age, who are coming to nothing.

Valentinians believed that God could never be directly observed or experienced. Neither could God be fully understood, directly known, described or explained. He is eternal. He is the origin of all things.

The Godhead manifests itself through a process of unfolding wherein various parts or qualities were manifested, all the while maintaining its unity. In certain instances, the expressions of God in turn had expressions, such as the Christ Spirit or Son, which was an expression or emanation, which in turn had expressions or emanations, like circles within circles.

Valentinians believed that God is androgynous and contained within God was as a male-female dyad. We see this in the fact that the Hebrew word for the Spirit of God was Ruak (Ruach). The word and the spirit (Ruak) were presented in female form. It was through the constraint of language, as the translations went from Hebrew to Greek and from Greek to Latin, that the feminine gender of the Spirit was lost. However, in the beginning she "Brooded" over the waters.

Genesis 1:1-2 Amplified Bible (AMP)

1 In the beginning God (Elohim) created [by forming from nothing] the heavens and the earth. 2 The earth was formless and void or a waste and emptiness, and darkness was upon the face of the deep [primeval ocean that covered the unformed earth]. The Spirit of God was moving (hovering, brooding) over the face of the waters.

In the literal reading, it can be seen that God provides the universe with both male and female energies of form and substance. The feminine aspect of the deity is called Wisdom, Mercy, Silence, Grace and Thought. Silence is God's primordial state of tranquility and self-awareness She is also the active creative thought that gives substance to the powers or states of being, such as "Aeons". The first feminine energy of God is called the Divine Thought.

In some Gnostic systems she is called, Barbelo, the mother of all that is. There are differences concerning the Holy Spirit between various Gnostic groups. Some have the Spirit as a function of Barbelo, while others say it is through Sophia. The variations may depend on where and how the spirit is introduced. For example, according to Valentinus, Sophia gives the spiritual seed to those who hear the true word of He Who Is.

The masculine aspect of God is Depth, Power, Law, and Order. He is also called Ineffable, the All, and First Father. Depth is the most profound aspect of God. It is all-encompassing and can never be fully understood. He is essentially passive, yet when moved to action by his feminine energy, Thought, he gives the universe form. It was through the union of the masculine force of the ALL and Divine Thought that the Christ Spirit was brought forth.

Aeons are beings produced by an emanation of energy, like a fire produces light and heat. In many Gnostic systems, the various emanations of God, who is also known by such names as the One, the Monad, The All, and Depth emanated Aeons such as "Sophia" (wisdom) and Christos (Christ, the Anointed One). In turn, Sophia and Christ also have emanations and thus produced Aeons, Archons, and angels. In different Gnostic systems, these emanations are differently named, classified, and described, but the emanation theory itself is common to all forms of Gnosticism.

The origin of the universe is described as a process of emanation from the Godhead. As a fire does not intend to emanate light, but does so simply because of its nature, so does God emanate and produce. The male and female aspects of the Father, acting in conjunction, manifested themselves in the Son. The Son is depicted by Valentinians as a male-female dyad.

We will see that the Son, the Lord, claimed he is called by many names but God gave him two. These are male and female. But, the female energy or part should not be confused with a female person or being. Jesus tells James that he existed before the feminine. This is because God is unified, God is one, and the "aspects" of God do not exist apart from the oneness of God. Females were produced after the Christ spirit, so says the Son to James. After the Son came into being, he manifested himself in twenty-six spiritual entities or Aeons arranged into male-female pairs. Together they constitute the Fullness (pleroma) of the Godhead.

The Aeons who are manifested by the Son are conceived as having psychological autonomy. They lie within God or the sphere where God resides but are separated from him by a boundary. As a result, they do not know the one who brought them into being. The Aeons sensed that they were incomplete and long to know their origin.

According to Valentinus, all Powers and Aeons were made in pairs. All had a consort that balanced and perfected them. Sophia's consort was Christ. We see how Valentinus may have arrived at this conclusion by looking at the Catholic and Orthodox Bibles and the book of Wisdom, contained in the Apocrypha.

The Book of Wisdom uses personification. The Hebrew word chakmah, like its Greek (sophia) and Latin (sapientia) equivalents, is a noun with feminine gender.

"I will tell you what wisdom is and how she came to be, and I will hide no secrets from you, but I will trace her course from the beginning of creation, and make knowledge of her clear, and I will not pass by the truth" (Wisdom 6:22).

"With you is wisdom, she who knows your works and was present when you made the world; she understands what is pleasing in your sight and what is right according to your commandments" (Wisdom 9:9).

Wisdom is called the "fashioner of all things" (Wisdom 7:22).

She has a spirit that is intelligent, holy, unique, subtle, mobile, clear, unpolluted, distinct, invulnerable, loving the good, keen, irresistible, humane, steadfast, sure, and free from anxiety

(Wisdom 7:22-23).

Even in Proverbs 1-9 Wisdom is spoken of as a woman.

Sophia (Wisdom), the youngest of the Aeons, yearned to know the All, the parent of all beings. She attempted to know and understand him. Some stories have her capturing a divine creative spark from God and using it by herself, without her consort. As a result, she became separated from her consort. According to several Gnostic stories, the consort of Sophia was Christ himself. Being separated from him she fell into a state of deficiency and suffering. In such a state, her creation was deficient and monstrous. He is called the Demiurge, the half-maker, and the craftsman.

Sophia's fall into ignorance produced three creations. The first is "Illusion". This is the belief the material world is all there is. But there is always a deeper feeling there is something else lying beyond. Illusion is characterized by a material existence and suffering. The personification of this state is the Devil.

The second creation of the fallen Sophia is the Soul. It originated as ignorance begins to give way to knowledge. It is personified as the Craftsman or Demiurge who formed the material world. He is a creative force but is deficient and is usually seen as ignorant of his position, ignorant of the All, and lacking Gnosis.

The third creation is the "Spiritual Seed", which is born from her knowledge (gnosis) and is personified in the fallen Sophia herself.

Through the power of Limit, Sophia was divided into two parts. Her higher part was returned to her consort but her lower part was separated from the Fullness into a lower realm along with the deficiency and suffering. This lower realm is the material or physical world.

Valentinians envisioned the universe as series of spheres within spheres. The smallest and center sphere is the physical world or deficiency, where the fallen or lower Sophia was exiled. Enclosing this is a larger sphere of the Fullness (pleroma) where the Aeons are. The Aeons are enclosed within the Son, as his sphere is with the Father and encompasses all things. The largest sphere is where the Son resides with the Father (Depth and Silence).

There is a boundary or limit between God and the pleroma. There is a second boundary or limit between the pleroma and the material world. Just as the pleroma is a product of the Godhead and lies within it, so the realm of deficiency, which is the material world, is a product of the pleroma and is contained in a sphere lying within the sphere of the pleroma. The deficiency arose as result of ignorance and it will only be escaped or dissolved through knowledge (gnosis).

In Gnosticism "Limit" is a power or creation. Where the word "Limit or Boundary" are used, it can be an actual creation with the active ability to cleave, cut, separate, or contain.

Through the mediation of the Son, which is the knowledge of the true Father of All and how all beings were created and connected, the Aeons within the pleroma were given rest. All twenty-six of the Aeons then joined together in celebration and were spontaneously integrated back into the personality of the Son. The fully integrated Son is called the Savior. He is destined to be the male partner or bridegroom of the fallen Sophia. He is surrounded by angels who were brought forth in honor of the Aeons.

The fallen Sophia remained in ignorance, trapped in the fallen material sphere. She continued to suffer the emotional pain of grief, fear and confusion. Because of her confusion and ignorance, she was unable to distinguish what was real and what unreal. In her pain, she began to call out for help. She sought the light and she began to plead for help. Her consort responded. The Savior, and his assisting and attending angels descended through the Limit to her. Through his knowledge (gnosis) of the eternal realm he freed the fallen part of Sophia from her illusion and suffering.

Sophia rejoiced because of her Savior and consort and his angels. In her joy she produced spiritual substances or spiritual seeds in his image (some stories have her producing spiritual seeds in the images of the savior and his angels, others have her producing spiritual seeds in the image of the savior). This spiritual substance or seed are the spirits present in every Christian and collectively make up the spiritual Church. The Savior is the bridegroom of Sophia. In the end times his emanations, the angels, will be the bridegrooms of the spiritual seeds, which are the Christians making up the spiritual church.

In the act of salvation, it is Sophia who sows a spiritual seed in all who hear the message of Jesus. Those who accept and gain Gnosis are spiritual Christians.

Despite the fact that the fallen Sophia was no longer ignorant, the ignorance was not fully dissipated. The spiritual seeds were immature and needed training. For this purpose, the creation of the material world was necessary. The fallen Sophia and the Savior secretly influenced the Demiurge to create the material world in the image of the Fullness. The Demiurge is ignorant of his mother and the All. He thinks that he acts alone and is the only creative force, but he unconsciously acts as her agent.

The Demiurge created the material world and human beings. In addition to a physical body, Valentinians believed that people were composed of a demonic part (chous / dirt, dust), a rational soul (psyche / mind), and a spiritual seed (pneuma / spirit).

Because the Demiurge is the deficient, corrupt, and cruel creator of this world, Gnostic theology has answered many nagging questions, such as why there is suffering, why is there disease, and why do bad things happen to good people.

Human beings were divided into three categories, depending on which of the three natures they exhibited. Valentinus believed that the children of Adam and Eve metaphorically represented the three categories of humans. Cain represented the carnal (choic) Abel represented the animate (psychic), and Seth represented the spiritual (pneumatic).

The ultimate pinnacle of world history came in the ministry of Jesus. Jesus is the physical manifestation of the Son or Savior. Prior to his coming, the true God was unknown. Jesus came to bring knowledge (gnosis) to a suffering humanity that was desperately seeking the true God.

This is why the Old Testament God and New Testament God are so different. The Old Testament God, the Demiurge, was vengeful, jealous and cruel, and the New Testament God, who Jesus was sent to reveal to us, is kind and merciful.

By knowledge, the spiritual seed and their consorts or counterpart, the angels are joined. This union was foreshadowed by the reuniting of Sophia and Christ.

In Valentinian Gnosticism there is a distinction between the human Jesus and the divine Jesus. The human Jesus the son of Mary and Joseph. By grace his body was constructed of the same substance as

Sophia and her spiritual seed. When Jesus was thirty years old, he was baptized by John and as he went down into the water God sent the "Spirit of the Thought of the Father" in the form of a dove and it descended on him and he was born of the virgin spirit. According to Valentinus, this is the true "virgin birth" and resurrection from the dead.

Jesus taught the people in parables, so that only the matured and spiritually awake would understand. He revealed the full and plain truth about the fall of Sophia and the coming restoration of the Fullness only to his closest followers. According to Valentinus, Mary Magdalene was a member of this inner circle. She is seen as an image of the lower Sophia and is described as Jesus' consort in the Gospel of Philip.

The divine Jesus experienced all of the emotions of human beings including grief, fear and confusion in the Garden of Gethsemane but only the body suffered. The son of Mary and Joseph was crucified but the spiritual Jesus did not physically suffer death, for before the body suffered and died the spiritual Jesus ascended.

Following the crucifixion Jesus appeared and taught his disciples about the Father for eighteen months. After his ascension, he appeared in visions. This is how Paul and Valentinus experienced Jesus.

People who receive the knowledge of Jesus' teaching receive a spiritual seed from Sophia that will bear fruit by awakening them from their stupor to a mystical knowledge (gnosis). They recognize their own spiritual nature. With or because of this knowledge they are joined with their angel consorts who accompany the Savior. This is the true resurrection of the dead. It is the spirit that was dead and now resurrected. Resurrections does not take place after death. It must be experienced in the living present.

First, the person spiritually ascends above the realm of the Demiurge and this material world to join with their consort angel, Sophia and the Savior in the higher realm of the Fullness or pleroma. Then, rejoicing with all of the saved, the person is joined with their angel and enters the Fullness. The person continues to have a physical existence in the material world but they are an awakened spirit and are in the world but not of it. They come to understand this physical existence is an illusion to keep men enslaved and asleep.

We have explored an outline of the doctrine and cosmology of Valentinian Gnosticism so we may better understand the book of the Apocalypse of James. The storyline of James has Jesus teaching James regarding the coming crucifixion of Jesus and how the body of the man Jesus will be killed but the Savior, who is the Son, and the Christ Spirit will leave the body before death. Further, Jesus tells of James' soon coming martyrdom.

The Lord tells James he will be martyred and after he departs his body he will encounter "Powers" that will attempt to block his path back to "the Pre-Existent One". These are called toll-collectors, gate-keepers, and other such designators, according to the translation of the text. These beings wish to capture or control the soul for their own purposes. However, the gate-keepers can be controlled or defeated with the proper words. The proper words, terms, and answers are given by the Lord to James with instructions on their use. Properly performed, the knowledge is meant to confuse and misdirect the Powers so that James may avoid their bondage and ascend to the Pre-Existent One.

Twelve Books on the Apocalypse

The teaching given to James indicates salvation is in fact the liberation of the spirit from the earthly plane and fleshly body and the spirit's return to the place of its origin, the eternal beginning and its union with God.

After the Lord instructs James on how to apply the new teaching and knowledge, he then comments on the place of female disciples. The Lord mentions a dispute between James and the other apostles.

The Apocrypha of James was likely written by a Gnostic scholar with the intent of furthering Gnostic teaching. The rejection of an actual bodily or familial relationship between James and Jesus is used as a way of placing the Lord in a separate state, wherein he does not have to possess a fleshly, human body. The Lord tells James they are only spiritual brothers even though the Bible states that James was the brother of Jesus. This distinction and separation of fallen and inferior flesh not being compatible with pure spirit continues the line of Gnostic teachings.

(New International Version: Galatians 1:19 "I saw none of the other apostles--only James, the Lord's brother.") the Catholic and Orthodox doctrine, as well as some Anglicans and Lutherans, teach the perpetual virginity of Mary. Owning to this belief they teach that James and others that are referred to in the Bible as the brothers and sisters of Jesus were not the biological children of Mary, but were cousins of Jesus or step-brothers and step-sisters of Jesus by way of his mother's husband, Joseph from Joseph's previous marriage.

James died in martyrdom between 62 and 69 A.D., and was an important figure of the Apostolic Age. He was also referred to as James the Just, or James, brother of the Lord.

James is referred to as "James the Just", which was a Christian designation. It indicates the book was written after the title was established by the followers of Jesus. Here we see the influence of the Jewish Christian community.

Besides being a Gnostic gospel, one of the most curious features of the First Apocalypse of James is that the date of writing of the original text indicates it was written after the text of The Second Apocalypse of James, which we will examine later in this book.

Now, let us look into the fascinating text titled, The Apocalypse of James.

The First Apocalypse of James

The Lord himself spoke to me saying: "Look, this is the completion of my redemption. I have given you a sign of all these things, my brother, James. I called you my brother for a reason. For although you are not my earthly brother I know you and I know the things concerning you. Because of this I give you a sign so that you will hear and understand."

"Nothing existed except He Who Is. He cannot be named. He cannot be described. Likewise, I cannot be named, for I am from He Who Is. Yet, I have been given a great number of names, but two names are from He Who Is. And now I stand before you.

Twelve Books on the Apocalypse

(Author's Note: In the beginning, there was nothing but the indescribable God, called "He Who Is" and "The All". Gnostic theology describes God bringing forth from himself a female power. From these two came The Christ Spirit, who was born of both male and female energies.)

You asked me about the feminine so now I will speak to you about that. The feminine does exist, but it was not created first. When it came forth it (Sophia) created powers and gods for itself. Since I am the image of He Who Is, I was first and it did not exist when I came forth.

I brought into being the image of He Who Is so that His sons might know what things are theirs and what is alien to them. Be attentive and I will reveal everything about this mystery to you. They will seize me in two days, but my redemption will be near."

James said, "Teacher, you said, 'they will seize me.' What can I possibly do?" He said to me, "James, do not be afraid. They will capture you too. Leave Jerusalem, because it is she (Jerusalem) who always gives a bitter cup to the sons of light. She is the home to a large number of archons.

(Author's Note: Archons were created by and are servants to the Demiurge, who is the "creator god of this world". The Demiurge and the archons stand between the human race and a transcendent God (He Who Is). God can only be reached through gnosis. The gnosis reveals the fact that there is a higher God than the Demiurge and the path to reach the All, He Who Is. The Demiurge and his servants, the archons strive to keep man separated from and ignorant of He Who Is. They would generally equate to the devil and his demons in an orthodox Christian view.)

Your redemption will be protected from them. Listen and I will teach you so that you might understand who they are and what their nature is.

(Author's Note: Here the codex is corrupted or missing pieces. Some words or phrases cannot be completely read.)

They are not [...] but archons [...]. These twelve [...] down [...] archons [...] upon his own group of seven."

James said, "Teacher, are there really twelve groups of seven and not just seven as there are in the scriptures?" The Lord said, "James, the person who taught regarding this scripture had a limited understanding. However, I am going to reveal to you what was produced from him who is beyond numbers. I will give you a sign for the number that came from Him who cannot be numbered and I will give you a sign for the measurement that came from Him who cannot be measured."

James said, "Teacher, Look, I have received their number. They measure seventy-two!" The Lord said, "These are the seventy-two heavens, but they are under the control of the Archons. These are the Powers of all their strength. The heavens were established by them and they were distributed everywhere (together they inhabit all places here), and the twelve archons have authority over them. The inferior power among them (the Demiurge) produced angels and an innumerable host for itself.

(Author's Note: Yaldaboth, the Demiurge, created twelve Powers or Archons to assist him, giving each a portion of his power, which he took from Sophia.)

Nonetheless, He Who Is, has been given [...] on account of [...] He Who Is [...] they are innumerable. If it is your desire to number them now, you will have to you abandon your blind thought, which comes from the prison of flesh that encases (encircles) you. Only then you will reach He Who Is. Then you will no longer be James but you are (will realize you are) the one who is. And each of those who are innumerable will have been named."

James said, "Teacher, how can I reach He Who Is, since all these powers and the host are armed against me?" He said to me, "These powers are not armed against you personally. They are armed against another specifically. They are armed against me.

They are enforced with other powers. Judgement is their weapon against me. They did not give [...] in it to me [...] through them [...]. In this place [...] my suffering, I shall [...]. He will [...] and I shall not try to stop them. Inside me shall be a silence and a hidden mystery. I shall be timid in the face of their anger."

James said, "Teacher, if they arm themselves against you, then how can you be blamed?" You have come with knowledge, that you might destroy their forgetfulness. You have come with recollection (of where you came from), that you might destroy their ignorance.

I was worry about you because you descended into the great ignorance that is here, but you have not been defiled by anything in it.

You descended into this great mindlessness, but your memories remained.

You walked in this mud, but your clothes were not soiled, and you have not been buried in their filth. You have not been entrapped.

Even though I was not like them, I clothed myself with everything of theirs. Forgetfulness is within me, but still, I remember things that are not from them.

There is in me [....], and I am in their [...]. [...] knowledge [...] not in their sufferings [...]. But I am afraid of them, because they are the rulers here. What will they do (to me)? What will I be able to say (to them)? What word will I be able to say that will allow me to escape from them?"

The Lord said, "James, I admire your understanding and I understand your fear. If you must worry, do not concern yourself about anything other than your own redemption. Watch and see. I will complete my destiny upon this earth as I have announced from the heavens. And I shall show you your redemption."

James said, "Teacher, after they capture you and you complete your destiny you will go up to He Who is, so how will you appear to us again?

The Lord said, "James, after these things have happened I will reveal everything to you, not only for your sake but for the sake of the unbelieving men. I do this so that faith may be in them also. Through this a multitude will attain faith and they will increase in (number / strength?)[...]. After this I shall appear to condemn the archons. And I will show them he who cannot be seized. If they seize him, then he will overpower each one of them.

I shall go now. Remember the things I have spoken to you and let the knowledge precede you." James said,"Lord, I shall hurry to do as you have said." The Lord bade him farewell. And the Lord fulfilled all that was right to do."

When James heard of his suffering he was very distressed. They awaited the sign of his coming and he came several days later.

And James was walking on a mountain called "Gaugelan", with his (the Lord's) disciples. They were listening to James because they were distressed and he was [...] being a comforter, saying, "This is [...] the second [...]" After the crowd dispersed James remained [...] in prayer [...], as was his custom.

(Author's Note: Gaulgelan is probably Golgotha. In Syriac the name of the mount is Gagultha. However, there may be a link with Gaugal, a mountain near Amida, mentioned by Syriac writers. Amida was an ancient city in Mesopotamia located where modern Diyarbakır, Turkey now stands. The Roman writers Ammianus Marcellinus and Procopius consider it a city of Mesopotamia. The city was located on the right bank of the Tigris. The walls were high and substantial, and constructed of the recycled stones from older buildings.)

And the Lord appeared to him. Then he stopped praying and embraced the Lord. He kissed the Lord and said, "Teacher, I have found you. I heard about all the suffering you went through. I have been so distressed. You know my compassion.

(Author's Note: The word "compassion" is made up of two words. Together – Suffer. To have compassion is the suffer together.)

I was thinking and I was wishing that I would not have to see these people. They must be judged for the things they have done (to you). What they have done goes against what is right and proper."

The Lord said, "James, do not be concerned for me or for these people. I am he who was within me. I never suffered in any way. I have not been anxious or in any pain. These people have done me no harm.

(Author's Note: Jesus has shed his body and is now a spiritual being. He is "He Who Is". The spirit left the body before the torment began and the divine Jesus was not harmed or hurt. His death held no great meaning for Gnostic since it was his teaching and not his death that freed people and pointed their way to heaven. This divergence from the view of the crucifixion held by the orthodox church turned the church against Gnostics and in time lead to the murder of thousands of Gnostics by the church, culminating in the Cathar massacre. The Cathars were a Gnostic Christian community living in southern France, between the 12th and 14th centuries. In 1209 the crusaders came, sent by the Pope. The order was to kill every Gnostic in the area. Arnaud-Amaury, the Cistercian abbot-commander, is supposed to have been asked how to tell Cathars from Catholics. His reply, recalled by Caesarius of Heisterbach, a fellow Cistercian, thirty years later was "Caedite eos. Novit enim Dominus qui sunt eius" — "Kill them all, the Lord will recognise His own". The doors of the church of St Mary Magdalene were broken down and the refugees dragged out and slaughtered. At least 7,000 innocent men, women and children were killed there by Catholic forces. In the town Gnostic and Catholics were living together. There was no way to distinguish between the two Christian sects.

All were killed. Thousands were mutilated and murdered. Prisoners were blinded, dragged behind horses, and used for target practice. The permanent population of the town at that time was then probably no more than 5,000, but local refugees seeking shelter within the city walls could conceivably have increased the number to 20,000.)

These people existed as a symbol of the archons, and the symbol and type should be destroyed through them.

But [...] the archons, [...] who has [...] since it [...] angry with (you) [...] The just (one) [...] is his servant.

Therefore, now your name will be "James the Just". Did you realize how you became sober when you saw me? (You woke up.) You stopped your prayer. You embraced and kissed me. Now you are a just man of God. Because of these things, you have stirred up great anger and rage against yourself. But (this has happened) so that others might come to be (free)."

But James was afraid and anxious, and he wept. The Lord sat with him on a rock. And the Lord said to him, "James, you will undergo suffering, but do not be sad. The flesh is weak and it will receive what it has been destined to receive, but do not be weak or fearful". Then the Lord stopped speaking.

Then, when James heard these things, he wiped away the bitter tears from his eyes [...] which is [...].

The Lord said to him, "James, listen and I will reveal your redemption to you. When you are seized, and you are suffering, a multitude of arms will be (fight) against you they may seize you. Three arms in particular may capture you. They are the one who sit as gate keepers. Not only do they demand toll, but they also steal souls.

When you come are their captive, the one who is their guard will ask you, 'Who are you and where do you come from?' You are to say to him, 'I am a son, and I am from the Father.' Then he will ask you, 'What kind of son are you, and to what father do you belong?' You must say to him, 'I am from the Pre-existent Father, and I am a son within the Pre-existent One.' When he says to you, [...], you must say to him [...] in the [...] that I might [...]."

(When he asks) "[...] of alien things? You must to him, "They are not entirely alien, but they are from Achamoth, who is the female (fallen Spohia)."

(Author's Note: This section is not complete but the Archons may be asking about the feminine energies, females, and Sophia. In Gnostic tradition, Sophia is a feminine figure, analogous to the human soul but also simultaneously one of the feminine aspects of God. Gnostics held that she was the consort of balancing half of Jesus Christ and the Bride of Christ. She is occasionally referred to by the Hebrew equivalent of Achamoth, Ἀχαμώθ. James must explain that Sophia is an Aeon and is fallen but not alien. Although the higher Sophia remained in the pleroma, Achamoth is the lower or fallen Sophia, who descended into the physical realm. The name, Achamoth, is not associated with the higher Sophia in Valentinius Gnosticism. Since Achamoth is the fallen Sophia, and was half of Sophia when she was split into two parts when she fell, and the lower Sophia was rescued by Christ. Achamoth is seen as a female brought into being by a female with no male consort. This was done in the same way the Demiurge and the Archons were brought into being by Sophia without the consent or help of her consort, Jesus.)

"And these thing/beings she produced as she brought down the race (of Archons) from the Pre-existent One. Therefore, they are not alien, but they are ours. They belong to us because she who their mother is from the Pre-existent One. Yet, they are alien because the Pre-existent One did not have intercourse with her, when she produced them."

When he asks, 'Where will you go?', you must say to him, 'I shall return to the place I came from.' If you say these things, you will escape their attacks.

"But when you come to those three who would take you captive and steal your soul [...] these. You [...] are a vessel [...] of much more than [...] of the one whom you [...] for [...] her root.

Also, you must be cautious [...]. Then I will call upon the eternal, incorruptible knowledge, which is Sophia, who is in the Father and who is the mother / creator of Achamoth. Achamoth had no father nor was there a male consort who helped create her, but she is female produced from a female (alone).

She (Achamoth) produced you (James) without a male, since she (Achamoth) thought she was alone. She was living in ignorance. She did not know and was unaware of what lives through her mother because she thought that she alone existed. (She did not know that she came to exist through her mother.)

But I shall cry out to Achamoth's mother (the higher Sophia). And then they, the Archons, will become confused and they will blame their origins and the race of their mother (Achamoth). But you, James will ascend to what is yours [...] and you will [...] be with the Pre-existent One."

(Author's Note: According to Valentinus, Aeons were created in pairs, male and female energies, which balanced, completed, and fulfilled each other. Since the fall of Sophia produced the material world, man, and the Archons, as well as splitting Sophia and producing Achamoth, Christ must rescue Achamoth out of the chaos of the lower, material world in order to restore Sophia to wholeness and have his consort in the restored and intact Sophia. Meanwhile, it is the higher Sophia that places the spirit within man as Gnosis occurs and allows for his salvation.)

"They are a type of the twelve disciples and the twelve pairs, [...] (one of these is) Achamoth, which is translated 'Sophia'. I myself am one, (and) so is the imperishable (higher) Sophia. It is she through whom you will be redeemed, and these redeemed are all the sons of He Who Is. These things they have known and have hidden within them.

You also are to hide these things within you, and you are to keep silence. But you are to reveal them to Addai.

(Author's Note: Addai is the apostle Thaddeus, one of the seventy sent out by Jesus.)

When you depart, there will immediately be war in this land. Weep for those who dwells in Jerusalem. But let Addai take these things to heart.

In the tenth year let Addai sit down and record these things. And when he writes them down [...] then the records are to be give to [...] he has the [...] and he is called Levi. Then he is to bring [...] the word [...] from what I said earlier [...] to a woman [...] for Jerusalem is in her [...] and he will begat two sons through her. They are to inherit these things along with the understanding of him who [...] exalts. And they are to inherit [...] his intellect. Now, the younger of them will be greater than the older. These things will remain hidden in him until he is seventeen years old, then [...] beginning [...] through them.

The Archons will intently pursue him, since they are from his [...] companions. But he will become acknowledged through them, and they will proclaim this word. He will become a seed of [...]."

James said, "I am satisfied [...] and they are [...] my soul, but I have one more question. Who are the seven women who have been your disciples? I have seen that all women bless you. I am amazed at how strong a weak vessel become when they recognize what is contain in them."

The Lord said, "You [...] (see) well [...] (there is) a spirit of [...], a spirit of thought, a spirit of counsel of a [...], a spirit [...] a spirit of knowledge [...] of their fear. [...] when we had passed through the breath of an archon named Adonaios [...] him and [...] he was ignorant [...] when I came forth from him, he remembered that I am one of his sons. Because I am his son he was gracious to me at that time. But before I appeared here, he cast them down among this people. And from the place of heaven the prophets [...]."

(Author's Note: Adonaios is an offspring of Yaldaboth. He helped create the physical world. Jesus may be saying that his body, the material Jesus was created by Adonaios but because the Archon are "asleep" and ignorant, Jesus had to reveal to him that Jesus was his son. Adonaios is also a name referring to the entity and powers of the Father in the Construction of the Sethian-Valentinian creation story. He is part of the divine tripartite powers of Jesus, Father-Mother-Son. The word has Sethian-Mandaean roots and is used as Adonai-Sabaoth. Adonaios or Father is an Archon of the Pleroma. According to Origen's Contra Celsum, a sect called the Ophites posited the existence of seven archons, beginning with Yaldabaoth, who created the six that follow: Yao, Sabaoth, Adonaios, Elaios, Astaphanos, and Horaios. It is unclear as to what this prior text means. Adonaios was ignorant that Jesus was his son. This could refer to the fact that a flame is oblivious to the light it produces since it is the light and would not account for each ray. Yet, seeing a ray the light would know its own.)

James said, "Teacher, [...] I [...] completely [...] in them especially [...]." The Lord said, "James, I commend you [...] travel on the earth [...] the words while he [...] on the [...]. You should cast this cup of bitterness away from you. Some from [...] will set themselves against you now that you have begun to understand their roots from beginning to end.

Reject all lawlessness. And beware because they will envy you. When you communicate your new way of seeing things you should encourage these four: Salome and Mariam and Martha and Arsinoe. [...] since he takes some [...] to me he is [...] burnt offerings and [...]. But I [...] not in this way; but [...] first-fruits of the [...] upward [...] so that the power of God might appear.

The perishable has ascended to the eternal and the feminine has attained its male counterpart."

James said, "Teacher, now into these three (things), has their [...] been cast. They have been hated, and they have been persecuted [...]. Look [...] everything [...] from everyone [...]. You have attained [...] of knowledge. And [...] that is what the [...] go [...] you will discover [...]. Now I will go and will reveal things to those who believed in you so that they may be content with their blessing and salvation. In this way, your revelation will come to pass."

Then he went from there immediately and scolded and reprimanded the twelve and shocked them out of their contentment with their (old) knowledge [...].

[...]. The majority of them [...] took in the messenger [...]. The others [...] said, "[...] wipe him from this earth. He is not worth living." Others were afraid. They fled saying, "We want no part in this blood. Is it right that a just man should perish through injustice?"

So, James departed. And they that [...] look [...] for we [...] him.

Information on
The Second Apocalypse of James

Although no Greek manuscript has been found, there is linguistic evidence in the extant Coptic text that the Second Apocalypse of James goes back to a translation from a Greek text. The occasional appearance of a name or a word of Greek origin or influence is an indication of a translation from the Greek. This can prove helpful in our understanding of the Coptic text.

The Coptic translation was likely accomplished as early as the second half of the 3rd century. The Greek text was probably written in middle of the 2nd century, although there is little evidence in the text or in any historical record to be certain.

The Second Apocalypse of James is an apocalyptic text of the Nag Hammadi library. It was placed directly after the First Apocalypse of James of what is now known as Codex V. The text narrates the martyrdom of James the Just.

The gnostic text contains many Jewish-Christian themes, making many scholars think it may be one of the earlier texts and was likely written before The First Apocalypse of James.

The prominent role of James the Lord's brother appears to speak for the geographical area of Syria and Palestine rather than for any other.

The text is clearly gnostic in character but the specific Gnostic system of the writer is uncertain. The author has knowledge of Jewish and Christian traditions, or the traditions of the Jewish converts to the Christian sect, and uses the name of James, who held a position of leadership and special prominence in Jewish-Christian circles, and in the Christian church. In the text, James is given a special revelation from Jesus. In both the First Apocalypse and the Second Apocalypse of James, James is given a role of prominence in the gnostic tradition like that of Peter in the orthodox tradition.

As Peter is supposed to be the rock upon which the church is built and the holder of the keys to the kingdom, according to Catholic tradition, in the Gnostic line James is the person who was given the keys in the Second Apocalypse to guide the Gnostic believers through the traps of the Archons and through the door into the heavenly kingdom.

In the text, the name of James' father and Mary's husband is given not as Joseph but as Theudas. The text reads, 'he (Jesus) is a brother of yours (James'). Unlike the First Apocalypse of James, the writer does not go out of his or her way to reject a bodily, material, or brotherhood relationship between Jesus and James. The text states that James and Jesus were nourished from the same milk. This reference to mother's milk could easily be taken as spiritually metaphorical.

The wife of Theudas is named Mary, but whether this Mary is the same woman as the mother of Jesus is not clear from the text.

The text features a kiss between James and Jesus, on the lips, in the way Jesus kissed Mary Magdalene in other gnostic texts. A kiss is a metaphor for the passing of gnosis and nothing more.

The text ends with the death of James by stoning, possibly reflecting an early oral tradition of what became of James.

The text can be broken down into four sections, having a hymn like quality. In the third section, James is described as performing the function of gnostic redeemer. After James' function is articulated the final section is the prayer of James set just before his death.

There are issues with the flow and clarity of texts, not the least of which is that the resurrected Jesus speaks in several places without being announced and without any sign of transition from one narrator or character to the next. We only pick up on this fact because Jesus is the only voice fitting the context. In these places, he refers to James in the second person (as "you"). The story line then switches back and forth from Jesus speak to James or about James and back to the voice of James preaching to the people. All the while we cannot forget the story of James was witnessed and recorded by Meriem, the priest and told to Theuda, the father of James. Meriem's place in the story is only evident in the first and last paragraphs of the text. Author's notes have been added to assist the reader in the difficult transitions and theological meanings in the text.

The Second Apocalypse of James

This regards the lesson that James the Just preached in Jerusalem, which Mereim, one of the priests, wrote down and told to Theuda, who is the father of (James) the Just One, because he was a relative of James.

He (Meriem) said, "Come quickly! Bring Mary, your wife, and also your relatives [...] the reason is [...] of this [...] to him. He will understand.

You will see that a large group is upset over his [...]. They are very angry at him. [...] and they pray [...]. He is telling them the same thing he often told others.

He (James) used to preach while people were gathered and seated. But this time he came in and did not sit down in the place, as he usually did. Instead he sat above them on the fifth story, which is reserved for honored guest. Then all our people [...] (heard) his words [...]."

"He (James) said, [...]. I am he who received a revelation from the Eternal Pleroma. I am the one who was first summoned by the great one. And I obeyed the Lord as he passed through the worlds [...]. It was he who [...]. He stripped himself and went about naked and he was seen in a transitory state, though he was about to ascend into an eternal state. This same Lord who is with us came as a son who sees, and as a brother was he search for. He will come to [...] that he produced him because [...] and he unites [...] to make him free [...] in [...] and he who came to [...]."

"Once again I am rich in knowledge. I understanding like no other, because this understanding could only be produced from above. The [...] comes from a [...]. I am the [...] the person I knew. The things revealed to me are hidden from everyone and can be revealed only through Him.

These two who see me, they have already proclaimed through the words: He shall be judged with those who are unrighteous. He who has lived without blaspheming died by blasphemy (from others). He who was rejected, they [...]."

[...] in the flesh. But it is by gnosis that I shall come forth from the flesh. I am certainly going to die, but I shall be found in life. I came to this place so that they could judge [...] I shall come out in [...] as judge [...] but I will not lay blame on any of his servants [...].

I hurry to free them. I wish to bring them with me and ascend over the one who wants to rule over them here. I am their secret brother who wants to help them. It is I who prayed to the Father until he [...] in [...] reign [...] eternally [...] first in [...].

(Author's Note: Jesus speaks in the following hymn-like sequence.)

I am the firstborn son. Father will destroy all of them (the Demiurge and archons) and their control and their kingdom.

I am the beloved one. I am the one who is righteous. I am the only son of the Father.

I have spoken what I have heard. I have commanded as I heard the command. I have shown you what I have found.

Listen as I speak so that I may come forth (in you).

Be attentive to me so that you may (really) see me.

If I have come manifested, who am I? I did not come here as I (really) am, and I would not have appeared as I (truly) am. I exist (here) for a short period of time [...]."

(Author's Note: James carries on from here.)

"Once when I was sitting and meditating, the one you hated and persecuted (Jesus) came in to me. He opened the door and said to me, "Hello, my brother. My brother, hello." I raised my face and stared at him. Then my mother said to me, "Do not be afraid because he called you 'my brother', my son. Because you both were nourished with the same milk he calls me "My mother". He is no stranger to us. He is your step-brother [...]."

(Author's Note: We assume this milk refers to mother's milk from their earthy mother who suckled both of them, but it is unclear and may refer to a metaphorical spiritual milk. Jesus begins speaking. He refers to James as "you".)

"[...] these words [...] great [...] I will find them, and they will come out. However, I am the stranger, and they have no idea or thought of me in their minds, but they know me in this place. However, it was right that others gain gnosis through you.

" Hear and understand, I say to you. A multitude will hear but they will be slow witted. But you understand what I will be able to tell you. Your father is not my father. But my father has become a father to you.

(Author's Note: James' father can be seen as either his parent or Yaldaboth the Demiurge, who made his world. The father of Jesus is He Who Is, the All. Jesus is saying that through Gnosis the ALL has become James' father.)

"You have heard about this particular virgin. This is how [...] virgin [...] specifically this virgin. [...], how [...] to me for [...] to understand [...] not as [...] whom I [...]. For this man [...] to him, and this will benefit you. You know your Father is rich. He will grant your inheritance, which is all these things that you see.

"Preach these words that I shall now speak to you. When you hear, listen closely and understand, then apply it as it was intended. You are the reason that they (the Archons) come by, and it was initiated by the glorious one.

And if they want to disturb you and take possession [...] he began [...] not, and not those who are coming, who were sent forth by (the Demiurge) him that formed this present creation. After these things happen, he will be ashamed and he will be disturbed that his labor is far inferior (to the Aeons) and amounts to nothing. He will see the inheritance he boasted of as being so great will seem small. His gifts are not blessings. His promises are evil conspiracies. You are not the recipient of his compassion, but he uses you to do violence. He never wants to treat you or I fairly or with justice. He will enforce his rule throughout the time he is given.

"But now understand and become familiar with the Father who is compassionate. He did not receive an inheritance that was unlimited. His inheritance is not limited in duration. It is as the eternal day [...] it is [...] perceive [...]. And he used [...].

(Author's Note: The Demiurge received his power from Sophia. This was his inheritance. The world and all the things he created are transient and unstable, limited in lifespan and duration. The true Father, the ALL did not inherit anything. He is everything and his kingdom in eternal and incorruptible.)

The fact is, he (the Demiurge) did not come from them and he is despised. So, he boasts, because he does not want to be scolded, chastised, or punished. He is superior to those below him, those who looked down on you. He captures ones from the Father and imprisons them and then he molds them into his image and they continue their existence with him.

(Author's Note: James speaks.)

"I saw this all happen as if I was high above, watching. I have explained to you how it all happened. They were in another form when they were visited and while I watched they became familiar with me through those I know."

(Author's Note: Jesus speaks. The "you" I the text now refers to James. Here we see James being assigned the role of guide and a type of spiritual leader. Some go so far as to say this makes James a Gnostic messiah.)

"Before these things come to pass they will make a [...]. I realized how they tried to come down here to get close to [...] the small children, but now I desire to reveal the spirit of power through you so that he might be revealed to those who are yours.

Those who desire to enter in and wish to walk in the path that is before the door will open this blessed door through you. They will follow you inside and you will be their escort when they are inside. And you will allow each that is ready to receive a reward.

Even though you are not THE redeemer or the helper of strangers, you are one who shines a light and A redeemer of those who are mine, and now a redeemer of those who are yours. You will let them see and you will bring good to all of them. Because of all your powerful deeds they will admire you. The heavens bless you. He, (the Demiurge) who calls himself Lord, will envy you.

I am the [...] of those who have been taught these things along with you.

For your sake, they will be taught these things so that they can rest.

For your sake, they will become kings and reign.

For your sake, they will have compassion on those they choose to pity.

As you were first to have clothed yourself (taken on this body, been born), you will be the first to strip himself (of his body), and you will become like you were before you were stripped."

(Author's Note: Gnostics believe we are held prisoners in this world by our bodies. The ultimate freedom is to lay down the body in death and thus gain freedom for our spirits. Our spirits, being the real beings, ascend to reunite with the Divine All. Jesus now stops speaking and James describes what happens next.)

"And he (Jesus) kissed my mouth. He held me and said, "My beloved, look and I will reveal to you those things that neither the heavens nor their archons have known.

(Author's Note: A kiss is symbolic of Gnosis passing from teacher to student. Jesus speaks again.)

Watch and I will reveal to you these things. He (the Demiurge), who did not understand but boasted by saying, "[...] there is no other except me. Am I not alive? Because I am a father, do I not have power for everything?"

Look, my beloved, I shall reveal everything to you. Understand and know them, so that you can come forth just as I am. Look and I will reveal to you him who is hidden. Reach out now and hold on to me."

(Author's Note: James speaks.)

"And then I reached out but he was not there like I thought he would be. Then I heard him saying, "Understand and take hold of me." I understood and I was afraid and filled with joy at the same time.

"Now I say to you judges, you have been judged. You did not spare anyone from your judgement and so you will not be spared either.

Be on guard and watch [...] you did not know. He (Jesus) was that one that he who created the heaven and the earth and dwelled in it (the Demiurge), did not see. (The Demiurge, who created this heaven and earth did not see or know Jesus.) He (Jesus) is the one who is the life. He was the light. He was that one who will come to be. He will be the way for what has begun (here) to end and this end is about to begin. He was the Holy Spirit and the Invisible One who did not descend upon the earth.

He was the virgin (spirit), and the things he intends, happens to him. That which he wills, comes about for him [...]. I saw that he was naked, and no garment (body) clothed him.

Renounce this difficult and unstable way, and walk with me according to the teaching of the one who desires to have you ascend above every dominion to make you free with me. He will not judge you for those things that you did (here). He will have mercy on you. It was not you that did those things. It was your Lord. He (He Who Is) is not wrath, but he is a kind Father."

The reason you remain in bondage is that you have judged yourselves. You oppress yourselves. You will repent and change your mind but (by that time) it will do you no good. You must see the one who speaks and look for the one who is silent. Know the one who came here, and understand the one who went out from this place.

I am the Just One who does not judge. I am not a master. I am a helper. He was cast out before he could reach out his hand (to save you). I [...]. [...] and now he allows me to hear. So, go ahead and play your trumpets, flutes and harps is this place. The Lord (of this place) has taken you captive from the (true) Lord, because he closed your ears, that they may not hear the sound of my word. However, you will still be able to be attentive in your hearts. Because of this you will call me 'the Just One.'"

(Author's Note: Jesus now speaks.)

Look, I have told you I gave you your house, which you say that God has made. It is the house through which he promised you would attain your inheritance. This house I have doomed to be destroyed, because it is contemptable and those in it are ignorant. Look. The judges are now deliberating [...]."

(Author's Note: The house is the physical body. The Demiurge, in the place of God, promises reward or inheritance for following him, but it is a lie. He, his kingdom, and all things physical will end. Jesus ends his speech and Meriem begins to describe the scene.)

At that time, the crowd of people were not convinced and became very upset. So, he got up and left but continues to preach like he had previously. He came again on the same day and spoke for a few hours.

I (Mereim) was with the priests but I did not tell him I was related or knew James since all of them were in agreement, saying, 'Come on, let us stone the Just One.' Then they got up and said, 'Yes, let us kill him and get him out of our midst. He is worthless.'

(Author's Note: It is easy to forget this story was recorded by Mereim the priest and told to Theuda, the father of James. Mereim continues by telling Theuda how James, is son, died.)

They went there and found him standing beside the columns of the temple beside the large corner stone. And they decided to throw him down from that high place, and they threw him down. Then they [...] they [...] and they grabbed him and struck him as they dragged him on the ground. They stretched him out and placed a stone on his stomach. They all stood on him, yelling 'You have sinned!'

But he was still alive so made him stand up and they made him dig a hole. They made him stand in the hole he dug. Then they buried him up to his chest and they stoned him.

Then James raised his hands and said this prayer, which is different from the way he normally prays:

'My God and my father, who saved me while my hope was dead, you enlivened me through the mystery your will. Now, do not let my days in this world be prolonged. The light of your day [...] remains in [...] salvation. Now, deliver me from my sojourn in this place. Do not let your grace be left behind in my body, but let your grace become pure. Save me from a death of defilement and bring me out of my tomb alive. I know your grace and love live in me for the purpose of fulfilling your work. Save me from this sinful flesh. I trust in you with all the strength I have. You are the life in all things living. Do not let the enemy humiliate me. Do not turn me over to a judge who deals with sin so severely. Forgive me all my sins in my life because I live in you and your grace lives in me. I have left everyone and I have confessed (my faith in) you. Save me from this evil sickness! This is the time and the hour. Holy Spirit, bring me salvation [...] the light [...] the light [...] in the power [...].'

"After he spoke (these words), he remained silent [...] word [...] after [...] this discourse [...]."

Information on the Apocalypse of Thomas

A. de Santos Otero comments (New Testament Apocrypha, vol. 2, pp. 748-749):

For centuries the Apocalypse of Thomas was known only through the notice of it in the Decretum Gelasianum (Item 27, cf. vol. 1, p. 39). In 1908 C. Frick (ZNW 9, 1908, 172) drew attention to another reference which is contained in the Chronicle of Jerome of the Codex Philippsianus No. 1829 in Berlin. In this it says in reference to the 18th year of Tiberius Caesar: in libro quodam apocrypho qui dicitur Thomae apostoli scriptum est dominum iesum ad eum dixisse ab ascensu suo ad celum usque in secundum adventum eius novem iobeleus contineri.

Today two versions of the Apocalypse of Thomas exist.

The longer is represented by: a) Cod. Clm 4585 fol. 66-67 (9th cent.) of Benediktbeuern. This text has been edited by Fr. Wilhelm in his book: Deutsche Legenden und Legendare, 1907; b) a manuscript from the Library of the Chapter of Verona (8th cent.) which has been published by M. R. James in JTS 11, 1910, 288-290; c) Cod. Vatic. Palat. no. 220, discovered by E. v. Dobschütz and used by Bihlmeyer in his edition of Cod. Clm 4563. An early English form of this version is found in the fifteenth sermon of the famous Anglo-

Saxon manuscript of Vercelli (9th cent.), cf. M.R. James, Apoc. NT, 556ff. This version consists of two different parts. The first is concerned with the events and signs which are to precede the last judgment. In this it reveals a close dependence on similar descriptions of other apocrypha of an apocalyptic nature, e.g. the Assumption of Moses, the Ascension of Isaiah and the Sibylline Books. This part should be regarded as an interpolation; its origin can be dated to the first or second half of the 5th century because of some historical references in the text (e.g. to the Emperor Theodosius and his two sons Arcadius and Honorius). Cf. Bihlmeyer in Rev. Bénéd. 28, 1911, 277.

The second part corresponds in range and content with the shorter version of the Apocalypse of Thomas. This version is represented by: a) Cod. Vindob. Palatinus 16 (formerly Bobbiensis) fol. 60r-60v from the 5th century. This text was first discovered by J. Bick (SWA 159, 1908, 90-100) and identified by E. Hauler (Wiener Studien 30, 1908, 308-340) as a fragment of the Apocalypse of Thomas. It is the oldest witness of all to our Apocalypse; b) Cod. Clm 4563 fol. 40r-40v (11th/12th century) from Benediktbeuern, discovered and edited by Bihlmeyer (Rev. Bénéd. 28, 1911, 272-276). This text agrees basically with Vindob. Palat. 16, has been fully preserved and reveals no interpolations.

The shorter version is our oldest witness to the original Apocalypse of Thomas, which should have been subject in the course of time to various orthodox and heretical revisions. We must associate this development above all with Manichean and Priscillianist currents of thought. In favour of that there is not only the mention of the Apocalypse of Thomas in the Decretum Gelasianum but also some parallel places in Priscillianist writings; cf. De Bruyne (Rev. Bénéd. 24, 1907, 318-335) and Bihlmeyer (ibid. 28, 1911, 279). Some typical Manichean ideas, e.g. that of light, appear again and again in our Apocalypse. In this connection Bihlmeyer (ibid. p. 282) points to the name Thomas which (according to the Acta Archelai of Hegemonius) was borne by one of the three greatest disciples of

Mani. Both the longer and shorter versions (Cod. Vindob. Palat. 16 dates from the 5th century) suggest the conjecture that the Apocalypse of Thomas originated prior to the 5th century. Closely dependent on the canonical Revelation of John, it is the only apocryphal apocalypse which apportions the events of the End into seven days. This clearly recalls the seven seals, the seven trumpets and the seven bowls of the Revelation of John (Rev. 5-8:2; 8:2-11; 16). The numerous variants of the Latin codices point to different versions of an original Greek text.

The basis of our translation is the Latin text of Cod. Clm 4563 in the edition of Bihlmeyer (Rev. Bénéd. 28, 1911, 272-276) in which he takes into account the variants of the other codices.

From "The Apocryphal New Testament"

M.R. James-Translation and Notes

Oxford: Clarendon Press, 1924

Introduction

The emergence of this book has been recent. The Gelasian Decree condemns the book 'called the Revelation of Thomas' as apocryphal, and that was all that was known of it. In 1908 a quotation in the Berlin MS. (eighth-ninth century) of Jerome's Chronicle was noticed by Dr. Frick. At the eighteenth year of Tiberius, the manuscript has this note:

In a certain apocryphal book, said to be of Thomas the apostle it is written that the Lord Jesus told him that from his ascension into heaven to his second advent the time comprised is nine jubilees.

This does not appear in any of the published texts. Already in 1907 F. Wilhelm had printed, in his Deutsche Legenden und Legendare, a text from a Munich MS. which attracted little attention, but was in fact the lost Apocalypse, or part of it.

In the same year E. Hauler showed that a leaf of a fifth-century palimpsest at Vienna -the same that contains a leaf of the Epistle of the Apostles- was a fragment of this book. Professor E. von Dobschutz had, before this, begun making preparation for an edition of the Apocalypse based on manuscripts at Munich and Rome which has not yet appeared. In the Journal of Theological Studies for 1910 I printed the beginning of the book from a Verona MS. (of eighth century). Maffei had noticed this, and in 1755 Dionisi had printed it in a forgotten volume. In 1911 Dom Bihlmeyer printed another 'uninterpolated' text from Munich in the Revue Benedictine. Yet more: in 1913 Max Forster (Studien z. engl. Phlilol.: Der Vercelli-Codex) showed that the fifteenth sermon in the famous Anglo-Saxon MS. at Vercelli is an Old English version of this Revelation; that a Hatton MS. and the Blickling Homilies also contain matter drawn from it: and that a shortened Latin form is to be found in a dialogue printed by Suchier (L'Enfant sage, 1910, p. 272). Lastly, there are quotations from it in some odd -I think Irish- homilies in a Reichenau MS. at Carlsruhe, printed by Domde Bruyneas 'Apocryphes Priscillianistes' in the Revue Bened., 1907.

There is, then, a quantity of material which we shall look to Professor Dohschutz to co-ordinate. Latin appears to have been the original language, and the data of the fuller text point to the days of Arcadius and Honorius. How much earlier the shorter text may be it is not easy to say: and I would not commit myself to the assertion that there is not a Greek document at the back of that.

Apocalypse of Thomas

A. Verona fragment (eighth century) and Wilhelm's text (Munich Clm. 4585, ninth century).

Here beginneth the epistle of the Lord unto Thomas.

Hear thou, Thomas, the things which must come to pass in the last times: there shall be famine and war and earthquakes in divers places, snow and ice and great drought shall there be and many dissensions among the peoples, blasphemy, iniquity, envy and villainy, indolence, pride and intemperance, so that every man shall speak that which pleaseth him. And my priests shall not have peace among themselves, but shall sacrifice unto me with deceitful mind: therefore will I not look upon them. Then shall the priests behold the people departing from the house of the Lord and turning unto the world (?) and setting up (or, transgressing) landmarks in the house of God. And they shall claim (vindicate) for themselves many [things and] places that were lost and that shall be subject unto Caesar (?) as also they were aforetime: giving poll-taxes of (for) the cities, even gold and silver and the chief men of the cities shall be condemned (here Verona ends: Munich continues) and their substance brought into the treasury of the kings, and they shall be filled.

For there shall be great disturbance throughout all the people, and death. The house of the Lord shall be desolate, and their altars shall be abhorred, so that spiders weave their webs therein. The place of holiness shall be corrupted, the priesthood polluted, distress (agony) shall increase, virtue shall be overcome, joy perish, and gladness depart. In those days evil shall abound: there shall be respecters of persons, hymns shall cease out of the house of the

Lord, truth shall be no more, covetousness shall abound among the priests; an upright man (al. an upright priesthood) shall not be found.

On a sudden there shall arise near the last time a king, a lover of the law, who shall hold rule not for long: he shall leave two sons. The first is named of the first letter (A, Arcadius), the second of the eighth (H, Honorius). The first shall die before the second (Arcadius died in 408- Honorius in 423).

Thereafter shall arise two princes to oppress the nations under whose hands there shall be a very great famine in the right-hand part of the east, so that nation shall rise up against nation and be driven out from their own borders.

Again another king shall arise, a crafty man (?), and shall command a golden image of Caesar (?) to be made (al. to be worshipped in the house of God), wherefore (?) martyrdoms shall abound. Then shall faith return unto the servants of the Lord, and holiness shall be multiplied and distress (agony) increase. The mountains shall the comforted and shall drop down sweetness of fire from the facet, that the number of the saints may be accomplished.

After a little space there shall arise a king out of the east, a lover of the law, who shall cause all good things and necessary to abound in the house of the Lord: he shall show mercy unto the widows and to the needy, and command a royal gift to be given unto the priests: in his days shall be abundance of all things.

And after that again a king shall arise in the south part of the world, and shall hold rule a little space: in whose days the treasury shall fail because of the wages of the Roman soldiers so that the substance of all the aged shall be commanded (to be taken) and given to the king to distribute.

Thereafter shall be plenty of corn and wine and oil, but great dearness of money, so that the substance of gold and silver shall be given for corn, and there shall be great dearth.

At that time shall be very great rising (?) of the sea, so that no man shall tell news to any man. The kings of the earth and the princes and the captains shall be troubled, and no man shall speak freely (boldly). Grey hairs shall be seen upon boys, and the young (?) shall not give place unto the aged.

After that shall arise another king, a crafty man, who shall hold rule for a short space: in whose days there shall be all manner of evils, even the death of the race of men from the east even unto Babylon. And thereafter death and famine and sword in the land of Chanaan even unto (Rome?). Then shall all the fountains of waters and wells boil over (?) and be turned into blood (or, into dust and blood). The heaven shall be moved, the stars shall fall upon the earth, the sun shall be cut in half like the moon, and the moon shall not give her light. There shall be great signs and wonders in those days when Antichrist draweth near. These are the signs unto them that dwell in the earth. In those days the pains of great travail shall come upon them. (al. In those days, when Antichrist now draweth near, these are the signs. Woe unto them that dwell on the earth; in those days great pains of travail shall come upon them.) Woe unto them that build, for they shall not inhabit. Woe unto them that break up the fallow, for they shall labour without cause. Woe unto them that make marriages, for unto famine and need shall they beget sons. Woe unto them that join house to house or field to field, for all things shall be consumed with fire. Woe unto them that look not unto (?) themselves while time alloweth, for hereafter shall they be condemned for ever. Woe unto them that turn away from the poor when he asketh.

[Here is a break: the text goes on: For I am of the high and powerful: I am the Father of all. (al. And know ye: I am the Father most high: I am the Father of all spirits.) This, as we shall see, is the beginning of the older(?) and shorter text, and of the Vienna fragment: only, in the latter, some words now unintelligible precede it: not the words, however, which are in Wilhelm's text. I will continue with Wilhelm.]

These are the seven signs the ending of this world. There shall be in all the earth famine and great pestilences and much distress: then shall all men be led captive among all nations and shall fall by the edge of the sword.

On the first day of the judgement will be a great marvel (or, the beginning shall be). At the third hour of the day shall be a great and mighty voice in the firmament of the heaven, and a great cloud of blood coming down out of the north, and great thunderings and mighty lightnings shall follow that cloud, and there shall be a rain of blood upon all the earth. These are the signs of the first day (Monday in the Anglo-Saxon, and so for the other days).

And on the second day there shall be a great voice in the firmament of the heaven, and the earth shall be moved out of its place: and the gates of heaven shall be opened in the firmament of heaven toward the east, and a great power shall be sent belched) forth by the gates of heaven and shall cover all the heaven even until evening (al. and there shall be fears and tremblings in the world). These are the signs of the second day.

And on the third day, about the second hour, shall be a voice in heaven, and the abysses of the earth shall utter their voice from the four corners of the world. The first heaven shall be rolled up like a book and shall straightway vanish. And because of the smoke and stench of the brimstone of the abyss the days shall be darkened unto the tenth hour. Then shall all men say: I think that the end draweth near, that we shall perish. These are the signs of the third day.

And on the fourth day at the first hour, the earth of the east shall speak, the abyss shall roar: then shall all the earth be moved by the strength of an earthquake. In that day shall all the idols of the heathen fall, and all the buildings of the earth. These are the signs of the fourth day.

And on the fifth day, at the sixth hour, there shall be great thunderings suddenly in the heaven, and the powers of light and the wheel of the sun shall be caught away, and there shall be great darkness over the world until evening, and the stars shall be turned away from their ministry. In that day all nations shall hate the world and despise the life of this world. These are the signs of the fifth day.

And on the sixth day there shall be signs in heaven. At the fourth hour the firmament of heaven shall be cloven from the east unto the west. And the angels of the heavens shall be looking forth upon the earth the opening of the heavens. And all men shall see above the earth the host of the angels looking forth out of heaven. Then shall all men flee.

(Here Wilhelm's text ends abruptly.)

B. Bihlmeyer's text, from Munich Clm. 4563 (eleventh to twelfth century, from Benedictbeuren): and the Vienna fragment.

Hear thou, O Thomas, for I am the Son of God the Father and I am the father of all spirits. Hear thou of me the signs which shall come to pass at the end of this world, when the end of the world shall be fulfilled (Vienna: that it pass away) before mine elect depart out of the world. I will tell thee that which shall come to pass openly unto men (or, will tell thee openly, &c.): but when these things shall be the princes of the angels know not, seeing it is now hidden from before

Then shall there be in the world sharings (participations) between king and king, and in all the earth shall be great famine great pestilences, and many distresses, and the sons of men shall be led captive among all nations and shall fall by the edge of the sword (and there shall be great commotion in the world: Vienna omits). Then after that when the hour of the end draweth nigh there shall be for seven days great signs in heaven, and the powers of the heavens shall be moved.

Then shall there be on the first day the beginning: at the third hour of the day a great and mighty voice in the firmament of heaven and a bloody cloud coming up (down, Vienna) out of the north, and great thunderings and mighty lightnings shall follow it, and it shall cover the whole heaven, and there shall be a rain of blood upon all the earth. These are the signs of the first day.

And on the second day there shall be a great voice in the firmament of heaven, and the earth shall be moved out of its place, and the gates of heaven shall be opened in the firmament of heaven toward the east, and the (smoke of a great fire shall break forth through the gates of heaven and shall cover all the heaven until evening. In that day there shall be fears and great terrors in the world. These are the signs of the second day. Vienna is defective here).

But on the third day about the third hour shall be a great voice in heaven, and the abysses of the earth (Vienna ends) shall roar from the four corners of the world; the pinnacles (so) of the firmament of heaven shall be opened, and all the air shall be filled with pillars of smoke. There shall be a stench of brimstone, very evil, until the tenth hour, and men shall say: We think the time draweth nigh that we perish. These are the signs of the third day.

And on the fourth day at the first hour, from the land of the east the abyss shall melt (so) and roar. Then shall all the earth be shaken by the might of an earthquake. In that day shall the ornaments of the heathen fall, and all the buildings of the earth, before the might of the earthquake. These are the signs of the fourth day.

But on the fifth day at the sixth hour, suddenly there shall be a great thunder in heaven, and the powers of light and the wheel of the sun shall be caught away (MS. opened), and there shall be great darkness in the world until evening, and the air shall be gloomy (sad) without sun or moon, and the stars shall cease from their ministry. In that day shall all nations behold as in a mirror (?) (or, behold it as sackcloth) and shall despise the life of this world. These are the signs of the fifth day.

And on the sixth day at the fourth hour there shall be a great voice in heaven, and the firmament of the heaven shall be cloven from the east unto the west, and the angels of the heavens shall be looking forth upon the earth by the openings of the heavens, and all these that are on the earth shall behold the host of the angels looking forth out of heaven. Then shall all men flee unto the monuments (mountains ?) and hide themselves from the face of the righteous angels, and say: Would that the earth would open and swallow us up! And such things shall come to pass as never were since this world was created.

Then shall they behold me coming from above in the light of my Father with the power and honour of the holy angels. Then at my coming shall the fence of fire of paradise be done away -because paradise is girt round about with fire. And this shall be that perpetual fire that shall consume the earth and all the elements of the world.

Then shall the spirits and souls of all men come forth from paradise and shall come upon all the earth: and every one of them shall go unto his own body, where it is laid up, and every one of them shall say: Here lieth my body. And when the great voice of those spirits shall be heard, then shall there be a great earthquake over all the world, and by the might thereof the mountains shall be cloven from above and the rocks from beneath. Then shall every spirit return into his own vessel and the bodies of the saints which have fallen asleep shall arise.

Then shall their bodies be changed into the image and likeness and the honour of the holy angels, and into the power of the image of mine holy Father. Then shall they be clothed with the vesture of life eternal, out of the cloud of light which hath never been seen in this world; for that cloud cometh down out of the highest realm of the heaven from the power of my Father. And that cloud shall compass about with the beauty thereof all the spirits that have believed in me.

Then shall they be clothed, and shall be borne by the hand of the holy angels like as I have told you aforetime. Then also shall they be lifted up into the air upon a cloud of light, and shall go with me rejoicing unto heaven, and then shall they continue in the light and honour of my Father. Then shall there be unto them great gladness with my Father and before the holy angels These are the signs of the sixth day.

And on the seventh day at the eighth hour there shall be voices in the four corners of the heaven. And all the air shall be shaken, and filled with holy angels, and they shall make war among them all the day long. And in that day shall mine elect be sought out by the holy angels from the destruction of the world. Then shall all men see that the hour of their destruction draweth near. These are the signs of the seventh day.

And when the seven days are passed by, on the eighth day at the sixth hour there shall be a sweet and tender voice in heaven from the east. Then shall that angel be revealed which hath power over the holy angels: and all the angels shall go forth with him, sitting upon chariots of the clouds of mine holy Father (so) rejoicing and running upon the air beneath the heaven to deliver the elect that have believed in me. And they shall rejoice that the destruction of this world hath come.

The words of the Saviour unto Thomas are ended, concerning the end of this world.

None of the Latin texts seem to be complete. But we see that Wilhelm's text is a blend of two sorts of Apocalypse -that akin to Daniel which, under the form of prophecy, describes events contemporary with the author and continues them into the future: and that which is more akin to John and describes the signs of the end.

Bihlmeyer's text has only the latter element, and as it agrees pretty closely with our oldest authority, the Vienna fragment (though in that, as I have said, something did precede Bihlmeyer's opening) I judge it to be the older of the two forms. The first part of Wilhelm's text with its clumsy indication of Arcadius and Honorius by means of their initials is much in the manner of the later Sibyllines, in which this particular trick is pushed to an absurd length, and used for quite imaginary personages as well as historic ones. In the second part Wilhelm's text departs widely from the Vienna fragment, and here again shows itself as probably inferior.

The Apocalypse, we see, was known in England in the ninth century at least: and I think it must probably be regarded as the ultimate parent of a little piece which is found in innumerable manuscripts and has often been printed: I mean Jerome on the Fifteen Signs of the last days before the judgement. The beginning of this states that Jerome found it 'in the annals of the Hebrews'. Its popularity was very great. Illustrations of the Fifteen Signs are occasionally to be found in manuscripts, and I have seen them on the alabaster tablets carved at Nottingham in the fourteenth and fifteenth centuries, but the best-known representation of them is in a window at All Saints', North Street, York, where they are accompanied by mottoes taken from the 'Prick of Conscience',which used to be attributed to Richard of Hampole.

The Anglo-Saxon version in the Vercelli Book (no. xv) begins thus:

We are told in this book how Saint Thomas the apostle of God asked our Lord when the time of Antichrist should be. Then the Lord spake unto him and said thus:

It behoveth that it be in the next days. Then shall be hunger and war, &c.:

The text conforms, generally speaking, to the longer recensions. The signs of the fifth day are omitted. The conclusion diverges from the

Latin and tells how the Virgin, Michael, and Peter successively intercede with the Judge, and he forgives a third part of the sinners at the prayer of each. But not all are pardoned: for we then have the sentences: Venite benedicti and Discedite maledicti as in Matt. xxv.

Quite recently (in Proc. R.I.A.) the Rev. St. J. Seymour has pointed out the probable dependence of the Saltair na Rann (eleventh century) on our apocalypse in its description of the Signs of the End.

Information of the Apocryphon of John

The Apocryphon, or "Secrets" of John forms the cornerstone of Gnostic mythology and cosmology. In this text we are introduced to the major entities of creation and lordship. We learn how the universe, including earth and man, came into being. The origin of evil, the creator god, and the material world are explained in detail. The story seems to be a mixture of various belief systems, including Chrithat of Plato, who seems to have borrowed freely from the format of Greek mythology, and Christianity. The story is loosely based on Genesis chapters 1 through 13 as a timeline.

The basic text of the Apocryphon of John existed in some form before 185 C.E. when A book called the Apocryphon of John was referred to by Irenaeus in his book, Against Heresies (Adversus Haereses), written in that year. Irenaeus reported about the Gnostic texts saying that teachers in 2nd century Christian communities were writing their own books to gain converts. He calls these books, "an indescribable number of secret and illegitimate writings, which they themselves have forged, to bewilder the minds of foolish people, who are ignorant of the true scriptures" (A.H. 1.20.1)

The Apocryphon of John continued to be circulated, expanded and embellished for the next seven hundred years. The document was reportedly in use during the eighth century by the Audians of Mesopotamia. Part of the mythology revealed in the Apocryphon of Jonh is also present in the Gnostic book, The Sophia (Wisdom) of Jesus as well as other Gnostic texts.

The specific document that so angered Irenaeus was lost and remained so until 1945, when a library of papyrus codices from the 4th century were found at Nag Hammadi in Egypt. The Apocryphon of John was among the texts,

Four versions have been found thus far. These are comprised of a long version, of which we have two identical Coptic manuscripts. A short version is also Coptic but differs from the others by eliminating certain details. A third, shorter Coptic manuscript had been found that differs slightly from the first shorter manuscript in style and vocabulary. A fragment has been found that shows some minor differences which distinguish it from the other.

Which, if any, of these texts are original have not been determined, however, it is the longer version that is presented here. This version was chosen because it contained more details and offered an overall cohesion of thought. This could be due to additions and embellishments sown through the shorter, less detailed versions.

Since we have already covered the general idea behind Gnostic mythology it need not be repeated her. However, a chart showing the main characters and their position on the divine family tree might serve us well. It is shown below.

Simplified Cast Of Characters

"Divine All", "Spirit" or "Father"
|
Divine Thought or Barbelo
_____
|
Fore-   Indestruct-   Fore-   Eternal   Truth
knowledge ability   thought   Life
_____
|
|
Christ, Self-created one, Perfect man
|
Sophia or wisdom
|
Elohim and Yaldaboth (who is also known as Yahweh)
|
|
Man and the material universe

The Apocryphon of John

The teaching of the savior, that will reveal the mysteries of things hidden which he taught John, his disciple, in silence.
On the day when John, the brother of James, the sons of Zebedee, had come to the temple, a Pharisee named Arimanius came up to him and said, "Where is your master whom you followed?" He said to him, He has gone back to the place he came from. The Pharisee said to him, This Nazarene deceived all of you with his deception. He filled your ears with lies, and closed your hearts and turned you all away from your fathers' traditions.

When I, John, heard these things I walked away from the temple into the desert. I grieved greatly in my heart, saying, How was the savior appointed, and why was he sent to the world by his Father, and who is his Father who sent him, and to which kingdom shall we go? What did he mean when he said to us, 'This kingdom which you will go to is an imperishable kingdom, but he did not teach us what kind it is.

Then, while I was meditating on these things, I saw the heavens open and the whole creation below heaven was shining and the world shook. I was afraid, and then I saw in the light a young man who stood by me. As I was looking at him he became like an old man. And he changed his visage again and become like a servant. There were not many beings in front of me, but there was a single being with many forms composed of light, and they could be seen through each other, and there were three forms within the one being.
He said to me, John, John, why do you doubt, and why are you afraid? (Mat. 28:17) Do you understand this image, do you not? Do not be afraid! I am the one who is with all of you always. I am the

Father and the Mother, and I am the Son. I am the undefiled and incorruptible one. I have come to teach you what is and what was and what will be, so that you may know the things visible and invisible, and to teach you concerning the upright, immutable (unshakable / unwavering) race of the perfect Man. Now, therefore, lift up your face, that you may receive the things that I shall teach you today, and may tell them to your fellow spirits who are from the upright, immutable (unwavering/ unshakable) race of the perfect Man. (Eph.4:13)

And I asked if I might understand it, and he said to me, The One God is a king with nothing above it. It is he who exists as God and Father of everything, the invisible One who rules over everything, who exists as incorruptible, which is in the pure light that no eye can look upon.
He is the invisible Spirit. It is not correct to think of him as a god, or anything similar. He is more than god, since there is nothing above him, for no one is above him. He does not exist within anything inferior to him, because everything exists within him. He has establishes himself. He is eternal, self-sufficient, and self-sustaining. He is complete perfection. He did not lack anything to be complete and he is continually perfect in light. He is unlimited, since there was no one before him to limit him. He is unknowable, since there exists no one prior to him to comprehend him. He is immeasurable, since there was no one before him to measure him. He is invisible, since no one has seen him. He is eternal, since he exists always. He is an enigma, since no one was able to apprehend him or explain him. He is unnamable, since there is no one came before him to give him a name.

He is One, immeasurable light, which is pure, holy and immaculate. He is too sacred to speak of, being perfect and incorruptible. He is beyond perfection, blessedness, and divinity, because he is vastly superior to them all. He is not corporeal nor is he incorporeal. He is

One and cannot be qualified or quantified, for no one can know him. He is not one among other beings; instead, he is far superior to all. He is so superior to all things that his essence is not part of the kingdoms, nor is he part of time. He who is a kingdom was created beforehand. Time does not matter to him, since he does not receive anything from another, for it would be received on loan. He who comes first needs nothing from anyone. Such a one expectantly beholds himself in his own light. He is majestic perfection. He is pure, immeasurable mind. He is a kingdom that gives the kingdoms their kingdom. He is life that gives life. He is the blessed One that blesses. He is knowledge and he gives knowledge. He is goodness that gives goodness. He is mercy and redemption and he bestows mercy. He is grace that gives grace. He does not give because he has these things but he gives the immeasurable, incomprehensible light from which all things flow.

How am I to speak with you about him? His kingdom is indestructible, at peace and existing in silence, at rest before everything was. He is the head of all the kingdoms (kingdoms), and he gives them strength in his goodness. For we know not the things that are unspeakably sacred, and we do not understand that which cannot be measured, except for him who was created from him, namely from the Father. It is he alone who told it to us.

He who beholds himself in the light which surrounds him and comes from him is the spring of the water of life. It is he who sustains the entire kingdom in every way, and it is he who gazes upon the image which he sees in the spring of the Spirit. It is he who puts his desire in the liquid light which is in the spring of the pure liquid light which surrounds him.
The Father's thought performed a deed and she was created from it. It is she who had appeared before him in the shining of his light. This is the first power which was before all of them and which was created from his mind. She is the Thought of the All and her light

shines like his light. It is the perfect power which is the visage of the invisible. She is the pure, undefiled Spirit who is perfect. She is the first power, the glory of Barbelo, the perfect glory of the kingdom (kingdoms), the glory revealed. She glorified the pure, undefiled Spirit and it was she who praised him, because thanks to him she had come forth. She is the first thought, his image; she became the womb of everything, for it is she who preceded them all. She is the Mother-Father, the first man, the Holy Spirit, the threefold male, the triple power, the androgynous one with three names, and the eternal kingdom among the invisible ones, and the first to come forth.

She asked the invisible, pure, undefiled Spirit, Barbelo, to give her Foreknowledge, and the Spirit agreed. And when he had agreed, the Foreknowledge was created, and it stood by the Thought; it originates from the thought of the invisible, pure, undefiled Spirit. It glorified him and his perfect power, Barbelo. It was for it was because of her that it had been created.

And she asked again to grant her indestructibility, and he agreed. When he had agreed, indestructibility was created, and it stood by the Divine Thought and the Foreknowledge. It glorified the invisible One and Barbelo, the one because of whom they had been created.

And Barbelo asked to grant her Eternal Life. And the invisible Spirit agreed. And when he had agreed, Eternal Life was created, and they attended and glorified the invisible Spirit and Barbelo, the one because of whom they had been created.

And she asked again to grant her truth. And the invisible Spirit agreed. And when he had agreed, Truth was created, and they attended and glorified the invisible, excellent Spirit and his Barbelo, the one because of whom they had been created.

This is the five-fold creation of the kingdom of the Father, which is the first man and the image of the invisible Spirit, which came from Barbelo, who was the divine Thought; Forethought, Foreknowledge, Indestructibility, Eternal life, and Truth.

This is the androgynous five-fold being of the kingdom, which is the ten types of kingdoms, which is the Father.
(Five, being both male and female, or neither male nor female, become ten)

And he looked at Barbelo with his pure light which surrounds the invisible Spirit, and his sparks, and she was impregnated by him. And a spark of light produced a light resembling his blessedness but it did not equal his greatness. This was the only-begotten child of the Mother-Father which had come forth. It is the only offspring and the only begotten of the Father, the pure Light.
And the invisible, pure, undefiled Spirit rejoiced over the light which was created, that which was produced by the first power of his Thought, which is Barbelo. And he poured his goodness over it until it became perfect and did not lack in any goodness, because he had anointed the child with the goodness of the invisible Spirit. It was his child and the child was there with him and he poured upon the child an anointing. And immediately when the child had received the Spirit, it glorified the Holy Spirit and the perfect Divine Thought, because the child owed these its existence.
And it asked to be given Mind as a fellow worker, and he agreed gladly. And when the invisible Spirit had agreed, the Mind was created, and it attended the anointed one (Christ), glorifying him and Barbelo. And all these were created in silence.

And Mind wanted to initiate and action through the word of the invisible Spirit. Thus, his will became an action and it appeared with the mind; and the light glorified it. And the word followed the will. It was because of the word that Christ, the divine self-created one, created everything. And Eternal Life and his will and Mind and Foreknowledge attended and glorified the invisible Spirit and Barbelo, because of whom they had been created.

And the Holy Spirit perfected and matured the divine Self-created one, and brought the son, together with Barbelo, so that he might present himself to the mighty and invisible, pure, undefiled Spirit as the divine Self-created one, the Christ (the anointed one) who loudly proclaimed honor to the spirit. He was created through Forethought. And the invisible, pure, undefiled Spirit placed the divine Self-created one of truth over everything. And he caused every authority to be subject to him and to Truth, which is in him, so that he may know the name of the "All," whose name is exalted above every name. That name will only be spoken to those who are worthy of it.

From the light, which is the Christ, there is incorruptibleness and through the gift of the Spirit four lights shone from the divine Self-created one. He wished that they might be with him. And the three are will, thought, and life. And the four powers are Understanding, Grace, Perception, and Thoughtfulness.

And Grace belongs to the everlasting realm of the luminary Harmozel, which is the first angel. And there are three other kingdoms with this everlasting kingdom: Grace, Truth, and Form. And the second luminary is Oriel, who has authority over the second everlasting realm. And there are three other kingdoms with him: Conception, Perception, and Memory. And the third luminary is Daveithai, who has authority over the third everlasting realm. And there are three other kingdoms with him: Understanding, Love, and Idea. And the fourth luminary, Eleleth, was given authority over the fourth everlasting realm. And there are three other kingdoms with him: Perfection, Peace, and Wisdom (Sophia). These are the four luminaries which serve the divine Self-created one. These are the twelve kingdoms which serve the child of god, the Self-created one, the Christ. They serve him through the will and the grace of the invisible Spirit. The twelve kingdoms belong to the child of the Self-created one. All things were established by the will of the Holy Spirit through the Self-created one.

From the Foreknowledge of the perfect mind, through the expression of the will of the invisible Spirit and the will of the Self-created one, the perfect Man came into being. He was the first revelation and the truth. The pure, undefiled Spirit called him "Adam, The Stranger" (not of the earthly realm, but belonging to the divine realm). The spirit placed him over the first realm with the mighty one, the Self-created one, the Christ, by the authority of the first luminary, Harmozel; and with him are his powers. And the invisible one gave Adam The Stranger an invincible spiritual power. And Adam The Stranger spoke, glorifying and praising the invisible Spirit, saying, "It is because of you that everything has been created and therefore, everything will return to you. I shall praise and glorify you and the Self-created one and all the realms, the three: the Father, the Mother, and the Son, who make up the perfect power."

And Adam The Stranger placed his son Seth over the second realm in which the second luminary Oriel is present. And in the third realm the children of Seth were established over the third luminary, Daveithai. And the souls of the saints were lodged there. In the fourth realm the souls are kept of those who do not know the Pleroma and who did not repent at once. These are they who persisted for a while and repented afterwards; they are in the area of the fourth luminary, Eleleth. They are those which glorify the invisible Spirit.

And the Sophia of the eternal realm manifested a thought from herself through the invisible Spirit and Foreknowledge. She wanted to produce a likeness of herself out of herself without the consent of the Spirit, but he had not approved. She attempted this act without her male consort, and without his permission. She had no male approval thus, she had not found her agreement. She had considered this without the consent of the Spirit and the knowledge of her compliment, but she brought forth her creation anyway. Because of the invincible power she possessed her thought did not remain idle, and something came out of her which was imperfect and different from her appearance because she had produced it without her compliment. It did not look like its mother because it has another form.

As she beheld the results of her desire, it changed into a form of a lion-faced serpent. Its eyes were like fire-like lightning which flashed. When she saw it she cast it away from her and threw it outside the realm so that none of the immortal ones might see it, for she had created it in ignorance. She surrounded it with a brightly glowing cloud and she put a throne in the middle of the cloud that no one might see it except the Holy Spirit who is called the mother of all that lives. And she called his name Yaldaboth.

This is the first Archon who took great power from his mother. And he left her and moved away from the realm in which he was born. He became strong and created for himself other kingdoms with a flame of glowing fire which still existed. And he mated with his own mindless ego that he had with him (he masturbated / or he was like is mother and did the same act of creation by himself) and brought into existence authorities for himself.

The name of the first one is Athoth, whom the generations call the reaper.
The second one is Harmas, who is the eye of envy.
The third one is Kalila-Oumbri.
The fourth one is Yabel.
The fifth one is Adonaiou, who is called Sabaoth (fool or chaos).
The sixth one is Cain, whom the generations of humans call the sun.
The seventh is Abel.

The eighth is Abrisene.
The ninth is Yobel.
The tenth is Armoupieel.
The eleventh is Melceir-Adonein.
The twelfth is Belias, it is he who is over the depth of Hades.
(These could be the 12 stations of the zodiac.)

There he placed seven kings corresponding to the sections of heaven to reign over the seven heavens and he placed five to reign over the depth of the abyss. (There were 7 known planets at the time of writing.) And he shared his fire with them, but he did not relinquish any power of the light which he had taken from his mother, for he is ignorant darkness.

And when light is added to darkness, it made the darkness bright. When darkness is added to light, it dims the light and it became neither light nor dark, but it became like dusk.

Now the Archon who is like the gloaming (gloom) has three names. The first name is Yaldaboth (fool / son of chaos), the second is Saklas, and the third is Samael. And he is evil in the arrogance and thoughtlessness that is in him. For he said, "I am God and there is no other God beside me" (Isaiah chapters 45 and 46). He said this because he did not know where his strength originated, nor from where he himself had come.

And the Archons created seven powers for themselves, and the powers created for themselves six angels for each one until they became 365 angels (the number of days in the solar year). And these are the bodies belonging with the names:
The first is Athoth, a he has a sheep's face;
The second is Eloaiou, he has a donkey's face;
The third is Astaphaios, he has a hyena's face;
The fourth is Yao, he has a snake face with seven heads;

The fifth is Sabaoth, he has a dragon's face;
The sixth is Adonin, he had a ape face;
The seventh is Sabbede (or Sabbadaios), he has a face that shone like fire.
This is the nature of seven types within the week.

But Yaldaboth had a plethora of faces, more than all of them, so that he could exhibit any face he wished to any of them, when he is in the midst of seraphim (seraphim plural of seraph. Seraphim are a class or type of angel of which, according to this text, Yaldaboth seems to be the head). He shared his fire with them and became their lord. He called himself God because of the power of the glory (brightness) he possessed that was taken from his mother's light. He rebelled against the place from which he came.

And he united the seven powers of his thoughts with the authorities that were with him. And when he spoke it became (happened).

And he named each power beginning with the highest:
The first is goodness with the first authority, Athoth;
The second is Foreknowledge with the second power, Eloaio; The third is divinity with the third one, Astraphaio);
The fourth is lordship with the fourth power, Yao;
The fifth is kingdom with the fifth one, Sabaoth;
The sixth is envy with the sixth one, Adonein;
The seventh is understanding with the seventh one, Sabbateon.
And these each has a kingdom (sphere on influence) within the realm (kingdom of heaven).
They were given names according to the glory belonging to heaven for the powers of their destructiveness. And there was power in the names given to them by their creator. But the names they were given according to the glory of heaven would mean their loss of power and their destruction. Thus they have two names.

He (Yaldaboth) created all things and structured things after the model of the first kingdom created so that he might create things in an incorruptible manner. It was not because he had ever seen the indestructible ones, but the power in him, which he had taken from his mother, produced in him the image of the order of the universe. And when he saw the creation surrounding him the innumerable amount of angels around him that had come from him, he said to them, "I am a jealous God, and there is no other God beside me." (Exodus 20:3) But by announcing this he had let the angels who were with him know that there is another God. If there were no other god, why would he be jealous?

Then the mother began to move here and there. She realized she has lost part of herself when the brightness of her light dimmed. And she became darker because her partner had not consorted with her.

I (John) said, Lord, what does it mean that she moved here and there? The lord smiled and said, "Do not think happened the way that Moses said it did 'above the waters'." (Genesis 1:2) No, it did not, but when she had seen the wickedness which had happened, and the fact her son had stolen from her, she repented. In the darkness of ignorance began to forget and to be ashamed. She did not dare to go back there, but she was restless. This restlessness was the moving here and there.

And the prideful one stole power from his mother. For he was ignorant and thought that there was no other in existence except his mother. When he saw innumerable angels he had created he exalted himself above them. When the mother recognized that the cloak (body) of darkness was imperfect, and she knew that her partner had not consorted with her, she repented and wept greatly. The entire pleroma heard the prayer of her repentance, and they praised the invisible, pure, undefiled Spirit on her behalf. And the Spirit agreed and when he agreed the Holy Spirit anointed her from the entire pleroma. For her consort did not come to her alone, but he brought to her through the pleroma that which was needed to restore what she was lacking. And she was allowed to ascend, not to her own kingdom but to the kingdom above her son, that she could remain in the ninth (heaven / kingdom) until she restored what she lacked in herself.

And a voice called from the highest kingdom of heaven: "The Man exists and the son of Man." And the head Archon, Yaldaboth, heard it and thought that the voice had come from his mother. He did not know whence it came. He taught them, the holy and perfect Mother-Father, the complete Foreknowledge, the image of the invisible one who is the Father of the all things and through whom everything came into being, the first Man. He is the one who revealed his image in human form.

And the whole kingdom of the first (head) Archon quaked, and the foundations of the abyss shook. And the underside of waters, which are above material world, were illuminated by the appearance of his image which had been revealed. When all the authorities and the head Archon looked, they saw the whole region of the underside (of the waters) that was illuminated. And through the light they saw the form of the image (reflected) in the water.

And he (Yaldaboth) said to the authorities him, "Come, let us make a man using the image of God as a template to our likeness, that his image may become a light for us." And they created by the means of their various powers matching the features which were given to them. And each authority supplied a feature in the form of the image which Yaldaboth had seen in its natural form. He created a being according to the likeness of the first, perfect Man. And they said, "Let us call him Adam (man), that his name may be a power of light for us."

And the powers began to create.
The first one, Goodness, created a bone essence; and the second, Foreknowledge, created a sinew essence; the third, Divinity, created a flesh essence; and the fourth, the Lordship, created a marrow essence; the fifth, Kingdom created a blood essence; the sixth, Envy, created a skin essence; the seventh, Understanding, created a hair essence. And the multitude of the angels were with him and they received from the powers the seven elements of the natural (form) so they could create the proportions of the limbs and the proportion of the buttocks and correct functioning of each of the parts together.

The first one began to create the head. Eteraphaope-Abron created his head; Meniggesstroeth created the brain; Asterechme created the right eye; Thaspomocha, the left eye; Yeronumos, the right ear; Bissoum, the left ear; Akioreim, the nose; Banen-Ephroum, the lips; Amen, the teeth; Ibikan, the molars; Basiliademe, the tonsils; Achcha, the uvula; Adaban, the neck; Chaaman, the vertebrae; Dearcho, the throat; Tebar, the right shoulder; the left shoulder; Mniarcon, the right elbow; the left elbow; Abitrion, the right underarm; Evanthen, the left underarm; Krys, the right hand; Beluai, the left hand; Treneu, the fingers of the right hand; Balbel, the fingers of the left hand; Kriman, the nails of the hands; Astrops, the right breast; Barroph, the left breast; Baoum, the right shoulder joint; Ararim, the left shoulder joint; Areche, the belly; Phthave, the navel; Senaphim, the abdomen; Arachethopi, the right ribs; Zabedo, the left ribs; Barias, the right hip; Phnouth the left hip; Abenlenarchei, the marrow; Chnoumeninorin, the bones; Gesole, the stomach; Agromauna, the heart; Bano, the lungs; Sostrapal, the liver; Anesimalar, the spleen; Thopithro, the intestines; Biblo, the kidneys; Roeror, the sinews; Taphreo, the spine of the body; Ipouspoboba, the veins; Bineborin, the arteries; Atoimenpsephei, theirs are the breaths which are in all the limbs; Entholleia, all the flesh; Bedouk, the right buttock; Arabeei, the penis; Eilo, the testicles; Sorma, the genitals; Gorma-Kaiochlabar, the right thigh;

Nebrith, the left thigh; Pserem, the kidneys of the right leg; Asaklas, the left kidney; Ormaoth, the right leg; Emenun, the left leg; Knyx, the right shin-bone; Tupelon, the left shin-bone; Achiel, the right knee; Phnene, the left knee; Phiouthrom, the right foot; Boabel, its toes; Trachoun, the left foot; Phikna, its toes; Miamai, the nails of the feet; Labernioum.

And those who were appointed over all of these are: Zathoth, Armas, Kalila, Jabel, (Sabaoth, Cain, Abel). And those who are particularly active in the limbs are the head Diolimodraza, the neck Yammeax, the right shoulder Yakouib, the left shoulder Verton, the right hand Oudidi, the left one Arbao, the fingers of the right hand Lampno, the fingers of the left hand Leekaphar, the right breast Barbar, the left breast Imae, the chest Pisandriaptes, the right shoulder joint Koade, the left shoulder joint Odeor, the right ribs Asphixix, the left ribs Synogchouta, the belly Arouph, the womb Sabalo, the right thigh Charcharb, the left thigh Chthaon, all the genitals Bathinoth, the right leg Choux, the left leg Charcha, the right shin-bone Aroer, the left shin-bone Toechtha, the right knee Aol, the left knee Charaner, the right foot Bastan, its toes Archentechtha, the left foot Marephnounth, its toes Abrana.

Seven have power over all of these: Michael, Ouriel, Asmenedas, Saphasatoel, Aarmouriam, Richram, Amiorps. And the ones who are in charge of the senses are Archendekta; and he who is in charge of the receptions is Deitharbathas; and he who is in charge over the imagination is Oummaa; and he who is over creativity Aachiaram, and he who is over the whole impulse Riaramnacho.

The origin of the demons that are in the entire body is known to be these four: heat, cold, wetness, and dryness. And the mother of all of them is the material creation. And he who rules over the heat is Phloxopha; and he who rules over the cold is Oroorrothos; and he who rules over what is dry is Erimacho; and he who rules over the wetness is Athuro. And the mother of all of these is

Onorthochrasaei, who stands in with them without limits, and she covorts with all of them. She is truly material and they are sustained by her.

The four ruling demons are: Ephememphi, who is attached to pleasure,
Yoko, who is attached to desire,
Nenentophni, who is attached to grief,
Blaomen, who is attached to fear,
and the mother of them all is Aesthesis-Ouch-Epi-Ptoe.
And from the four demons passions was created. And grief spawned envy, jealousy, distress, trouble, pain, callousness, anxiety, mourning, and more. Pleasure spawned wickedness, vanity, pride, and similar things. Desire spawned anger, wrath, and bitterness, and driving passion, the inability to be satisfied, and similar things. Fear spawned dread, subservience, agony, and shame. These are both good and evil, but the understanding of their nature is attributed to Anaro, who is over the material soul. It belongs with the seven senses, which are controlled by Ouch-Epi-Ptoe.

This is the number of the angels: together they are 365. They all worked on it from limb to limb, until the physical (material) body was completed by them. Now there are other ones in charge over the remaining passions whom I did not mention to you. But if you wish to know them, it is written in the book of Zoroaster. And all the angels and demons worked until they had constructed (fashioned) the physical body. And their creation was completely devoid of activity and was motionless for a long time.

And when the mother (Sophia) wanted to recapture the power which was taken from her by the head Archon, she prayed to the Mother-Father of the All, who is most merciful. He sent a holy decree containing the five lights down to the place where the angels of the head Archon reside. They advised him (Yaldaboth) that he should bring forth the power of the mother. And they said to Yaldaboth, "Blow some of your spirit into his face and his body will arise." And he blew the spirit power of the mother into his (Adam's) face. (Genesis 2:7) Yaldaboth did not know to do this because he existed in ignorance. And the power of the mother went out of Yaldaboth into Adam's physical body, which they had fashioned after the image of the one who exists from the beginning. The body moved and gained strength, and it was enlightened.

And in that instant the other powers became jealous, although he (Adam) had been created through all of them. They were jealous because they had given Adam their power and now he was more intelligent than those who had made him, and his mind was greater than that of the head Archon. And when they recognized that he was enlightened, and that he could think better than they, and that he was free of evil, they took him and threw him into the lowest material realm.

But the blessed One, the Mother-Father, the giving and gracious One, had mercy on the power of the mother which had been transmitted from the head Archon because he did not want the Archons to gain power over the material body again. Therefore, he sent, a helper to Adam through his giving Spirit and his great compassion. The enlighted Afterthought which comes out of him is called "Life" (Zoe means life and is the name of Eve in certain Greek texts and the Septuagint). And she assists the whole creature, by working with him and restoring him to his fullness and by teaching him about the descent (flaws) of his seed and by teaching him about the way of ascent (to go upward again), which is based on the way he came down. (Rom. 8:22)

And the enlightened Afterthought was hidden within Adam so that the Archons would not know she was there, but that the

Afterthought might restore (correct) what was lacking of the mother.

And the man was revealed because of the shadow of light in him. And his thinking was higher to all those who had made him. When they looked up and realized that his thinking was superior. And they conspired with the entire force of Archons and angels. They took fire and earth and water as a mixture and added the four fiery winds. And they worked them together and caused a great noise. And they brought Adam into the shadow of death so that that they might re-make him from earth, water, fire and the spirit (wind) which make up matter. This was the ignorance of their darkness and desire, and their lying (false) spirit. This is the tomb of the reformed body that the thieves had clothed Adam in. It contained the bonds of forgetfulness and cause him to become a mortal entity. He is the first one who came down, and the first to be separated (from the Divine All). Now, it is up to the Afterthought of the light which was in him to awaken his thinking.

And the Archons took him and placed him in paradise. And they said to him, "Eat at your leisure," (Genesis 2:16) for their pleasure is bitter and their beauty is twisted. Their pleasure is entrapment and their trees lack any holiness and their fruit is deadly poison and their promise is death. And the tree of their life they had placed in the center of paradise (Genesis 2:9).

And I (Jesus) shall teach all of you the mystery of their life. It is the plan that they made together, which is made from the template of their spirit. The root of this tree is bitter and its branches are death, its shadow is hate. Its leaves are a trap, and its blossom is the ointment of evil. Its fruit is death and its seed is desire. It sprouts (blooms) in darkness. Those who taste it dwell in Hades, and they rest in darkness.

But what they call "the tree of knowledge of good and evil" is the Afterthought of the light. They stationed themselves in front of it so that Adam might not understand his fullness and recognize his nakedness and be ashamed. But it was I (Jesus) who made them decide what they ate.

And to I said to the savior, Lord, wasn't it the serpent that instructed Adam to eat? The savior smiled and said, The serpent instructed them to eat because of it's evil desire to produced sexual lust and destruction so that Adam would be useful to him. Adam knew that he was disobedient to Yaldaboth because the light of the Afterthought lived in him and made him stronger and more accurate in his thinking than the head Archon. Yaldaboth wanted to harvest the power that he himself had given Adam. And he caused Adam to forget.

And I said to the savior, "What is this forgetfulness?" He said, "It is not how Moses wrote and it is not how you have heard. He wrote in his first book, 'He put him to sleep' (Genesis 2:21), but that was how Adam perceived it. For also he said through the prophet, 'I will make their minds heavy, that they may not perceive nor understand.' (Isaiah 6:10)."

The Afterthought of the light hid herself in Adam. The head Archon wanted to bring her out through his rib but the Afterthought of the light cannot be apprehended. Although darkness pursued her, it did not catch her. Yaldaboth brought out part of Adam's power and he created another and formed a woman, using the template of the Afterthought which he had seen. The power he had taken from the Adam was formed into the female. This is what happened and not as Moses said, 'She was formed from the bone of his rib.' (Genesis 2:21)

Adam saw the woman beside him. In that instant the enlightened Afterthought appeared. She lifted the veil which occluded his mind. Adam sobered from the drunkenness of darkness and recognized his counterpart (compliment / agreement) , and he said, 'This is indeed bone of my bones and flesh of my flesh.' (Genesis 2:23) Therefore the man will leave his father and his mother, and he will cleave to his wife, and they will both be one flesh. (Genesis 2:24) For his partner will be sent to him and he will leave his father and his mother .

Our sister Sophia is the one who came down innocently in order to reclaim what she has lost. That is why she was called Life, because she is the mother of the living, by the Foreknowledge of the sovereignty of heaven. Through her they that live have tasted the perfect Knowledge. I (Jesus) appeared in the form of an eagle on the tree of knowledge, which is the Afterthought from the Foreknowledge of the pure light. I did this so that I might teach them and wake them from them the deep sleep. For they were both in a fallen state, and they recognized they were naked. The Afterthought appeared to them in the form of light and she awakened their minds.

When Yaldaboth noticed that they fled from him, he cursed the earth he has made. He found the woman as she was preparing herself for her husband. He was lord over her, though he did not know the mystery was instated through the holy plan, so they were afraid to rebel against Yaldaboth. And he demonstrated to his angels the ignorance in him by casting them out of paradise, and he clothed them in darkening blackness.

And the head Archon saw the virgin standing beside Adam, and that the enlightened Afterthought of life had appeared in her Yaldaboth was ignorant. But when the Foreknowledge of All noticed it, she sent agents and they quickly stole the life (Zoe) out of Eve.

Then, the head Archon seduced her and he conceived two sons in her. The first is Eloim and the second is Yahweh. Eloim has a face like a bear and Yahweh has a face like a cat. The one is righteous but the other is unjust. (Yahweh is related to the New Testament and is considered a more just and kind God. Eloim is related to the Old Testament and is considered a jealous, revengeful, wrathful God.) He set Yahweh over fire and wind, and he set Eloim over water and earth. And he name them Cain and Abel in an attempt to deceive.

Sexual intercourse continues to this very day because of the head Archon. He instilled sexual desire in the woman who belongs to Adam. And Adam, through intercourse caused bodies to be replicated, and Yaldaboth breathed into them with his fraudulent spirit.

And he set the two Archons (Elohim and Yehweh) over principal elements, so that they might rule over the tomb (body). When Adam recognized the image of his own Foreknowledge, he begot the image of the son of man (Jesus) and he called him Seth, according to the fashion of the divine race living in the ethereal kingdoms. The mother (Sophia) sent her spirit also. It was in her image and a was a replica of those who are in the pleroma. In this way she will prepare a dwelling place for the kingdoms to come.

Yaldaboth made them drink water of forgetfulness that he had made so that they might not remember from where they came. The seed remained with man for a while to assist him so that when the Spirit comes out from the holy kingdoms, he may raise up and heal him of his lack so the whole pleroma may again become holy and complete.

And I said to the savior, Lord, will all the souls be led safely into the pure light? He answered me and said, "Great things have arisen in your mind, and it is difficult to explain them to anyone except those from the race that cannot be moved. These are they on whom the Spirit of life will descend and with whom will be with the Power. They will be saved and become complete, perfect and worthy of greatness. They will be purified from all wickedness and evil actions. Then they will have no other care other than the incorruption, on which they shall focus their attention from here on, without anger or envy or jealousy or desire and greed for anything. They are affected by nothing except existing in the flesh, which they bear while looking expectantly for the time when they will be met by those who will receive them (their body). Such ones are worthy of the (incorruptible) imperishable, eternal life and the calling. They endure everything and bear up under everything, that they may finish the good fight (wrestling contest) and inherit eternal life. (Cor. 13:7)

I said to him, Lord, will the souls of those who did not do these works (things) but on whom the power and Spirit descended, be rejected? He answered and said to me, "If the Spirit descended upon them, they will certainly be saved, and they will be changed. The power will descend on every man, for without it no one could stand. And after they are born, when the Spirit of life grows in them and the power comes and strengthens that soul, no one can be led astray with evil deeds, but those on whom the false spirit falls are drawn astray by him.

I said, Lord, where will the souls go when they shed their flesh? And he laughed (smiled) and said to me, "The soul in which the power will become stronger than the false spirit is strong and she (the soul) turns and runs from evil and through the intervention of the incorruptible one, she is saved taken up to the kingdoms and will rest there.

And I said, "Lord, what about those who do not know to whom they belong, where will their souls go?" And he said to me, "Those, the spoiled (double-minded) spirit has gained strength while they went astray and that casts a burden on the soul and draws her towards the deeds of evil, and he throws her down into forgetfulness. After she comes out of the body, it is handed over to the authorities that came into being through the Archon. They bind her with chains and cast her into prison, and hound her until she is set free from the forgetfulness and acquires knowledge. If she becomes perfected she is saved.

And I said, Lord, how can the soul become young again and return to its mother's womb or into (another) man? (This is a question regarding reincarnation.) He was glad when I asked him this, and he said to me, "You are blessed because you have understood!" That soul is made to follow another, since the Spirit of life is in it. It is saved through that soul. It is not forced into another flesh (body) again.

And I said, Lord, "Where will the souls go form those who gained knowledge but afterward turned away?" Then he said to me, "They will go to the place where the angels of misery (abject poverty) go. This is the place where there is no repentance (escape). There they will be kept with those who have blasphemed the spirit. They will be tortured and punished forever and ever. (Heb 6:4-8 and Heb 12:17-31)

I said, "Lord, from where did the false (evil) spirit come?" Then he said to me, "The Mother-Father, who is the gracious and holy of Spirit, the One who is merciful and who has compassion for all, the Afterthought of the Foreknowledge of light raised up the child of the perfect race and their thought was the eternal light of man.

When the head Archon realized that these people were exalted above him and their minds were stronger than him he wanted to capture their thought. He did not know that their minds were stronger and that he would not be able to capture their thoughts.

He made a plan with his agents, his powers, and they raped (committed adultery together (all of them) with) Sophia, and unbearable imprisonment (bitter fate) was born through them, which is the last unbreakable bondage. It is the kind that is unpredictable fate. This fate is harder and stronger than the gods, angels and demons and all the generations until this day together have seen. It imprisoned all through periods, seasons, and times. From that fate every sin, unrighteousness, blasphemy, forgetfulness, and ignorance and every oppressive command, and carnal sins and fear emerged. From this the whole creation was blinded, so that they may not know the God who is above them all. And because of the chain of forgetfulness, their sins were hidden from them. They are bound with measures, seasons, and time since fate is lord over everything.

When the head Archon repented for everything which had been created through him, he sought to cause a flood to destroy the works of man (Genesis 6:6). But the great light, the Foreknowledge, told Noah, and Noah announced it to all the children, the sons of men. But those who were estranged from him did not listen to him. It is not as Moses said, "They hid themselves in an ark" (Genesis 7: 7), but they hid in a certain place. Noah hid and also many other people from the immutable race. They went to a certain place and hid in a shining, glowing (enlightened) cloud. Noah understood his authority because she who is part of the light was with him. She enlightened them because the head Archon darkened the entire earth.

And he planned with his agents to send his emissaries (angels) to the daughters of men so that they might take some (as wives) for themselves and raise offspring (children) for their personal enjoyment. At first they had no success so they came together again and laid a plan. They made a false spirit (like themselves), but who looked like the Spirit which had come down to them. In this way they could defile souls through it.

And the emissaries (angels) transformed themselves into the image of the husbands of the women (the daughters of men). They filled them with the spirit of darkness, which was an evil concoction they had made for them. They brought gold and silver and a gift and copper and iron and metal and all kinds of things to the angels. And they led those who followed them away into great turmoil with their lies. The people grew old without enjoying life. They died before finding truth and without knowing the God of truth. This way the entire creation was enslaved forever, from the beginning of the world until now.

And they took wives and produced children of darkness born in the image of their spirit. To this day, they closed their minds, and they hardened their hearts through the intractability of the false spirit.

I, the perfect Aeon of the All, changed myself into my own child (seed), for I existed first and have traveled every path. I am the fullness of the light. I am the remembrance of the pleroma. I sojourned to the kingdom of darkness and endured so I could I entered into the midst of this prison. The foundations of chaos shook. I disguised myself from the wicked ones, and they did not recognize me.

I returned for the second time, and I journeyed here and there. I was created from those who belong to the light, and I am that light, the perfect Aeon. I entered into the midst of darkness and depths of

Hades to accomplish my task. And the foundations of chaos shook so hard they could have fallen down and killed those in chaos. I sought to root them in light so that they might not be destroyed before the time was complete.

Still for a third time I went - I am the light which exists in the light, I am the remembrance of the perfect Aeon. I entered into the midst of darkness and the depths of Hades. I filled my face with light so I could perfect (complete) their kingdom. I came into the midst of their prison, which is the prison of the body (flesh). I announced, "He who hears, let him wake up from the deep sleep." And he wept and shed tears. He wiped away bitter tears from himself and he said, "Who is it that calls my name, and from where has this hope come to me, while I am in the chains of the prison?" And I said, 'I am the perfect Aeon of the pure light; I am the thought of the pure, undefiled Spirit, who raised you up to the place of honor. Stand and remember that it is you who heard and sought your own beginnings, which is I, the merciful one. Guard yourself against the angels of bitter providence and the demons of chaos and all those who seek to entrap you Guard against of the deep sleep and the cage of Hades.

And I stood him up and sealed him in the light of the water with five seals so that death might not have power over him ever again. Now I shall go ascend to the perfect kingdom. I have told you all I have to say. And I have said everything to you that you might write it down and give them secretly to your fellow spirits. It is the mystery of the immutable race.

And the savior gave these things to John so that he might write them down and keep them intact. And he said to him, Cursed is everyone who will trade these things for a gift or for food or for water or clothing or anything. These things were presented to him in a mystery, and immediately he disappeared from him. And he

went to his fellow disciples and told them what the savior had told him.
Jesus Christ, Amen.

Information on Coptic Apocalypse of Peter

Andreas Werner writes (New Testament Apocrypha, vol. 2, p. 702):

The manuscript of Codex VII probably derives from the 4th century (middle or end?); at this period a translation must therefore already have been available. Since it has evidently been transcribed before, we may assume an earlier time of origin, which is further confirmed by the assumption of translation from the Greek. If the text itself, with its mention of the name 'Hermas' at p. 78.18, engages in polemic against the possibility of repentance advocated in the Shepherd of Hermas, this would yield a terminus post quem on grounds of content in the middle of the 2nd century. Apoc. Pet. presupposes and criticizes the structures of a Great Church in process of consolidation, and the appropriation of Peter as the inaugurator of Gnosis is probably also directed against this; these points together with the controversy with other gnostics suggest placing the document at the end of the 2nd century or the beginning of the 3rd.

James Brashler writes (The Nag Hammadi Library in English, pp. 372-373): "The Apocalypse of Peter is significant in several respects. It contains important source material for a gnostic Christology that understands Jesus as a docetic redeemer. The view of the Gnostic community, including its relationship to Peter as its originator, is another key theme of this document. Of considerable interest are the identity of the gnostic group to which the writing is addressed, and the stage of the controversy, between emerging orthodoxy and heresy, presupposed by the tractate. It would appear that the Apocalypse of Peter was written in the third century, when this distinction between orthodoxy and heresy was rather clearly drawn."

Coptic Apocalypse of Peter

Translated by James Brashler and Roger A. Bullard

As the Savior was sitting in the temple in the three hundredth (year) of the covenant and the agreement of the tenth pillar, and being satisfied with the number of the living, incorruptible Majesty, he said to me, "Peter, blessed are those above belonging to the Father, who revealed life to those who are from the life, through me, since I reminded they who are built on what is strong, that they may hear my word, and distinguish words of unrighteousness and transgression of law from righteousness, as being from the height of every word of this Pleroma of truth, having been enlightened in good pleasure by him whom the principalities sought. But they did not find him, nor was he mentioned among any generation of the prophets. He has now appeared among these, in him who appeared, who is the Son of Man, who is exalted above the heavens in a fear of men of like essence. But you yourself, Peter, become perfect in accordance with your name with myself, the one who chose you, because from you I have established a base for the remnant whom I have summoned to knowledge. Therefore be strong until the imitation of righteousness - of him who had summoned you, having summoned you to know him in a way which is worth doing because of the rejection which happened to him, and the sinews of his hands and his feet, and the crowning by those of the middle region, and the body of his radiance which they bring in hope of service because of a reward of honor - as he was about to reprove you three times in this night."

And as he was saying these things, I saw the priests and the people running up to us with stones, as if they would kill us; and I was afraid that we were going to die.

And he said to me, "Peter, I have told you many times that they are blind ones who have no guide. If you want to know their blindness, put your hands upon (your) eyes - your robe - and say what you see."

But when I had done it, I did not see anything. I said "No one sees (this way)."

Again he told me, "Do it again."

And there came in me fear with joy, for I saw a new light greater than the light of day. Then it came down upon the Savior. And I told him about those things which I saw.

And he said to me again, "Lift up your hands and listen to what the priests and the people are saying."

And I listened to the priests as they sat with the scribes. The multitudes were shouting with their voice.

When he heard these things from me he said to me, "Prick up your ears and listen to the things they are saying."

And I listened again, "As you sit, they are praising you".

And when I said these things, the Savior said, "I have told you that these (people) are blind and deaf. Now then, listen to the things which they are telling you in a mystery, and guard them, Do not tell them to the sons of this age. For they shall blaspheme you in these ages since they are ignorant of you, but they will praise you in knowledge."

"For many will accept our teaching in the beginning. And they will turn from them again by the will of the Father of their error, because they have done what he wanted. And he will reveal them in his judgment, i.e., the servants of the Word. But those who became mingled with these shall become their prisoners, since they are without perception. And the guileless, good, pure one they push to the worker of death, and to the kingdom of those who praise Christ in a restoration. And they praise the men of the propagation of falsehood, those who will come after you. And they will cleave to the name of a dead man, thinking that they will become pure. But they will become greatly defiled and they will fall into a name of error, and into the hand of an evil, cunning man and a manifold dogma, and they will be ruled without law."

"For some of them will blaspheme the truth and proclaim evil teaching. And they will say evil things against each other. Some will be named: (those) who stand in (the) strength of the archons, of a man and a naked woman who is manifold and subject to much suffering. And those who say these things will ask about dreams. And if they say that a dream came from a demon worthy of their error, then they shall be given perdition instead of incorruption."

"For evil cannot produce good fruit. For the place from which each of them is produces that which is like itself; for not every soul is of the truth, nor of immortality. For every soul of these ages has death assigned to it in our view, because it is always a slave, since it is created for its desires and their eternal destruction, in which they are and from which they are. They love the creatures of the matter which came forth with them."

"But the immortal souls are not like these, O Peter. But indeed, as long as the hour is not yet come, it (the immortal soul) shall resemble a mortal one. But it shall not reveal its nature, that it alone is the immortal one, and thinks about immortality, having faith, and desiring to renounce these things."

"For people do not gather figs from thorns or from thorn trees, if they are wise, nor grapes from thistles. For, on the one hand, that which is always becoming is in that from which it is, being from what is not good, which becomes destruction for it and death. But that which comes to be in the Eternal One is in the One of the life and the immortality of the life which they resemble."

"Therefore all that which exists not will dissolve into what exists not. For deaf and blind ones join only with their own kind."

"But others shall change from evil words and misleading mysteries. Some who do not understand mystery speak of things which they do not understand, but they will boast that the mystery of the truth is theirs alone. And in haughtiness they shall grasp at pride, to envy the immortal soul which has become a pledge. For every authority, rule, and power of the aeons wishes to be with these in the creation of the world, in order that those who are not, having been forgotten by those that are, may praise them, though they have not been saved, nor have they been brought to the Way by them, always wishing that they may become imperishable ones. For if the immortal soul receives power in an intellectual spirit -. But immediately they join with one of those who misled them."

"But many others, who oppose the truth and are the messengers of error, will set up their error and their law against these pure thoughts of mine, as looking out from one (perspective) thinking that good and evil are from one (source). They do business in my word. And they will propagate harsh fate. The race of immortal souls will go in it in vain, until my Parousia. For they shall come out of them - and my forgiveness of their transgressions, into which they fell through their adversaries, whose ransom I got from the slavery in which they were, to give them freedom that they may create an imitation remnant in the name of a dead man, who is Hermas, of the first-born of unrighteousness, in order that the light which exists may not believed by the little ones. But those of this sort are the workers who will be cast into the outer darkness, away from the sons of light. For neither will they enter, nor do they permit those who are going up to their approval for their release."

"And still others of them who suffer think that they will perfect the wisdom of the brotherhood which really exists, which is the spiritual fellowship of those united in communion, through which the wedding of incorruptibility shall be revealed. The kindred race of the sisterhood will appear as an imitation. These are the ones who oppress their brothers, saying to them, "Through this our God has pity, since salvation comes to us through this," not knowing the punishment of those who are made glad by those who have done this thing to the little ones whom they saw, (and) whom they took prisoner."

"And there shall be others of those who are outside our number who name themselves bishop and also deacons, as if they have received their authority from God. They bend themselves under the judgment of the leaders. Those people are dry canals."

But I said " I am afraid because of what you have told me, that indeed little (ones) are, in our view, the counterfeit ones, indeed, that there are multitudes that will mislead other multitudes of living ones, and destroy them among themselves. And when they speak your name they will be believed."

The Savior said, "For a time determined for them in proportion to their error they will rule over the little ones. And after the completion of the error, the never-aging one of the immortal understanding shall become young, and they (the little ones) shall rule over those who are their rulers. The root of their error he shall pluck out, and he shall put it to shame so that it shall be manifest in all the impudence which it has assumed to itself. And such ones shall become unchangeable, O Peter."

"Come therefore, let us go on with the completion of the will of the incorruptible Father. For behold, those who will bring them judgment are coming, and they will put them to shame. But me they cannot touch. And you, O Peter, shall stand in their midst. Do not be afraid because of your cowardice. Their minds shall be closed, for the invisible one has opposed them."

When he had said those things, I saw him seemingly being seized by them. And I said "What do I see, O Lord? That it is you yourself whom they take, and that you are grasping me? Or who is this one, glad and laughing on the tree? And is it another one whose feet and hands they are striking?"

The Savior said to me, "He whom you saw on the tree, glad and laughing, this is the living Jesus. But this one into whose hands and feet they drive the nails is his fleshly part, which is the substitute being put to shame, the one who came into being in his likeness. But look at him and me."

But I, when I had looked, said "Lord, no one is looking at you. Let us flee this place."

But he said to me, "I have told you, 'Leave the blind alone!'. And you, see how they do not know what they are saying. For the son of their glory instead of my servant, they have put to shame."

And I saw someone about to approach us resembling him, even him who was laughing on the tree. And he was <filled> with a Holy Spirit, and he is the Savior. And there was a great, ineffable light around them, and the multitude of ineffable and invisible angels blessing them. And when I looked at him, the one who gives praise was revealed.

And he said to me, "Be strong, for you are the one to whom these mysteries have been given, to know them through revelation, that he whom they crucified is the first-born, and the home of demons, and the stony vessel in which they dwell, of Elohim, of the cross, which is under the Law. But he who stands near him is the living Savior, the first in him, whom they seized and released, who stands joyfully looking at those who did him violence, while they are divided among themselves. Therefore he laughs at their lack of perception, knowing that they are born blind. So then the one susceptible to suffering shall come, since the body is the substitute. But what they released was my incorporeal body. But I am the intellectual Spirit filled with radiant light. He whom you saw coming to me is our intellectual Pleroma, which unites the perfect light with my Holy Spirit."

"These things, then, which you saw you shall present to those of another race who are not of this age. For there will be no honor in any man who is not immortal, but only (in) those who were chosen from an immortal substance, which has shown that it is able to contain him who gives his abundance. Therefore I said, 'Every one who has, it will be given to him, and he will have plenty.' But he who does not have, that is, the man of this place, who is completely dead, who is removed from the planting of the creation of what is begotten, whom, if one of the immortal essence appears, they think that they possess him - it will be taken from him and be added to the one who is. You, therefore, be courageous and do not fear at all.

For I shall be with you in order that none of your enemies may prevail unto you. Peace be to you, Be strong!"

When he (Jesus) had said these things, he (Peter) came to himself.

Information on Thunder, Perfect Mind

"Thunder, Perfect Mind" is a powerful and enigmatic poem that has captured the imagination of scholars, theologians, and spiritual seekers since its discovery among the Gnostic texts in the Nag Hammadi library in the 20th century. This ancient text, often attributed to the Gnostic tradition, provides a unique and poetic exploration of divine identity, feminine wisdom, and the paradoxical nature of existence.

The origin of "Thunder, Perfect Mind" is shrouded in mystery, much like many other Gnostic texts. The Nag Hammadi library, discovered in Egypt in 1945, contained a collection of Gnostic scriptures that were hidden away in the 4th century to escape destruction during the suppression of non-canonical Christian writings. Most of the texts were written on papyrus and were written in the Coptic language. Some date to the first century C.E.

The Gnostic tradition itself was a diverse and mystical movement within early Christianity that emphasized direct spiritual experience, inner knowledge (gnosis), and the pursuit of divine understanding beyond the confines of orthodox doctrine.

It has been theorized that the text was originally composed in Greek due to its meter and phrasing, and it has been dated to a period of time before 350 C.E., the date of the Coptic manuscript from which the text originates. The paradoxical lines resemble Greek identity riddles, a common poetic form in the Mediterranean during the period.

Despite being associated with Gnostic Christianity, the specific origins of "Thunder, Perfect Mind" remain uncertain. The authorship of the text is unknown, and it is unclear whether it was composed by a single individual or emerged from a community of believers.

The title "Thunder, Perfect Mind" suggests a powerful and transcendent force. The word "thunder" evokes a sense of divine authority and awe, while "perfect mind" implies a wisdom that surpasses human understanding. The poem is written in the first person, with the speaker expressing a series of paradoxical statements that challenge conventional notions of divinity, gender, and identity. One can see the structure using doublets in a contradictory, paradoxical way, as if to say to the reader, God can be opposites at the same time. This same structure is used to augment a description of God, as if to say, God to great, and even greater than that.

One of the striking features of "Thunder, Perfect Mind" is the fluid and shape-shifting nature of the speaker's identity. The speaker identifies as both the divine and the marginalized, the exalted and the debased. This dynamic interplay of opposites reflects the Gnostic belief in the dualistic nature of the material world and the transcendent realm of the divine. The speaker declares, "I am the first and the last. I am the honored one and the scorned one. I am the whore and the holy one." This paradoxical self-description challenges traditional religious categories and invites the reader to contemplate the complexity of divine existence.

The feminine aspect of the divine is a prominent theme in "Thunder, Perfect Mind." The speaker identifies as a feminine presence, claiming, "For I am the wisdom of the Greeks and the knowledge of the barbarians (foreigners / aliens). I am the judgment of the Greeks and the foreigner, alien, or barbarians. I am the one whose image is great in Egypt." This portrayal of divine wisdom as feminine challenges the prevailing patriarchal interpretations of religious texts and highlights the multifaceted nature of the divine. Yet, toward the end of the text there are statements made in a male voice, showing both listeners and God are both.

The form of writing, in paradoxical doublets, is found in works such as, The Psalms of Thomas". It also reminds one of the Tao Te Ching. As an example, "Those who know do not speak and those who speak do not know." This leads one to look at "Thunder, Perfect Mind" in the same light as an extended koan, which challenges the mind and reminds one that The Way (Tao) or God cannot be articulated.

"Thunder, Perfect Mind" also calls to mind an approach to the divine labeled "apophatic theology" found in books such as "The Cloud of Unknowing". This approach does not try to explain God, but instead rips away all preconceived ideas to reveal the truth that anything that can be experienced, expressed, or conceived is not God, but simply an expression or idea of God. Instead Thunder, Perfect Mind takes an opposite approach, presenting the reader with ideas so contradictory that one could say God is everything at once, Gnosis is everything and everywhere, and therefore as incomprehensible as the very idea of nothingness.

The poem also explores the idea of divine immanence and transcendence. The speaker declares, "I am the one who is hated everywhere and loved everywhere. I am the one whom they call Life, and you have called Death." This statement encapsulates the paradoxical nature of the divine, simultaneously present in all aspects of existence and yet often misunderstood or rejected by humanity.

The meaning of "Thunder, Perfect Mind" is open to interpretation, and scholars have offered various readings of its significance. Some see it as a hymn celebrating the divine feminine, challenging traditional gender roles and hierarchies. Others view it as a mystical expression of the Gnostic understanding of the divine as both immanent and transcendent, beyond human comprehension. The poem's rich symbolism and evocative language invite readers to delve into its depths and explore the mysteries it presents.

"Thunder, Perfect Mind" stands as a testament to the complexity and depth of the Gnostic tradition. Its enigmatic verses challenge conventional religious narratives, inviting readers to contemplate the paradoxes of existence, the fluidity of divine identity, and the wisdom that transcends human understanding. As we engage with this ancient text, we are reminded of the enduring power of poetry to inspire contemplation and exploration of the profound mysteries of life and spirituality.

Because of the age of the text, there is damage and some letters, words, and lines cannot be read. At these points, we indicate the missing text in brackets [...]. When there are various ways of translating the text we indicate alternate wording in parentheses ( ).

Thunder: Perfect Mind

I was sent forth from the Power

And I have come to those who meditate upon me.

And I have been found among those who pursue me.

Gaze upon me, all you who meditate on me;

And you who listen, hear me!

You who abide (tarry) for me, take me into yourselves.

And do not turn your gaze away from me.

And do not make your voice hate me (do not say you hate me), nor your hearing (nor hate my sound when you hear it).

Do not be ignorant of me at any place or any time (Do not stop thinking of me at any place or during any time).

Be on guard!

Do not take your mind off me.

For I am the first and the last.

I am the honored and the scorned,

I am the whore and the holy one.

I am the wife and the virgin.

I am the mother and the daughter.

I am the members of my mother's family.

I am the barren one and the one with many sons.

I am she who had many marriages, and I have not taken a husband.

I am the midwife and she who does not give birth.

I am the place of comfort from labor pains.

I am the bride and the bridegroom.

It is my husband who brought me forth.

I am the mother of my father and the sister of my husband (grandfather and sister-in-law).

And he (my husband) is my offspring.

I am the slave of him who prepared me and I am the king of my offspring.

But he is the one who brought me forth before the time on a day of birth

and he is my offspring in (the fullness of) time.

My power is from him.

I am the rod of his power in his youth

and he is the rod of my old age.

And whatever he wills shall happen to me.

I am the silence that cannot be comprehended,

and I am the thought that repeats in your mind.

I am the voice of many sounds and the word (logos) whose appearance takes many forms.

I am the vocalization (sound / utterance) of my name (I am the manifestation of my name uttered).

You who hate me, why do you love me

And why do you hate those who love me?

You who deny me, proclaim (confess) me,

And you who proclaim (confess) me, deny me.

You who speak the truth about me, tell lies about me,

And you who have lied about me, speak the truth about me.

You who know me, become ignorant of me,

and those who have been ignorant of me, will come to know me.

For I am knowledge and ignorance.

I am timidity (shame) and boldness.

I am unashamed, I am ashamed.

I am strength and I am fear.

I am war and peace.

Give heed to me.

I am disgraced and the exalted one.

Give notice of my poverty and my wealth.

Do not look down on me when I am discarded upon the ground (earth),

And you will find me among those who are to come.

And when you see me on the garbage-heap, do not leave me there discarded.

And you will find me in the kingdoms.

And do not look upon me now laugh at me when I am thrown away with those who are disgraced and in the lowest (least) places.

And do not discard me (cast me down) among those who are killed violently.

I am merciful and I am cruel.

So be on your guard!

Do not hate my obedience,

And do not love my self-control.

 Do not forsake me in my (time of) weakness.

And do not be afraid of my power.

Why then do you despise my fear

And curse my pride?

I am she who exists in all fears and in boldness and in trembling.

I am she who is weak, and I do well in a place of pleasure.

I am foolish (senseless – beyond your senses) and I am wise.

Why have you hated me in your places of discussion and debate (counsels)?

For this reason I shall be silent among those who are silent,

And then I shall appear and speak?

Why have you hated me, you Greeks?

Because I am a non-Greek among non-Greeks?

For I am the Wisdom (Sophia) of the Greeks

And the Gnosis (Knowledge) of foreigners (non-Greeks / barbarians).

I am the judgment for Greeks and foreigners (non-Greeks / barbarians).

I am the one whose multiple images are in Egypt. (the one whose image is great in Egypt)

And the one who has no image among foreigners (non-Greeks / barbarians).

I am she who has been hated everywhere

and she who has been loved everywhere.

I am she who is called Life and you have called Death.

I am she who is called Law and you have called Lawlessness.

I am the one you have pursued, and I am the one you have caught (seized / restrained).

I am the one you have scattered and the one you have gathered together.

Before me you have been ashamed and you have been shameless to me (unashamed).

I am she who observes no holy days (festival) and I am she whose holy days (festivals) are many.

I am the one who is godless and I am she whose God is great (multiple).

I am the one you meditate one and the one whom you have rejected (scorned).

I am ignorant, and yet it is from me they learn.

I am she whom you have despised but it is me you think of.

I am the one you hide from, yet you appear to me (are made manifest to me).

But whenever you hide yourselves, I will be made manifest.

For whenever you are manifest, I will hide myself from you.

[NOTE: Here, the codex is damaged and the some of the text is missing.]

Those who have […] to it

[…]

[…] senselessly

Take me […] understanding out of grief (pain),

and receive me to yourselves in understanding and in grief (pain).

Receive me to yourselves in disgraceful places and places in ruin.

And seize (take / rob) from me those (things) which are good even though in disgrace.

Note: Another rendering could be: Lay hold on me from those who are good, even though you do so in disgrace.

Out of shame, receive me to yourselves without shame.

And out of shamelessness and shame, blame my members among yourselves.

And come toward (closer to) to me, you who know me and who know my members.

Establish the mighty ones from among the small first creatures.

Come forward into childhood and do not hate it because it is tiny and small.

And do not turn your back even slightly on greatnesses (which are) in parts from smallnesses,

for the things of smallness are known from the things of greatness.

Why do you curse me and honor me?

You have wounded and you have had mercy.

Do not separate me from the first ones whom you have known.

And do not cast anyone out and do not bring anyone back [...]

(Note: Here the codex is damaged and letters are missing.)

...Throw you away (brought you back)

and ... know him not.

[I...] what is mine

[...]

I know the first ones and those after them know me.

But I am the perfect mind and the respite of the [...]

I am the gnosis of my seeking, and the discovery of those who seek me.

And the command of those who inquire of me.

And the power of the powers by my gnosis

of the angels who have been sent at my logos (word/command),

And the gods in their seasons (times) by my command,

And it is of (with) me that the spirits of all humans exist,

and it is within me that women live.

I am she who is honored and praised

and who is scornfully hated.

I am peace but because of me war has come.

And I am a foreigner and a citizen.

I am substance and she who has no substance.

Those who come into being from my synousia (intercourse – congress – social interaction)

are ignorant of me,

And those who are in my substance know me.

Those who are close to me have been ignorant of me

And those who are far from me have known me.

On the day when I am close, you are far away from me

And on the day when I am far away from you, I am close to you.

I am [....] within.

[I am] ..... of the natures.

I am [......] of the creation of spirits ....inquiry of the souls.

I am controlled and unrestraint.

I am union and disintegration.

I am the enduring and I am the releasing (letting go / cease).

I am the one below and they ascend to me.

I am the judgment and the acquittal.

I am the one who is sinless and the root of sin initiates (evolves, springs, develops) from me.

I am desire and lust in outward manifestation (appearance)

and inner self-control exists within me.

I am the hearing which everyone is able to understand

255

and the utterance that cannot be understood (unable to be grasped).

I am a silent mute and great is the multitude of my words (utterances).

Hear me in gentleness (softness) and learn from me in harshness.

I am she who cries out,

And I am thrown out upon the face of the earth.

I prepare the bread and my mind within.

I am the gnosis of my name.

I am she who shouts and I am the one who listens.

I appear and [...] walk in [...] seal of my [...]... sign of the

I am [...] the defense.

I am she who is called Truth. And sin (lies / iniquity / violence) [...].

You honor me [...] (with your words) and you whisper against me.

You who are defeated, judge those who defeated you before they judge you,

Because judgement (the judge) and prejudice exist within you.

If you are condemned by this one, who will acquit you?

Or if you are acquitted by him, who will be able to detain (arrest) you?

Whatever is inside of you is also what is outside of you.

And the one who fashioned you on the outside is also the one who has molded the inside of you.

And that which you see outside of you, you see inside of you.

It is manifest (visible) and it is your garment.

Hear me, listeners, and be taught my word, you who know me!

I am the hearing that is able to be understood (acceptable) in all matters;

I am the words (sound) that cannot be held back (restrained / grasped).

I am the name of the sound (voice) and the sound (voice) of the name.

I am the sign (shape) of writing (letters) and the existence of separation (visage of difference).

(Note: the codex is damaged here and three lines are missing. Also note the change is gender here as the subject shifts from female to male.)

And I …

[…] light […] and […]

[…] listeners […] to you.

[…] the great power.

And […] will not move the name.

[…] the one who created me.

But I shall speak his name.

Behold, his words and all the writings that have been completed.

Give heed you listeners, and you also, you angels who have been sent,

And you, spirits who have arisen from the dead,

For I am the one who singularly exists (alone exists).

I have no one who will judge me.

Many sweet and desirable forms exist in numerous sins,

And unrestrained indulgent acts and disgraceful passions, and passing (temporal) pleasures,

Which men hold on to (grasp) until they become sober

And go up to their place of rest.

And they will find me there,

And they will live and they will not die again.

Information on The Apocalypse of Baruch's

Apocalyptic is the literature of suffering. The Syriac Apocalypse of Baruch (2 Baruch) was probably written between 70 CE and 132 CE, the period between the destruction of the Temple and the failed Bar Kokhba revolt; it is a direct response to the Roman destruction of Jerusalem in 70 C.E — a time of great suffering for the Jewish population of Palestine. The eschatology and language of 2 Baruch betray its origins in the period when Judaism and Christianity still overlap. Portions of 2 Baruch were included in the lectionaries of the Syriac Church, which preserved the whole of the work when the Hebrew original was lost and/or fell out of usage in Judaism. The paper takes up the first of two laments in 2 Baruch: 10: 6-19, which asks God the age-old question about suffering: Why? A part of God's extended answer to Baruch and his community is: "the present time, sweltering in blood and (corrupted) by evil, will be forgotten")t4Y8BB lPLPMd)$hd)NBzL nrKwd)wh)Lw (2 Baruch 44:9c). The paper also examines the eschatologies of 2 Baruch to show how there is an inner confusion about the exact nature of the end of time when suffering will be no more, particularly in relation to 2 Baruch's thinking about the Law and the Messiah.

The Syriac Apocalypse of Baruch (2 Baruch) responds to the Roman destruction of Jerusalem of 70 C.E, a time of great suffering for the Jewish population of Palestine. The paper takes up the first (of two) laments in 2 Baruch: 10: 6-19, which ask God the age-old question about suffering: Why? The thesis of the paper is that the first lament presents the problem of suffering to God in order to introduce God's extended answer to Baruch and his community: hold on to Torah — this suffering will be forgotten: "the present time, sweltering in blood and (corrupted) by evil, will be forgotten" (44: 9). Furthermore, the eschatology of 2 Baruch betrays an inner confusion about the exact nature of the end of time when suffering will be no more.

A. F. J. Klijn writes: "Until recently the Apocalypse of Baruch was only known from a Syriac manuscript dating from the sixth or seventh century AD. Since the beginning of this century two fragments have come to light in Greek (12:1-13:2 and 13:11-14:3) from the fourth or fifth century. Small fragments of the text, again in Syriac, have been discovered in lectionaries of the Jacobite Church. However, no fewer than thirty-six manuscripts of the letter at the end of this work (78:1 till the end) are known because it once belonged to the canon of Scriptures in the Syriac speaking Church. Not long ago the entire work was discovered in an Arabic manuscript on Mount Sinai. This text differs in many details from the Syriac which we already knew before. Nevertheless the Arabic translation appears to be a free rendering of an original Syriac version. This means that the contents are not very helpful in determining the original text of the somewhat corrupt Syriac translation." (Outside the Old Testament, p. 193)

James Charlesworth writes: "Most scholars have divided the book into seven sections, with some disagreement regarding borderline verses: an account of the destruction of Jerusalem (1-12); the impending judgment (13-20); the time of retribution and the subsequent messianic era (21-34); Baruch's lament and an allegory of the vine and the cedar (35-46); terrors of the last time, nature of the resurrected body, and teh features of Paradise and Sheol (47-52); Baruch's vision of a cloud (53-76); Baruch's letters to the nine and a half tribes and to the two and a half tribes (77-87). The pseudepigraphon is important for numerous theological concepts, e.g. the explanation that Jerusalem was destroyed not by enemies but by angels (7:1-8:5); the preoccupation with the origin of sin (15:5f., 23:4f., 48:42, 54:15, 19; cf. 4Ezra 7:116-31); pessimism for the present (85:10); the contention that the end will not come until the number of those to be born is fulfilled (23:4-7; cf. 4Ezra 4:35-37); the description of the resurrected body (49:1-51:6); and the varied messianic concepts." (The Pseudepigrapha and Modern Research, p. 84)

Raymond F. Surburg writes: "The book divides itself into seven sections. It begins with the model of prophecy: 'The word of the Lord came to Baruch, the son of Neraiah, saying.' In the first section the fall of Jerusalem is announced, but Baruch is comforted by the promise that the overthrow of Isarel will only be 'for a season.' In the second section Baruch has a vision in which he is told to fast for seven days after which he is permitted to pour out his complaint before the Lord. Baruch is informed of the judgments which will come over the Gentiles and of the glory of the world to come, which is to exist especially for the righteous. The destruction of Jerusalem is described as the work of angels instead of the Chaldeans. In the third section Baruch raises the problem of the nature of evil, which is also the theme of 2 Esdras. In the fourth section the reader is assured that the future world is made for the righteous. In the fifth section Baruch complains about the delay of God's kingdom and is assured that first the number of the elect must be fulfilled. When this has happened, the Messiah will come. Section six gives the vision of the cedar and the vine, which symbolizes the Roman Empire and the triumph of the Messiah. Baruch asks who will share in the glory to come and is told, 'Those that believe.' The six 'black waters' described represent six evil periods in world history, and the 'six clear waters' denote the number of good periods. It is in this section that the doctrine of the resurrection of the body is set forth by the author." (Introduction to the Intertestamental Period, pp. 140-141)

Martin McNamara writes: "Baruch announces the destruction of Jerusalem and, in chap. 4 (which some regard as interpolated) is shown the heavenly Jerusalem. Like Ezra, Baruch is made to see that God's ways are incomprehensible. He is told that the holy city of Zion has been taken away so that God might hasten the day of judgment (20). God's final judgment will come in God's own time, that is when all the souls destined to be born have been born." (Intertestamental Literature, p. 79)

Emil Schürer writes: "My own opinion is that it is quite the converse of this, and that it would be nearer the truth to say that it is precisely in the case of Baruch that this problem is uppermost, viz. How is the calamity of Israel and the impunity of its oppressors possible and conceivable? while in the case of Ezra, though this problem concerns him too, still there is a question that almost lies yet nearer his heart, viz. Why is it that so many perish and so few are saved? The subordination of the former of these questions to the other, which is a purely theological one, appears to me rather to indicate that Ezra is of a later date than Baruch. Not only so, but it is decidedly of a more finished character, and is distinguished by greater maturity of thought and a greater degree of lucidity than the last-mentioned book. But this is a point in regard to which it is scarcely possible to arrive at a definite conclusion. And hence we are equally unable to say whether our book was written shortly after the destruction of Jerusalem (so Hilgenfeld, Fritzsche, Drummond), or during the reign of Domitian (so Ewald), or in the time of Trajan (so Langen, Wieseler, Renan, Dillmann). Undoubtedly the most probable supposition of all is that it was composed not long after the destruction of the holy city, when the question 'How could God permit such a disaster?' was still a burning one. It is older at all events than the time of Papias, whose chimerical fancies about the millennial kingdom (Irenaeus, v. 33. 3) are borrowed from our Apocalypse (xxix. 5)." (The Literature of the Jewish People in the Time of Jesus, pp. 90-91)

Leonhard Rost writes: "There is a reasonable consensus among scholars that the book was written around A.D. 90; the author looks back on the destruction of the Temple and the city in the year 70, but knows nothing of the revolt under Bar Kochba. This argument does not rule out R. H. Charles' theory: he views the three apocalypses 27-30:1; 36-40; 53-74 as earlier sections, written before A.D. 70. It still remains a matter of debate, however, in view of the many points of contact between the Apocalypse of Baruch and IV Ezra, whether the former or the latter is earlier. At present, the scales are tipped in favor of an earlier origin for IV Ezra. It is reasonably certain that the book was composed in Jerusalem. The author has points of contact with the Pharisees." (Judaism Outside the Hebrew Canon, pp. 128-129)

A. F. J. Klijn writes: "The work appears to have been written after the fall of Jerusalem in AD 70, like 4 Ezra, an apocalypse with which it has a number of points in common, and the Paraleipomena

Jeremiou in which Baruch also is an important figure. The work tries to give an answer to the burning question why God allowed his temple to be destroyed. The answer is that God himself sent his angels to destroy his sanctuary and that the time of this tribulation will be short. In other words, the destruction of the temple is God's final act before the day of judgment on which the enemies of Israel will be punished and God's people will be vindicated. Although, as the Apocalypse indicates, nothing is left but God and the Law, Israel may expect to be rescued from its enemies." (Outside the Old Testament, p. 194)

THE BOOK OF THE APOCALYPSE OF BARUCH THE SON OF NERIAH
Also called 2 Baruch

Translation from the Syriac by R. H. Charles

The Apocrypha and Pseudepigrapha of the Old Testament in English
(Oxford: Oxford University Press, 1913) 2: 481-524

1—4. Announcement of the coming Destruction of Jerusalem to Baruch

1 1 And it came to pass in the twenty-fifth year of Jeconiah, king of Judah, that the word of the Lord came to Baruch, the son of Neriah, and said to him: 2 'Have you seen all that this people are doing to Me, that the evils which these two tribes which remained have done are greater than (those of) the ten tribes which were carried away captive? 3 For the former tribes were forced by their kings to commit sin, but these two of themselves have been forcing and compelling their kings to commit sin. 4 For this reason, behold I bring evil upon this city, and upon its inhabitants, and it shall be removed from before Me for a time, and I will scatter this people among the Gentiles that they may do good to the Gentiles. And My people shall be chastened, and the time shall come when they will seek for the prosperity of their times.

2 1 For I have said these things to you that you may bid Jeremiah, and all those that are like you, to retire from this city.

2 For your works are to this city as a firm pillar,

And your prayers as a strong wall.'

3 1 And I said: 'O LORD, my Lord, have I come into the world for this purpose that I might see the evils of my mother? Not (so) my Lord. 2 If I have found grace in Your sight, first take my spirit that I may go to my fathers and not behold the destruction of my mother. For two things vehemently constrain me: for I cannot resist you, and my soul, moreover, cannot behold the evils of my mother. 4 But one thing I will say in Your presence, O Lord. 5 What, therefore, will there be after these things? for if you destroy Your city, and deliver up Your land to those that hate us, how shall the name of Israel be again remembered? 6 Or how shall one speak of Your praises? or to whom shall that which is in Your law be explained? Or shall the world return to its nature of aforetime), and the age revert to primeval silence? And shall the multitude of souls be taken away, and the nature of man not again be named? And where is all that which you did say regarding us?'

4 1 And the Lord said unto me:

'This city shall be delivered up for a time,

And the people shall be chastened during a time,

And the world will not be given over to oblivion.

4:2-7. The heavenly Jerusalem

2 [Dost you think that this is that city of which I said: "On the palms of My hands have I graven you"? 3 This building now built in your midst is not that which is revealed with Me, that which prepared beforehand here from the time when I took counsel to make Paradise, and showed Adam before he sinned, but when he transgressed the commandment it was removed from him, as also Paradise. 4 And after these things I showed it to My servant Abraham by night among the portions of the victims. 5 And again also I showed it to Moses on Mount Sinai when I showed to the likeness of the tabernacle and all its vessels. 6 And now, behold, it is preserved with Me, as Paradise. 7 Go, therefore, and do as I command you.']

5. Baruch's Complaint and God's Reassurance

5 1 And I answered and said:

'So then I am destined to grieve for Zion,

For your enemies will come to this place and pollute Your sanctuary,

And lead your inheritance into captivity,

And make themselves masters of those whom you have loved,

And they will depart again to the place of their idols,

And will boast before them:

And what will you do for Your great name?'

2   And the Lord said unto me:

'My name and My glory are unto all eternity;

And My judgment shall maintain its right in its own time.

3   And you shall see with your eyes

That the enemy will not overthrow Zion,

Nor shall they burn Jerusalem,

But be the ministers of the Judge for the time.

4   But do you go and do whatsoever I have said unto you.

5   And I went and took Jeremiah, and Adu, and Seriah, and Jabish, and Gedaliah, and all the honorable men of the people, and I led them to the valley of Kidron, and I narrated to them all that had been said to me. 6 And they lifted up their voice, and they all wept. 7 And we sat there and fasted until the evening.

6—8. Invasion of the Chaldeans and their Entrance into the City after the Sacred Vessels were hidden and the City's Walls overthrown by Angels

6 1 And it came to pass on the morrow that, lo! the army of the Chaldees surrounded the city, and at the time of the evening, I, Baruch, left the people, and I went forth and stood by the oak. 2 And I was grieving over Zion, and lamenting over the captivity which had come upon the people. 3 And lo! suddenly a strong spirit

raised me, and bore me aloft over the wall of Jerusalem. 4 And I beheld, and lo! four angels standing at the four corners of the city, each of them holding a torch of fire in his hands. 5 And another angel began to descend from heaven. and said unto them: 'Hold your lamps, and do not light them till I tell you. 6 For I am first sent to speak a word to the earth, and to place in it what the Lord the Most High has commanded me.' 7 And I saw him descend into the Holy of Holies, and take from there the veil, and holy ark, and the mercy-seat, and the two tables, and the holy raiment of the priests, and the altar of incense, and the forty-eight precious stones, wherewith the priest was adorned and all the holy vessels of the tabernacle. 8 And he spoke to the earth with a loud voice:

'Earth, earth, earth, hear the word of the mighty God,

And receive what I commit to you,

And guard them until the last times,

So that, when you are ordered, you may restore them,

So that strangers may not get possession of them.

9 For the time comes when Jerusalem also will be delivered for a time,

Until it is said, that it is again restored for ever.'

10 And the earth opened its mouth and swallowed them up.

7 1 And after these things I heard that angel saying unto those angels who held the lamps: 'Destroy, therefore, and overthrow its wall to its foundations, lest the enemy should boast and say:

> " We have overthrown the wall of Zion,
>
> And we have burnt the place of the mighty God."'

2   And they have seized the place where I had been standing before.

8 1 Now the angels did as he had commanded them, and when they had broken up the corners of the walls, a voice was heard from the interior of the temple, after the wall had fall saying:

2   'Enter, you enemies,

> And come, you adversaries;
>
> For he who kept the house has forsaken (it).'

3   And I, Baruch, departed. 4 And it came to pass after these things that the army of the Chaldees entered and seized the house, and all that was around it. And they led the people away captive and slew some of them, and bound Zedekiah the king, and sent him to the king of Babylon.

9—12. First Fast of seven Days: Baruch to remain amid the Ruins of Jerusalem and Jeremiah to accompany the Exiles to Babylon. Baruch's Dirge over Jerusalem

9 1 And I, Baruch, came, and Jeremiah, whose heart was found pure from sins, who had not been captured in the seizure of the City. 2 And we rent our garments, we wept, and mourned, and fasted seven days.

10 1 And it came to pass after seven days, that the word of God carne to me, and said unto me: 2 'Tell Jeremiah to go and support the captivity of the people unto Babylon. But do you remain here amid the desolation of Zion, and I will show to you after these days 'what will befall at the end of days.' And I said to Jeremiah as the Lord commanded me. And he, indeed, departed with the people, but I, Baruch, returned and sat before the gates of the temple, and I lamented with the following lamentation over Zion and said:

6 'Blessed is he who was not born,

Or he, who having been born, has died.

7 But as for us who live, woe unto us,

Because we see the afflictions of Zion,

And what has befallen Jerusalem.

8 I will call the Sirens from the sea,

And you Lilin, come you from the desert,

And you Shedim and dragons from the forests:

Awake and gird up your loins unto mourning,

And take up with me the dirges,

And make lamentation with me.

9   Ye husbandmen, sow not again;

    And, O earth, wherefore give you your harvest fruits?

    Keep within you the sweets of your sustenance.

10 And thou, vine, why further do you give your wine;

    For an offering will not again be made from there in Zion,

    Nor will first-fruits again be offered.

11 And do ye, O heavens, 'withhold your dew,

    And open not the treasuries of rain:

12 And do thou, O sun withhold the light of your rays.

    And do thou, O moon, extinguish the multitude of your light;

    For why should light rise again

    Where the light of Zion is darkened?

13 And you, you bridegrooms, enter not in,

    And let not the brides adorn themselves with garlands;

    And, you women, pray not that you may bear.

14 For the barren shall above all rejoice,

    And those who have no sons shall be glad,

    And those who have sons shall have anguish.

15 For why should they bear in pain,

Only to bury in grief?

16 Or why, again, should mankind have sons?

Or why should the seed of their kind again be named,

Where this mother is desolate,

And her sons are led into captivity?

17 From this time forward speak not of beauty,

And discourse not of gracefulness.

18 Moreover, you priests) take you the keys of the sanctuary,

And cast them into the height of heaven,

And give them to the Lord and say:

"Guard Your house Thyself,

For lo! we are found false stewards."

19 And you, you virgins; who weave fine linen

And silk with gold of Ophir,

Take with haste all (these) things

And cast (them) into the fire,

That it may bear them to Him who made them,

And the flame send them to Him who created them,

Lest the enemy get possession of them.'

11 1 Moreover, I, Baruch, say this against you, Babylon:

'If you had prospered,

And Zion had dwelt in her glory,

Yet the grief to us had been great

That you should be equal to Zion.

2 But now, lo! the grief is infinite,

And the lamentation measureless,

For lo! you are prospered

And Zion desolate.

3 Who will be judge regarding these things?

Or to whom shall we complain regarding that which has befallen us?

O Lord, how have you borne (it)?

4 Our fathers went to rest without grief,

And lo! the righteous sleep in the earth in tranquility;

5 For they knew not this anguish,

Nor yet had they heard of that which had befallen us.

6 Would that you had ears, O earth,

And that you had a heart, O dust:

That you might go and announce in Sheol,

And say to the dead:

7 "Blessed are you more than we who live."'

OXYRHYNCHUS GREEK FRAGMENT, from Grenfell and Hunt's Oxyrhynchus Papyri, vol. iii. 3-7, 1903.

Verso.

12 1 But I will say this as I think.

And I will speak against you, O land, which alt prospering.

2 The noonday does not always burn.

Nor do the rays of the sun constantly give light.

3 Do not expect Land hope] that you will always he prosperous and rejoicing.

And be not greatly up lifted and boastful.

4 For assuredly in its own season shall the (divine) wrath awake against you.

Which now in long-suffering is held in as it were by reins.

(2-5) 12 1 But I will say this as 1 think,

And speak against you, the land that is prospering.

2   Not always does the noonday burn,

   Nor do the rays of the sun constantly give light.

(6-8) 3 And do not you expect to

   rejoice,

Nor condemn greatly.

(8-10) 4 For assuredly in its season shall the (divine) wrath be awakened against you,

Which is now restrained by long-suffering as it were by a rein.

12:5 – 13. Second Fast. Revelation as to the coming judgment on the Heathen.

5 And when I had said these things, I fasted seven days.

13 1 And it came to pass after these things, that I, Baruch, was standing upon Mount Zion, and lo! a voice came from the height and said unto me: 2 'Stand upon your feet, Baruch, and hear the word of the mighty God.'

(10-16) 5 And having said these things I fasted seven days.

13 1 And it came to pass after these things that I, Baruch, was standing upon Mount Zion, and lo a voice came forth from the height and said unto me:

2 'Stand upon your feet, Baruch, and hear the word of the mighty God.'

3 Because you have been astonished at what has befallen Zion, you shall therefore be assuredly preserved to the consummation of the times, that you may be for a testimony. 4 So that, if ever those prosperous cities say: 5 'Why hath the mighty God brought upon us this retribution?' Say you to them, you and those like you who shall have seen this evil: '(This is the evil) and retribution which is coming upon you and upon your people in its (destined) time that the nations may be thoroughly smitten. 6 And then they shall be in anguish. 7 And if they say at that time:

8   For how long? you will say to them:

"Ye who have drunk the strained wine,

Drink you also of its dregs,

The judgment of the Lofty One

Who has no respect of persons."'

9   On this account he had aforetime no mercy on His own sons,

But afflicted them as His enemies, because they sinned,

10   Then therefore were they chastened

That they might be sanctified.

OXYRHYNCHUS GREEK FRAGMENT Recto

11   But now, you peoples and nations, you are guilty

      Because you have always trodden down the earth,

      And used the creation unrighteously.

12   For I have always benefited you.

      And you have always been ungrateful for the beneficence.

(19-20) 11 (Ye) peoples and . . .

      (Ye) have trodden down the earth

      And misused the created things

in it.

(21-22) 12 For you were always being benefited

      But you were always ungrateful.

14–19. The Righteousness of the Righteous has profited neither them nor their City; God's Judgments are incomprehensible; the World was made for the Righteous, yet they pass and the World remains (14). Answer—Man knows God's Judgments and has sinned willingly. This World is a Weariness to the Righteous but the next is theirs (15), to be won through Character whether a Man's

Time here be long or short (16—17). Final Weal or Woe—the supreme Question (18—19).

OXYRHYNCHUS GREEK FRAGMENT Recto

14 1 And I answered and said: 'Lo! you have shown me the method of the times, and that which shall be after these things, and you have said unto me, that the retribution, which has been spoken of by you, shall come upon the nations. 2 And now I know that those who have sinned are many, and they have lived in prosperity,' and departed from the world, but the few nations will be left in those times, to whom those words shall he said which you did say. 3 For what advantage is there in this, or what (evil), worse than what' we have seen befall us, are we to expect to see?

(23-25) 14 1 And I answered and said: 'Behold, you have shown me the methods of the times, and that which shall be.

(25-27) And you have said unto me that the retribution which was spoken of by you shall be endured by the nations.

(27-32) 2 And now I know that those who have sinned are many, and they have lived . . . , and departed from the world, but that few nations will be left in those times to whom . . . the words (which) you did say.

(32-33) 3 And what advantage (is there) in this or what worse than (these?)

4 But again I will speak in Your presence: 5 What have they profited who had knowledge before you and have not walked in vanity as the rest of the nations, and have not said to the dead: "Give us life," but always feared you, and have not left Your ways? 6 And lo! they

have been carried off, nor on their account have you had mercy on Zion. 7 And if others did evil, it was due to Zion that on account of the works of those who wrought good works she should be forgiven, and should not be overwhelmed on account of the works of those who wrought unrighteousness. 8 But who, O LORD, my Lord, will comprehend Your judgment,

> Or who will search out the profoundness of Your way?
>
> Or who will think out the weight of Your path?
>
> 9 Or who will be able to think out Your incomprehensible counsel?
>
> Or who of those that are born has ever found
>
> The beginning or end of Your wisdom?

10 For we have all been made like a breath. 11 For as the breath ascends involuntarily, and again dies, so it is with the nature of men, who depart not according to their own will, and know not what will befall them in the end. 12 For the righteous justly hope for the end, and without fear depart from this habitation, because they have with you a store of works preserved in treasuries. 13 On this account also these without fear leave this world, and trusting with joy they hope to receive the world which you have promised them. 14 But as for us — woe to us, who also are now shamefully entreated, and at that time look forward (only) to evils. 15 But you know accurately what you have done by means of Your servants; for we are not able to understand that which is good as you art, our Creator. 16 But again I will speak in Your presence, O LORD, my Lord. 17 When of old there was no world with its inhabitants, you did devise and speak with a word, and forthwith the works of creation stood before you. 18 And you did say that you wouldst make for Your world man as the administrator of Your works, that it might be known that he was by no means made on account of the

world, but the world on account of him. 19 And now I see that as for the world which was made on account of us, lo! it abides; but we, on account of whom it was made, depart.'

15 1 And the Lord answered and said unto me: 'You are rightly astonished regarding the departure of man, but you have not judged well regarding the evils which befall those who sin. 2 And as regards what you have said, that the righteous are carried off and the impious are prospered, 3 And as regards what you have said: "Man knows not Your judgment " — On this account hear, and I will speak to you, and hearken, and I will cause you to hear My words. 5 Man would not rightly have understood My judgment, unless he had accepted the law, and I had instructed him in understanding. 6 But now, because he transgressed wittingly, yea, just on this ground that he knows (about it), he shall be tormented.

7 And as regards what you did say touching the righteous, that on account of them has this world come, so also again shall that, which is to come, come on their account. 8 For this world is to them a strife and a labor with much trouble; and that accordingly which is to come, a crown with great glory.'

16 1 And I answered and said: 'O LORD, my Lord, lo! the years of this time are few and evil, and who is able in his little time to acquire that which is measureless?'

17 1 And the Lord answered and said unto me: 'With the Most High account is not taken of time nor of a few years. 2 For what did it profit Adam that he lived nine hundred and thirty years and transgressed that which he was commanded? Therefore the multitude of time that he lived did not profit him, but brought

death and cut off the years of those who were born from him. wherein did Moses suffer loss in that he lived only one hundred and twenty years, and, inasmuch he was subject to Him who formed him, brought the law to the seed of Jacob, and lighted a lamp for the nation of Israel?'

18 1 And I answered and said: 'He that lighted has taken from the light, and there are but few that have imitated him. But those many whom he has lighted have taken from the darkness of Adam and have not rejoiced in the light of the lamp.'

19 And He answered and said unto me: 'Wherefore at that time he appointed for them a covenant and said:

"Behold I have placed before you life and death,"

And he called heaven and earth to witness against them.

2   For he knew that his time was but short,

But that heaven and earth endure always.

3   But after his death they sinned and transgressed,

Though they knew that they had the law reproving (them),

And the light in which nothing could err,

Also the spheres which testify, and Me.

4 Now regarding everything that is, it is I that judge, but do not you take counsel in your soul regarding these things, nor afflict thyself because of those which have been. 5 For now it is the consummation of time that should be considered, whether of business, or of prosperity, or of shame and not the beginning thereof. 6 Because if a man be prospered in his beginnings and shamefully entreated in his old age, he forgets all the prosperity that he had. 7 And again, if a man is shamefully entreated in his beginnings, and at his end is prospered, he remembers not again his evil entreatment. 8 And again hearken: though each one were prospered all that time — all the time from the day on which death was decreed against those who transgress — and in his end was destroyed, in vain would have been everything.'

20. Zion has been taken away to hasten the Advent of the Judgment

20 1   'Therefore, behold! the days come,

And the times shall hasten more than the former,

And the seasons shall speed on more than those that are past,

And the years shall pass more quickly than the present (years).

2 Therefore have I now taken away Zion,

That I may the more speedily visit the world in its season.

3   Now therefore hold fast in your heart everything that I command you,

And seal it in the recesses of your mind.

4 And then I will show you the judgment of My might,

And My ways which are unsearchable.

5 Go therefore and sanctify thyself seven days, and eat no bread, nor drink water, nor speak to anyone. 6 And afterwards come to that place and I will reveal Myself to you, and speak true things with you, and I will give you commandment regarding the method of the times; for they are coming and tarry not.'

21:1-11. Fast of seven Days: Baruch's Prayer: God's Answer

The Prayer of Baruch the Son of Neriah.

21 1 And I went there and sat in the valley of Kidron in a cave of the earth, and I sanctified my soul there, and I ate no bread, yet I was not hungry, and I drank no water, yet I thirsted not, and I was there till the seventh day, as He had commanded me. 2 And afterwards I came to that place where He had spoken with me. 3 And it came to pass at sunset that my soul took much thought, and I began to speak in the presence of the Mighty One, and said: 4 'O you that have made the earth, hear me, that have fixed the firmament by the word, and have made firm the height of the heaven by the spirit, that have called from the beginning of the world that which did not yet exist, and they obey you. 5 you that have commanded the air by Your nod, and have seen those things which are to be as those things which you are doing. 6 you that rule with great thought the hosts that stand before you: also the countless holy beings, which you did make from the beginning, of flame and fire, which stand

around Your throne you rule with indignation. 7 To you only does this belong that you should do forthwith whatsoever you do wish. 8 Who causes the drops of rain to rain by number upon the earth, and alone knows the consummation of the times before they come; have respect unto my prayer. For 9 you alone are able to sustain all who are, and those who have passed away, and those who are to be, those who sin, and those who are to righteous [as living (and) being past finding out]. For you alone do live immortal and past finding out, and know the number of mankind. And if in time many have sinned, yet others not a few have been righteous.

21:12-18. Baruch's Depreciation of this Life.

12 you know where you preserve the end of those who have sinned, or the consummation of those who have been righteous. 2 For if there were this life only, which belongs to all men, nothing could be more bitter than this.

14   For of what profit is strength that turns to sickness,

Or fullness of food that turns to famine,

Or beauty that turns to ugliness.

15 For the nature of man is always changeable. 16 For what we were formerly now we no longer are and what we now are we shall not afterwards remain. 16 For if a consummation had not been prepared for all, in vain would have been their beginning. But

regarding everything that comes from you do you inform me, and regarding everything about which I ask you, do you enlighten me.

21:19-25. Baruch prays to God to hasten the Judgment and fulfill His Promise

19 How long will that which is corruptible remain, and how long will the time of mortals be prospered, and until what time will those who transgress in the world be polluted with much wickedness? 20 Command therefore in mercy and accomplish all that you saidst you wouldst bring, that Your might may be made known to those who think that Your long-suffering is weakness. 21 And show to those who know not, that everything that has befallen us and our city until now has been according to the long-suffering of Your power, because on account of Your name you have called us a beloved people. 22 Bring to an end therefore henceforth mortality. 23 And reprove accordingly the angel of death, and let Your glory appear, and let the might of Your beauty be known, and let Sheol be sealed so that from this time forward it may not receive the dead, and let the treasuries of souls restore those which are enclosed in them. 24 For there have been many years like those that are desolate from the days of Abraham and Isaac and Jacob, and of all those who are like them, who sleep in the earth, on whose account you did say that you had created the world. 25 And now quickly show Your glory, and do not defer what has been promised by you.' 26 And (when) I had completed the words of this prayer I was greatly weakened.

22–23. God's Reply to Baruch's Prayer. He will fulfill His Promise: Time needed for its Accomplishment: Things must be judged in the Light of their Consummation (22). Till all Souls are born the End cannot come (23).

22 1 And it came to pass after these things that lo! the heavens were opened, and I saw, and power was given to me, and a voice was beard from on high, and it said unto me: 2 Baruch, Baruch, why are you troubled? 3 He who travels by a road but does not complete it, or who departs by sea but does not arrive at the port, can he be comforted? 4 Or he who promises to give a present to another, but does not fulfill it, is it not robbery? 5 Or he who sows the earth, but does not reap its fruit in its season, does he not lose everything? 6 Or he who plants a plant unless it grows till the time suitable to it, does he who planted it expect to receive fruit from it? 7 Or a woman who has conceived, if she bring forth untimely, does she not assuredly slay her infant? 8 Or he who builds a house, if he does not roof it and complete it, can it be called a house? Tell Me that first.'

23 1 And I answered and said: Not so, O LORD, my Lord.' 2 And He answered and said unto me: 'Why therefore are you troubled about that which you know not, and why are you ill at ease about things in which you are ignorant? 3 For as you have not forgotten the people who now are and those who have passed away, so I remember those who are appointed to come. 4 Because when Adam sinned and death was decreed against those who should be born, then the multitude of those who should be born was numbered, and for that number a place was prepared where the living might dwell and the dead might be guarded. Before therefore the number aforesaid is fulfilled, the creature will not live again [for My spirit is the creator of life], and Sheol will receive the dead. 6 And again it is given to you to hear what things are to come after these times. 7 For truly My redemption has drawn nigh, and is not far distant as aforetime.

24. The coming Judgment

24 1 'For behold! the days come and the books shall be opened in which are written the sins of all those who have sinned, and again also the treasuries in which the righteousness of all those who have been righteous in creation is gathered. 2 For it shall come to pass at that time that you shall see—and the many that are with you—the long-suffering of the Most High, which has been throughout all generations, who has been long-suffering towards all who are born, (alike) those who sin and (those who) are righteous.' 3 And I answered and said: 'But, behold! O Lord, no one knows the number of those things which have passed nor yet of those things which are to come. 4 For I know indeed that which has befallen us, but what will happen to our enemies I know not, and when you will visit Your works.'

25 – 26. Sign of the coming Judgment

25 1 And He answered and said unto me: 'You too shall be preserved till that time till that sign which the Most High will work for the inhabitants of the earth in the end of days. 2 This therefore shall be the sign. 3 When a stupor shall seize the inhabitants of the earth, and they shall fall into many tribulations, and again when they shall fall into great torments. And it will come to pass when they say in their thoughts by reason of their much tribulation: "The Mighty 'One doth no longer remember the earth"—yes, it will come to pass when they abandon hope, that the time will then awake.'

26 1 And I answered and said: 'Will that tribulation which is to be continue a long time, and will that necessity embrace many years?'

26-30. The Twelve Woes that are to Come upon the Earth: The Messiah and the temporary Messianic Kingdom

27 1 And He answered and said unto me: 'Into twelve parts is that time divided, and each one of them is reserved for that which is appointed for it. 2 In the first part there shall be the beginning of commotions. 3 And in the second part (there shall be) slayings of the great ones. 4 And in the third part the fall of many by death. 5 And in the fourth part the sending of the sword. 6 And in the fifth part famine and the withholding of rain. 7 And in the sixth part earthquakes and terrors. 8 [Wanting.] 9 And in the eighth part a multitude of specters and attacks of the Shedim. 10 And in the ninth part the fall of fire. 11 And in the tenth part rapine and much oppression. 12 And in the eleventh part wickedness and unchastity. 13 And in the twelfth part confusion from the mingling together of all those things aforesaid. 14 For these parts of that time are reserved, and shall be mingled one with another and minister one to another. 15 For some shall leave out some of their own, and receive (in its stead) from others, and some complete their own and that of others, so that those may not understand who are upon the earth in those days that this is the consummation of the times.

28 1 Nevertheless, whoever understands shall then be wise. 2 For the measure and reckoning of that time are two parts a week of seven weeks.' 3 And I answered and said: 'It is good for a man to

come and behold, but it is better that he should not come lest he fall. 4 [But I will say this also: 5 Will he who is incorruptible despise those things which are corruptible, and whatever befalls in the case of those things which are corruptible, so that he might look only to those things which are not corruptible?] 6 But if; O Lord, those things shall assuredly come to pass which you have foretold to me, so do you show this also unto me if indeed I have found grace in Your sight. 7 Is it in one place or in one of the parts of the earth that those things are come to pass, or will the whole earth experience (them) ?'

29 1 And He answered and said unto me: 'Whatever will then befall (will befall) the whole earth; therefore all who live will experience (them). 2 For at that time I will protect only those who are found in those self-same days in this land. 3 And it shall come to pass when all is accomplished that was to come to pass in those parts, that the Messiah shall then begin to be revealed. 4 And Behemoth shall be revealed from his place and Leviathan shall ascend from the sea, those two great monsters which I created on the fifth day of creation, and shall have kept until that time; and then they shall be for food for all that are left. 5 The earth also shall yield its fruit ten-thousandfold and on each (?) vine there shall be a thousand branches, and each branch shall produce a thousand clusters, and each cluster produce a thousand grapes, and each grape produce a cor of wine. 6 And those who have hungered shall rejoice: moreover, also, they shall behold marvels every day. 7 For winds shall go forth from before Me to bring every morning the fragrance of aromatic fruits, and at the close of the day clouds distilling the dew of health. 8 And it shall come to pass at that self-same time that the treasury of manna shall again descend from on high, and they will eat of it in those years, because these are they who have come to the consummation of time.

30 1 And it shall come to pass after these things, when the time of the advent of the Messiah is fulfilled, that He shall return in glory.

30:2-5. The Resurrection

2 Then all who have fallen asleep in hope of Him shall rise again. And it shall come to pass at that time that the treasuries will be opened in which is preserved the number of the souls of the righteous, and they shall come forth, and a multitude of souls shall be seen together in one assemblage of one thought, and the first shall rejoice and the last shall not be grieved. 3 For they know that the time has come of which it is said, that it is the consummation of the times. 4 But the souls of the wicked, when they behold all these things, shall then waste away the more. 5 For they shall know that their torment has come and their perdition has arrived.'

31—33. Baruch exhorts the People to prepare themselves for worse Evils

31 1 And it came to pass after these things: that I went to the people and said unto them: 'Assemble unto me all your elders and I will speak words unto them.' 2 And they all assembled in the valley of the Kidron. 3 And I answered and said unto them:

Hear, O Israel, and I will speak to you,

And give ear, O seed of Jacob, and I will instruct you.

4 Forget not Zion,

But hold in remembrance the anguish of Jerusalem.

5 For lo! the days come,

When everything that is shall become the prey of corruption

And be as though it had not been.

32 1 'But as for you, if you prepare your hearts, so as to sow in them the fruits of the law, it shall protect you in that time in which the Mighty One is to shake the whole creation. 2 [Because after a little time the building of Zion will be shaken in order that it may be built again. But that building will not remain, but will again after a time be rooted out, and will remain desolate until the time. 4 And afterwards it must be renewed in glory, and perfected for evermore.] 5 Therefore we should not be distressed so much over the evil which has now come as over that which is still to be. 6 For there will be a greater trial than these two tribulations when the Mighty One will renew His creation. 7 And now do not draw near to me for a few days, nor seek me till I come to you.' 8 And it came to pass when I had spoken to them all these words, that I, Baruch, went my way, and when the people saw me setting out, they lifted up their voice and lamented and said : 9 To where are you departing from us, Baruch, and are you forsaking us as a father who forsakes his orphan children, and departs from them?

33 1 'Are these the commands which your companion, Jeremiah the prophet, commanded you, and said unto you: "Look to this people till I go and make ready the rest of the brethren in Babylon against whom has gone forth the sentence that they should be led into captivity"? And now if you also forsake us, it were good for us all to die before you, and then that you should withdraw from us.'

34–35. Lament of Baruch

34 And I answered and said unto the people: 'Far be it from me to forsake you or to withdraw from you, but I will only go unto the Holy of Holies to inquire of the Mighty One concerning you and concerning Zion, if in some respect I should receive more illumination: and after these things I will return to you.

35 1 And I, Baruch, went to the holy place, and sat down upon the ruins and wept, and said:

2   'O that mine eyes were springs,

And mine eyelids a fount of tears.

3   For how shall I lament for Zion,

And how shall I mourn for Jerusalem?

4   Because in that place where I am now prostrate,

Of old the high priest offered holy sacrifices,

And placed thereon an incense of fragrant odors.

5   But now our glorying has been made into dust,

And the desire of our soul into sand.'

36—37. The Vision of the Forest, the Vine, the Fountain and the Cedar

36 1 And when I had said these things I fell asleep there, and I saw a vision in the night. 2 And lo! a forest of trees planted on the plain, and lofty and rugged rocky mountains surrounded it, and that forest occupied much space. 3 And lo! over against it arose a vine, and from under it there went forth a fountain peacefully. 4 Now that fountain came to the forest and was (stirred) into great waves, and those waves submerged that forest, and suddenly they rooted out the greater part of that forest, and overthrew all the mountains which were round about it. 5 And the height of the forest began to be made low, and the top of the mountains was made low and that fountain prevailed greatly, so that it left nothing of that great forest save one cedar only. 6 Also when it had cast it down and had destroyed and rooted out the greater part of that forest, so that nothing was left of it, nor could its place be recognized, then that vine began to come with the fountain in peace and great tranquility, and it came to a place which was not far from that cedar, and they brought the cedar which had been cast down to it. 7 And I beheld and lo! that vine opened its mouth and spoke and said to that cedar: Art you not that cedar which was left of the forest of wickedness, and by whose means wickedness persisted, and was wrought all those years, and goodness never. 8 And you kept conquering that which was not yours, and to that which was your you did never show compassion, and you did keep extending your power over those who were far from you, and those who drew near you, you did hold fast in the toils of your wickedness, and you did uplift thyself always as one that could not be rooted out! 9 But now your time has sped and your hour is come. 10 Do you also therefore depart, O cedar, after the forest, which departed before you, and become dust with it, and let your ashes be mingled together. 11 And

now recline in anguish and rest in torment till your last time come, in which you will come again, and be tormented still more.'

37 And after these things I saw that cedar burning, and the vine growing, itself and all around it, the plain full of unfading flowers. And I indeed awoke and arose.

38–40. Interpretation of the Vision

38 1 And I prayed and said: 'O LORD, my Lord, you do always enlighten those who are led by understanding. 2 Your law is life, and Your wisdom is right guidance. 3 Make known to me therefore the interpretation of this vision. 4 For you know that my soul hath always walked in Your law, and from my (earliest) days I departed not from Your wisdom.'

39 1 And He answered and said unto me: 'Baruch, this is the interpretation of the vision which you have seen. 2 As you have seen the great forest which lofty and rugged mountains surrounded, this is the word. 3 Behold! the days come, and this kingdom will be destroyed which once destroyed Zion, and it will be subjected to that which comes after it. 4 Moreover, that also again after a time will be destroyed, and another, a third, will arise, and that also will have dominion for its time, and will be destroyed. 5 And after these things a fourth kingdom will arise, whose power will be harsh and evil far beyond those which were before it, and it will rule many times as the forests on the plain, and it will hold fast for times, and will exalt itself more than the cedars of Lebanon. 6 And by it the truth will be hidden, and all those who are polluted

with iniquity will flee to it, as evil beasts flee and creep into the forest. 7 And it will come to pass when the time of its consummation that it should fall has approached, then the principate of My Messiah will be revealed, which is like the fountain and the vine, and when it is revealed it will root out the multitude of its host. 8 And as touching that which you have seen, the lofty cedar, which was left of that forest, and the fact, that the vine spoke those words with it which you did hear, this is the word.

40 1 The last leader of that time will be left alive, when the multitude of his hosts will be put to the sword, and he will be bound, and they will take him up to Mount Zion, and My Messiah will convict him of all his impieties, and will gather and set before him all the works of his hosts. 2 And afterwards he will put him to death, and protect the rest of My people which shall be found in the place which I have chosen. 3 And his principate will stand for ever, until the world of corruption is at an end, and until the times aforesaid are fulfilled. 4 This is your vision, and this is its interpretation.'

41—42. The Destiny of the Apostates and of the Proselytes

41 1 And I answered and said: 'For whom and for how many shall these things be? or who will be worthy to live at that time? 2 For I will speak before you everything that I think, and I will ask of you regarding those things which I meditate. 3 For lo! I see many of Your people who have withdrawn from Your covenant, and cast from them the yoke of Your law. 4 But others again I have seen who have forsaken their vanity, and fled for refuge beneath Your wings. 5 What therefore will be to them? or how will the last time receive

them? 6 Or perhaps the time of these will assuredly be weighed, and as the beam inclines will they be judged accordingly?'

42 1 And He answered and said unto me: 'These things also will I show unto you. 2 As for what you did say — "To whom will these things be, and how many (will they be)? " — to those who have believed there shall be the good which was spoken of aforetime, and to those who despise there shall be the contrary of these things. 3 And as for what you did say regarding those who have drawn near and those who have withdrawn this in the word. 4 As for those who were before subject, and afterwards withdrew and mingled themselves with the seed of mingled peoples, the time of these was the former, and was accounted as something exalted. 5 And as for those who before knew not but afterwards knew life, and mingled (only) with the seed of the people which had separated itself, the time of these (is) the latter, and is accounted as something exalted. 6 And time shall succeed to time and season to season, and one shall receive from another, and then with a view to the consummation shall everything be compared according to the measure of the times and the hours of the seasons. 7 For corruption shall take those that belong to it, and life those that belong to it. 8 And the dust shall be called, and there shall be said to it: "Give back that which is not yours, and raise up all that you have kept until its time".'

43. Baruch told of his Death and bidden to give his last Commands to the People

43 1   But, do thou, Baruch, direct your heart to that which has been said to you,

And understand those things which have been shown to you;

For there are many eternal consolations for you.

2   For you shall depart from this place,

And you shall pass from the regions which are now seen by you,

And you shall forget whatever is corruptible,

And shall not again recall those things which happen among mortals.

3 Go therefore and command your people, and come to this place, and afterwards fast seven days, and then I will come to you and speak with you.'

44:1-8; 45—46. Baruch tells the Elders of his impending Death, but encourages them to expect the Consolation of Zion

44 1 And I, Baruch, went from thence, and came to my people, and I called my first-born son and [the Gedaliahs] my friends, and seven of the elders of the people, and I said unto them:

>   Behold, I go unto my fathers

According to the way of all the earth.

3   But withdraw you not from the way of the law,

But guard and admonish the people which remain,

Lest they withdraw from the commandments of the Mighty One.

4   For you see that He whom we serve is just,

And our Creator is no respecter of persons.

5   And see you what hath befallen Zion,

And what hath happened to Jerusalem.

6   For the judgment of the Mighty One shall (thereby) be made known,

And His ways, which, though past finding out, are right.

7   For if you endure and persevere in His fear,

And do not forget His law,

The times shall change over you for good.

And you shall see the consolation of Zion.

8, 9   Because whatever is now is nothing,

But that which shall be is very great.

For everything that is corruptible shall pass away,

And everything that dies shall depart,

And all the present time shall be forgotten,

Nor shall there be any remembrance of the present time, which is defiled with evils.

10   For that which runs now runs unto vanity,

And that which prospers shall quickly fall and be humiliated.

11   For that which is to be shall be the object of desire,

And for that which comes afterwards shall we hope;

For it is a time that passes not away,

12   And the hour comes which abides for ever.

And the new world (comes) which does not turn to corruption those who depart to its blessedness,

And has no mercy on those who depart to torment,

And leads not to perdition those who live in it.

13   For these are they who shall inherit that time which has been spoken of,

>   And theirs is the inheritance of the promised time.

14   These are they who have acquired for themselves treasures of wisdom,

>   And with them are found stores of understanding,
>
>   And from mercy have they not withdrawn,
>
>   And the truth of the law I have they preserved.

15   For to them shall be given the world to come,

But the dwelling of the rest who are many shall be in the fire.'

45 2 'Do you therefore so far as you are able instruct the people, for that labor is ours. For if you teach them, you will quicken them.'

46 1 And my son and the elders of the people answered and said unto me:

'Has the Mighty One humiliated us to such a degree

As to take you from us quickly?

2   And truly we shall be in darkness,

And there shall be no light to the people who are left,

3   For where again shall we seek the law,

Or who will distinguish for us between death and life?'

4   And I said unto them: 'The throne of the Mighty One I cannot resist;

Nevertheless, there shall not be wanting to Israel a wise man

Nor a son of the law to the race of Jacob.

5   But only prepare you your hearts, that you may obey the law,

And be subject to those who in fear are wise and understanding;

And prepare your souls that you may not depart from them.

6   For if you do these things, Good tidings shall come unto you.

[Which I before told you of; nor shall you fall into the torment, of which I testified to you before.' 7 But with regard to the word that I was to be taken I did not make (it) known to them or to my son.]

47 1 And when I had gone forth and dismissed them, I went there and said unto them: 'Behold! I go to Hebron: for thither the Mighty One hath sent me.' 2 And I came to that place where the word had been spoken unto me, and I sat there, and fasted seven days.

48:1-47. PRAYER OF BARUCH

48 1 And it came to pass after the seventh day, that I prayed before the Mighty One and said

2 'O my Lord, you summon the advent of the times,

And they stand before you;

You cause the power of the ages to pass away,

And they do not resist you;

    You arrange the method of the seasons,

And they obey you.

3   You alone know the duration of the generations,

And you reveal not Your mysteries to many.

4   You make known the multitude of the fire,

And you weigh the lightness of the wind.

5   You explore the limit of the heights,

And you scrutinize the depths of the darkness.

6   You care for the number which pass away that they may be preserved, And you prepare an abode for those that are to be.

7   You remember the beginning which you have made,

And the destruction that is to be You forget not.

8   With nods of fear and indignation You command the flames,

And they change into spirits,

And with a word you quicken that which was not,

And with mighty power you hold that which has not yet come.

9   You instruct created things in the understanding of you,

And you make wise the spheres so as to minister in their orders.

10   Armies innumerable stand before you

And minister in their orders quietly at Your nod.

11   Hear Your servant

And give ear to my petition.

12   For in a little time are we born,

        And in a little time do we return.

13 But with you hours are as a time,

   And days as generations.

14 Be not therefore wroth with man; for he is nothing

15 And take not account of our works; For what are we?

For lo! by Your gift do we come into the world,

   And we depart not of our own will.

16 For we said not to our parents, "Beget us,

Nor did we send to Sheol and say, "Receive us."

17 What therefore is our strength that we should bear Your wrath,

Or what are we that we should endure Your judgment?

18 Protect us in Your compassions,

   And in Your mercy help us.

19 Behold the little ones that are subject unto you,

   And save all that draw near unto you:

   And destroy not the hope of our people,

   And cut not short the times of our aid.

20 For this is the nation which you have chosen,

   And these are the people, to whom you find no equal.

21 But I will speak now before you,

And I will say as my heart thinks.

22   In you do we trust, for lo! Your law is with us,

And we know that we shall not fall so long as we keep Your statutes.

23   [To all time are we blessed at all events in this that we have not mingled with the Gentiles.]

24   For we are all one celebrated people,

Who have received one law from One:

And the law which is amongst us will aid us,

And the surpassing wisdom which is in us will help us.'

25 And when I had prayed and said these things, I was greatly weakened. 26 And He answered and said unto me:

'You have prayed simply, O Baruch,

And all your words have been heard.

27   But My judgment exacts its own

And My law exacts its rights.

28   For from your words I will answer you,

And from your prayer I will speak to you.

29 For this is as follows: he that is corrupted is not at all; he has both wrought iniquity so far as lie could do anything, and has not remembered My goodness, nor accepted My long-suffering. 30 Therefore you shall surely be taken up, as I before told you. 31 For that time shall arise which brings affliction; for it shall come and pass by with quick vehemence, and it shall be turbulent coming in the heat of indignation. 32 And it shall come to pass in those days that all the inhabitants of the earth shall be moved one against another, because they know not that My judgment has drawn nigh.

33   For there shall not be found many wise at that time,

   And the intelligent shall be but a few:

   Moreover, even those who know shall most of all be silent.

34   And there shall be many rumors and tidings not a few,

   And the doing of phantasms shall be manifest,

   And promises not a few be recounted,

   Some of them (shall prove) idle,

   And some of them shall be confirmed.

35   And honor shall be turned into shame,

   And strength humiliated into contempt,

And probity destroyed,

And beauty shall become ugliness.

36   And many shall say to many at that time:

"Where hath the multitude of intelligence hidden itself,

And whither hath the multitude of wisdom removed itself?"

37   And whilst they are meditating these things,

Then envy shall arise in those who had not thought aught of themselves (?)

And passion shall seize him that is peaceful,

And many shall be stirred up in anger to injure many,

And they shall rouse up armies in order to shed blood,

And in the end they shall perish together with them.

38   And it shall come to pass at the self-same time,

That a change of times shall manifestly appeal to every man,

Because in all those times they polluted themselves

And they practiced oppression,

And walked every man in his own works,

And remembered not the law of the Mighty One.

39   Therefore a fire shall consume their thoughts,

And in flame shall the meditations of their reins be tried;

For the Judge shall come and will not tarry.

40   Because each of the inhabitants of the earth knew when he was transgressing.

But My Law they knew not by reason of their pride.

41   But many shall then assuredly weep,

Yea, over the living more than over the dead.'

42   And I answered and said:

'O Adam, what have you done to all those who are born from you?

And what will be said to the first Eve who hearkened to the serpent?

43   For all this multitude are going to corruption,

Nor is there any numbering of those whom the fire devours.

44 But again I will speak in Your presence. 45 You, O LORD, my Lord, know what is in Your creature. 46 For you did of old command the dust to produce Adam, and you know the number of those who are born from him, and how far they have sinned before you, who have existed and not confessed you as their Creator. 47 And as regards all these their end shall convict them, and Your law which they have transgressed shall requite them on Your day.'

48:48-50. Fragment of an Address of Baruch to the People

48   ['But now let us dismiss the wicked and inquire about the righteous.

49   And I will recount their blessedness

And not be silent in celebrating their glory, which is reserved for them.

50   For assuredly as in a little time in this transitory world in which you live, you have endured much labor,

So in that world to which there is no end, you shall receive great light.']

49—52. The Nature of the Resurrection Body: the final Destinies of the Righteous

and the Wicked

49 1 'Nevertheless, I Will again ask from you, O Mighty One, yea, I will ask made all things.

2   "In what shape will those live who live in Your day?

Or how will the splendor of those who (are) after that time continue?

3   Will they then resume this form of the present,

And put on these entrammelling members,

Which are now involved in evils,

And in which evils are consummated,

Or will you perchance change these things which have been in the world

As also the world?"

50 1 And He answered and said unto me:

'Hear, Baruch, this word,

And write in the remembrance of your heart all that you shall learn.

2   For the earth shall then assuredly restore the dead,

[Which it now receives, in order to preserve them].

    It shall make no change in their form,

But as it has received, so shall it restore them,

And as I delivered them unto it, so also shall it raise them.

3 For then it will be necessary to show the living that the dead have come to life again, and that those who had departed have returned (again). 4 And it shall come to pass, when they have severally recognized those whom they now know, then judgment shall grow strong, and those things which before were spoken of shall come.

51 1 And it shall come to pass, when that appointed day has gone by, that then shall the aspect of those who are condemned be afterwards changed, and the glory of those who are justified. 2 For the aspect of those who now act wickedly shall become worse than it is, as they shall suffer torment. 3 Also (as for) the glory of those who have now been justified in My law, who have had understanding in their life, and who have planted in their heart the

root of wisdom, then their splendor shall be glorified in changes, and the form of their face shall be turned into the light of their beauty, that they may be able to acquire and receive the world which does not die, which is then promised to them. 4 For over this above all shall those who come then lament, that they rejected My law, and stopped their ears that they might not hear wisdom or receive understanding. 5 When therefore they see those, over whom they are now exalted, (but) who shall then be exalted and glorified more than they, they shall respectively be transformed, the latter into the splendor of angels, and the former shall yet more waste away in wonder at the visions and in the beholding of the forms. 6 For they shall first behold and afterwards depart to be tormented.

7 But those who have been saved by their works,

And to whom the law has been now a hope,

And understanding an expectation,

And wisdom a confidence,

Shall wonders appear in their time.

8 For they shall behold the world which is now invisible to them,

And they shall behold the time which is now hidden from them:

9 And time shall no longer age them.

10 For in the heights of that world shall they dwell,

And they shall be made like unto the angels,

And be made equal to the stars,

And they shall be changed into every form they desire,

From beauty into loveliness,

And from light into the splendor of glory.

11 For there shall be spread before them the extents of Paradise, and there shall be shown to them the beauty of the majesty of the living creatures which are beneath the throne, and all the armies of the angels, who are now held fast by My word, lest they should appear, and] are held fast by a command, that they may stand in their places till their advent comes. 12 Moreover, there shall then be excellency in the righteous surpassing that in the angels. 13 For the first shall receive the last, those whom they were expecting, and the last those of whom they used to hear that they had passed away.

14   For they have been delivered from this world of tribulation,

And laid down the burthen of anguish.

15   For what then have men lost their life,

And for what have those who were on the earth exchanged their soul?

16   For then they chose (not) for themselves this time,

Which, beyond the reach of anguish, could not pass away:

But they chose for themselves that time,

Whose issues are full of lamentations and evils,

And they denied the world which ages not those who come to it,

And they rejected the time of glory,

So that they shall not come to the honor of which I told you before.'

52 1 And I answered and said:

'How can we forget those for whom woe is then reserved?

2   And why therefore do we again mourn for those who die?

Or why do we weep for those who depart to Sheol?

3   Let lamentations be reserved for the beginning of that coming torment,

And let tears be laid up for the advent of the destruction of that time.

4   [But even in the face of these things will I speak.

5   And as for the righteous, what will they do now?

6   Rejoice you in the suffering which you now suffer:

For why do you look for the decline of your enemies?

7   Make ready your soul for that which is reserved for you,

And prepare your souls for the reward which is laid up for you.']

53–54. THE MESSIAH APOCALYPSE

53. The Vision of the Cloud with black and white Waters

53 1 And when I had said these things I fell asleep there, and I saw a vision, and lo! a cloud was ascending from a very great sea, and I kept gazing upon it) and lo! it was full of waters white and black, and there were many colors in those self-same waters, and as it were the likeness of great lightning was seen at its summit. 2 And I saw the cloud passing swiftly in quick courses, and it covered all the earth. 3 And it came to pass after these things that that cloud began to pour upon the earth the waters that were in it. 4 And I saw that there was not one and the same likeness in the waters which descended from it. 5 For in the first beginning they were black and many (Or a time, and afterwards I saw that the waters became bright, but they were not many, and after these things again I saw black (waters), and after these things again bright, and again black and again bright. 6 Now this was done twelve times, but the black were always more numerous than the bright. 7 And it came to pass at the end of the cloud, that lo! it rained black waters, and they were darker than had been all those waters that were before, and fire was mingled with them, and where those waters descended, they wrought devastation and destruction. 8 And after these things I saw how that lightning which I had seen on the summit of the cloud, seized hold of it and hurled it to the earth. 9 Now that lightning shone exceedingly, so as to illuminate the whole earth, and it healed those regions where the last waters had descended and wrought devastation. 10 And it took hold of the whole earth, and had dominion over it. 11 And I saw after these things, and lo! twelve rivers were ascending from the sea, and they began to surround that lightning and to become subject to it. 12 And by reason of my fear I awoke.

54–55. Baruch's Prayer for an Interpretation of the Vision: Ramiel's advent for

this Purpose

54 1 And I besought the Mighty One, and said:

'You alone, O Lord, know of aforetime the deep things of the world,

And the things which befall in their times You bring about by Your word, And against the works of the inhabitants of the earth you do hasten the beginnings of the times,

And the end of the seasons you alone know.

2   (You) for whom nothing is too hard,

But who do everything easily by a nod:

3   (You) to whom the depths come as the heights,

And whose word the beginnings of the ages serve:

4   (You) who reveal to those who fear you what is prepared for them,

That thenceforth they may be comforted.

5   You show great acts to those who know not;

You break up the enclosure of those who are ignorant,

And lightest up what is dark,

And reveal what is hidden to the pure,

[Who in faith have submitted themselves to you and Your law.]

6 You have shown to Your servant this vision;

Reveal to me also its interpretation.

7 For I know that as regards those things wherein I besought you, I have received a response,

And as regards what I besought, you did reveal to me with what voice I should praise you,

And from what members I should cause praises and hallelujahs to ascend to you.

8 For if my members were mouths,

And the hairs of my head voices,

Even so I could not give you the reward of praise,

Nor laud you as is befitting,

Nor could I recount Your praise,

Nor tell the glory of Your beauty.

9 For what am I amongst men,

Or why am I reckoned amongst those who are more excellent than I,

That I have heard all these marvelous things from the Most High,

And numberless promises from Him who created me?

10   Blessed be my mother among those that bear,

And praised among women be she that bare me.

11   For I will not be silent in praising the Mighty One,

And with the voice of praise I will recount His marvelous deeds.

12   For who doeth like unto Your marvelous deeds, O God,

Or who comprehend Your deep thought of life.

13   For with Your counsel you do govern all the creatures which Your right hand has created

And you have established every fountain of light beside you,

And the treasures of wisdom beneath Your throne have you prepared.

14   And justly do they perish who have not loved Your law,

And the torment of judgment shall await those who have not submitted themselves to Your power.

15   For though Adam first sinned

And brought untimely death upon all,

Yet of those who were born from him

Each one of them has prepared for his own soul torment to come,

And again each one of them has chosen for himself glories to come.

16   [For assuredly he who believeth will receive reward.

17   But now, as for you, you wicked that now are, turn you to destruction, because you shall speedily be visited, in that formerly you rejected the understanding of the Most High.

18   For His works have not taught you,

Nor has the skill of His creation which is at all times persuaded you.]

19   Adam is therefore not the cause, save only of his own soul,

But each of us has been the Adam of his own soul.

20   But do You, O Lord, expound to me regarding those things which you have revealed to me,

And inform me regarding that which I besought you.

21   For at the consummation of the world vengeance shall be taken upon those who have done wickedness according to their wickedness,

And you will glorify the faithful according to their faithfulness.

22   For those who are amongst your own you rule,

And those who sin you blot out from amongst your own.'

55 1 And it came to pass when I had finished speaking the words of this prayer, that I sat there under a tree, that I might rest in the shade of the branches. 2 And I wondered and was astonished, and pondered in my thoughts regarding the multitude of goodness which sinners who are upon the earth have rejected, and regarding the great torment which they have despised, though they knew that they should be tormented because of the sin they had committed.

And when I was pondering on these things and the like, lo! the angel Ramiel who presides over true visions was sent to me, and he said unto me:

4   'Why does your heart trouble you, Baruch,

and why does your thought disturb you?

5   For if owing to the report which you have only heard of judgment you are so moved,

What (wilt you be) when you shall see it manifestly with your eyes?

6   And if with the expectation wherewith you do expect the day of the Mighty One you are so overcome,

What (wilt you be) when you shall come to its advent?

7   And, if at the word of the announcement of the torment of those who have done foolishly you are so wholly distraught,

How much more when the event will reveal marvelous things?

8   And if you have heard tidings of the good and evil things which are then coming and are grieved,

What (wilt you be) when you shall behold what the majesty will reveal, Which shall convict these and cause those to rejoice.'

56–74. Interpretation of the Vision. The black and bright Waters symbolize the World's History from Adam to the Advent of the Messiah.

56 1 'Nevertheless, because you have besought the Most High to reveal to you the interpretation of the vision which you have seen, I have been sent to tell you. 2 And the Mighty One hath assuredly made known to you the methods of the times that have passed, and of those that are destined to pass in His world from the beginning of its creation even unto its consummation, of those things which (are) deceit and of those which (are) in truth. 3 For as you did see a great cloud which ascended from the sea, and went and covered the earth, this is the duration of the world (= αιων) which the Mighty One made when he took counsel to make the world. 4 And it came to pass when the word had gone forth from His presence, that the duration of the world had come into being in a small degree, and was established according to the multitude of the intelligence of Him who sent it. 5 And as you did previously see on the summit of the cloud black waters which descended previously on the earth, this is the transgression wherewith Adam the first man transgressed.

6   For [since] when he transgressed

Untimely death came into being,

Grief was named

And anguish was prepared,

And pain was created,

And trouble consummated,

And disease began to be established,

And Sheol kept demanding that it should be renewed in blood,

And the begetting of children was brought about,

And the passion of parents produced,

And the greatness of humanity was humiliated,

And goodness languished.

7 What therefore can be blacker or darker than these things? 8 This is the beginning of the black waters which you have seen. 9 And from these black (waters) again were black derived, and the darkness of darkness was produced. 10 For he became a danger to his own soul: even to the angels 11 For, moreover, at that time when he was created, they enjoyed liberty. 12 And became he a danger some of them descended, and mingled with the women. 13 And then those who did so were tormented in chains. 14 But the rest of the multitude of the angels, of which there is (no) number, restrained themselves. 15 And those who dwelt on the earth perished together (with them) through the waters of the deluge. 16 These are the black first waters.

57 1 And after these (waters) you did see bright waters: this is the fount of Abraham, also his generations and advent of his son, and of his son's son, and of those like them. 2 Because at that time the unwritten law was named amongst them,

And the works of the commandments were then fulfilled,

And belief in the coming judgment was then generated,

And hope of the world that was to be renewed was then built up,

And the promise of the life that should come hereafter was implanted.

3   These are the bright waters, which you have seen.

58 1 'And the black third waters which you have seen, these are the mingling of all sins, which the nations afterwards wrought after the death of those righteous men, and the wickedness of the land of Egypt, wherein they did wickedly in the service wherewith they made their sons to serve. 2 Nevertheless, these also perished at last.

59 1 'And the bright fourth waters which you have seen are the advent of Moses and Aaron and Miriam and Joshua the son of Nun and Caleb and of all those like them. 2 For at that time the lamp of the eternal law shone on all those who sat in darkness, which announced to them that believe the promise of their reward, and to them that deny, the torment of fire which is reserved for them. 3 But also the heavens at that time were shaken from their place, and those who were under the throne of the Mighty One were perturbed, when He was taking Moses unto Himself. 4 For He showed him many admonitions together with the principles of the law and the consummation of the times, as also to you, and likewise the pattern of Zion and its measures, in the pattern of which the sanctuary of the present time was to be made. 5 But then also He showed to him the measures of the fire, also the depths of the abyss, and the weight of the winds, and the number of the drops of rain: 6 And the suppression of anger, and the multitude of long-suffering, and the truth of judgment: 7 And the root of wisdom, and the riches of understanding, and the fount of knowledge: 8 And the height of the air, and the greatness of Paradise, and the consummation of the ages, and the beginning of the day of judgment: 9 And the number of the offerings, and the earths which have not yet come: 10 And the mouth of Gehenna, and the station of vengeance, and the place of faith, and the region of hope: And the likeness of future torment, and the multitude of innumerable angels, and the flaming hosts, and the splendor of the lightnings, and the voice of the thunders, and the orders of the chiefs of the angels, and the treasuries of light,

and the changes of the times, and the investigations of the law. 12 These are the bright fourth waters which you have seen.

60 1 And the black fifth waters which you have seen raining are the works which the Amorites wrought, and the spells of their incantations which they wrought, and the wickedness of their mysteries, and the mingling of their pollution. 2 But even Israel was then polluted by sins in the days of the judges, though they saw many signs which were from Him who made them.

61 1 And the bright sixth waters which thru did see, this is the time in which David and Solomon were born.

2   And there was at that time the building of Zion,

And the dedication of the sanctuary,

And the shedding of much blood of the nations that sinned then,

And many offerings which were offered then in the dedication of the sanctuary.

3   And peace and tranquility existed at that time,

4   And wisdom was heard in the assembly:

And the riches of understanding were magnified in the congregations,

5   And the holy festivals were fulfilled in blessedness and in much joy.

6   And the judgment of the rulers was then seen to be without guile,

And the righteousness of the precepts of the Mighty One was accomplished with truth.

7   And the land [which] was then beloved by the Lord,

And because its inhabitants sinned not, it was glorified beyond all lands, And the city Zion ruled then over all lands and regions.

8   These are the bright waters which you have seen.

62 1 And the black seventh waters which you have seen, this is the perversion (brought about) by the counsel of Jeroboam, who took counsel to make two calves of gold: 2 And all the iniquities which kings who were after him iniquitously wrought. 3 And the curse of Jezebel and the worship of idols which Israel practiced at that time. 4 And the withholding of rain, and the famines which occurred until women eat the fruit of their wombs. 5 And the time of their captivity which came upon the nine tribes and a half, because they were in many sins. 6 And Shalmanezzar king of Assyria came and led them away captive. 7 But regarding the Gentiles it were tedious to tell how they always wrought impiety and wickedness, and never wrought righteousness. 8 These are the black seventh waters which you have seen.

63 1 'And the bright eighth waters which you have seen, this is the rectitude and uprightness of Hezekiah king of Judah and the grace (of God) which came upon him. 2 For when Sennacherib was stirred up in order that he might perish, and his wrath troubled him in order that he might thereby perish, for the multitude also of the nations which were with him. 3 When, moreover, Hezekiah the king heard those things which the king of Assyria was devising, (i.e.) to come and seize him and destroy his people, the two and a half

tribes which remained: nay, more he wished to overthrow Zion also: then Hezekiah trusted in his works, and had hope in his righteousness, and spoke with the Mighty One and said: 4 "Behold, for lo! Sennacherib is prepared to destroy us, and he will be boastful and uplifted when he has destroyed Zion."

5   And the Mighty One heard him, for Hezekiah was wise,

And He had respect unto his prayer, because he was righteous.

6 And thereupon the Mighty One commanded Ramiel His angel who speaks with you. 7 And I went forth and destroyed their multitude, the number of whose chiefs only was a hundred and eighty-five thousand, and each one of them had an equal number (at his command). 8 And at that time I burned their bodies within, but their raiment and arms I preserved outwardly, in order that the still more wonderful deeds of the Mighty One might appear, and that thereby His name might be spoken of throughout the whole earth. 9 And Zion was saved and Jerusalem delivered: Israel also was freed from tribulation. 10 And all those who were in the holy land rejoiced, and the name of the Mighty One was glorified so that it was spoken of 11 These are the bright waters which you have seen.

64 1 'And the black ninth waters which you have seen, this is all the wickedness which was in the days of Manasseh the son of Hezekiah. 2 For he wrought much impiety, and he slew the righteous, and he wrested judgment, and he shed the blood of the innocent, and wedded women he violently polluted, and he overturned the altars, and destroyed their offerings, and drove forth their priests lest they should minister in the sanctuary. 3 And he made an image with five faces: four of them looked to the four winds, and the fifth on the summit of the image as ah adversary of

the zeal of the Mighty One. 4 And then wrath went forth from the presence of the Mighty One to the intent that Zion should be rooted out, as also it befell in your days. But also against the two tribes and a half went forth a decree that they should also be led away captive, as you have now seen. 5 And to such a degree did the impiety of Manasseh increase, that it removed the praise of the Most High from the sanctuary. 7 On this account Manasseh was at that time named 'the impious," and finally his abode was in the fire. 8 For though his prayer was heard with the Most High, finally, when he was cast into the brazen horse and the brazen horse was melted, it served as a sign unto him for the hour. 9 For he had not lived perfectly, for he was not worthy — but that thenceforward he might know by whom finally he should be tormented. 10 For he who is able to benefit is also able to torment.

65 1 'Thus, moreover, did Manasseh act impiously, and thought that in his time the Mighty One would not inquire into these things. 2 These are the black ninth waters which you have seen.

66 1 'And the bright tenth waters which you have seen: this is the purity of the generations of Josiah king of Judah, who was the only one at the time who submitted himself to the Mighty One with all his heart and with all his soul. 2 And he cleansed the land from idols, and hallowed all the vessels which had been polluted, and restored the offerings to the altar, and raised the horn of the holy, and exalted the righteous, and honored all that were wise in understanding, and brought back the priests to their ministry, and destroyed and removed the magicians and enchanters and necromancers from the land. 3 And not only did he slay the impious that were living, but they also took from the sepulchers the bones of the dead and burned them with fire. 4 [And the festivals and the Sabbaths he established in their sanctity], and their polluted ones he burnt in the fire, and the lying prophets which deceived the people, these also he burnt in the fire, and the people who listened to them when they were living, he cast them into the brook Kidron, and

heaped stones upon them. 5 And he was zealous with zeal for the Mighty One with all his soul, and he alone was firm in the law at that time, so that he left none that was uncircumcised, or that wrought impiety in all the land, all the days of his life. 6 Therefore he shall receive an eternal reward, and he shall be glorified with the Mighty One beyond many at a later time. 7 For on his account and on account of those who are like him were the honorable glories, of which you were told before, created and prepared. These arc the bright waters which you have seen.

67 1 'And the black eleventh waters which you have seen: this is the calamity which is now befalling "Zion.

2 Do you think that there is no anguish to the angels in the presence of the Mighty One,

That Zion was so delivered up,

And that lo! the Gentiles boast in their hearts,

And assemble before their idols and say,

"She is trodden down who oftentimes trod down,

And she has been reduced to servitude who reduced (others)"?

3 Dost you think that in these things the Most High rejoices,

Or that His name is glorified?

4 [But how will it serve towards His righteous judgment?]

5   Yet after these things shall the dispersed among the Gentiles be taken hold of by tribulation,

And in shame shall they dwell in every place.

6   Because so far as Zion is delivered up

And Jerusalem laid waste,

Shall idols prosper in the cities of the Gentiles,

And the vapor of the smoke of the incense of the righteousness which is by the law is extinguished in Zion,

And in the region of Zion in every place lo! there is the smoke of impiety.

7   But the king of Babylon will arise who has now destroyed Zion,

And he will boast over the people,

And he will speak great things in his heart in the presence of the Most High.

8   But he also shall fall at last. These are the black waters.

68 1 'And the bright twelfth waters which you have seen: this is the word. For after these things time will come when your people shall fall into distress, so that they shall all run the risk of perishing together. 3 Nevertheless, they will be saved, and their enemies will fall in their presence. 4 And they will have in (due) time much joy. 5 And at that time after a little interval Zion will again be rebuilt, and its offerings will again be restored, and the priests will return to their ministry, and also the Gentiles will come to glorify it. 6 Nevertheless, not fully as in the beginning. 7 But it will come to pass

after these things that there will be the fall of many nations. 8 These are the bright waters which you have seen.

69 1 'For the last waters which you have seen which were darker than all that were before them, those which were after the twelfth number, which were collected together, belong to the whole world. 2 For the Most High made division from the beginning, because He alone knows what will befall. 3 For as to the enormities and the impieties which should be wrought before Him, He foresaw six kinds of them. 4 And of the good works of the righteous which should be accomplished before Him, He foresaw six kinds of them, beyond those which He should work at the consummation of the age. 5 On his account there were not black waters with black, nor bright with bright; for it is the consummation.

70 1 'Hear therefore the interpretation of the last black waters which are to come [after the black]: this the word. 2 Behold! the days come, and it shall be when the time of the age has ripened,

And the harvest of its evil and good seeds has come,

That the Mighty One will bring upon the earth and its inhabitants and upon its rulers

Perturbation of spirit and stupor of heart.

3   And they shall hate one another,

And provoke one another to fight,

And the mean shall rule over the honorable,

And those of low degree shall be extolled above the famous.

4   And the many shall be delivered into the hands of the few,

And those who were nothing shall rule over the strong,

And the poor shall have abundance beyond the rich,

And the impious shall exalt themselves above the heroic.

5   And the wise shall be silent,

And the foolish shall speak,

Neither shall the thought of men be then confirmed,

Nor the counsel of the mighty,

Nor shall the hope of those who hope be confirmed.

6   And when those things which were predicted have come to pass,

Then shall confusion fall upon all men,

And some of them shall fall in battle,

And some of them shall perish in anguish,

7 And some of them shall be destroyed by their own. Then the Most High peoples whom He has prepared before,

And they shall come and make war with the leaders that shall then be left.

8   And it shall come to pass that whoever gets safe out of the war shall die in the earthquake,

And whoever gets safe out of the earthquake shall be burned by the fire,

And whoever gets safe out of the fire shall be destroyed by famine.

9 [And it shall come to pass that whoever of the victors and the vanquished gets safe out of and escapes all these things aforesaid will be delivered into the hands of My servant Messiah.] 10 For all the earth shall devour its inhabitants.

71 1 'And the holy land shall have mercy on its own, And it shall protect its inhabitants at that time. 2 This is the vision which you have seen, and this is the interpretation. 3 For I have come to tell you these things, because your prayer has been heard with the Most High.

72 'Hear now also regarding the bright lightning which is to come at the consummation after these black (waters): this is the word. 2 After the signs have come, of which you were told before, when the nations become turbulent, and the time of My Messiah is come, he shall both summon all the nations, and some of them he shall spare, and some of them he shall slay. 3 These things therefore shall come upon the nations which are to be spared by Him. 4 Every nation, which knows not Israel and has not trodden down the seed of Jacob, shall indeed be spared. 5 And this because some out of every nation shall be subjected to your people. 6 But all those who have ruled over you, or have known you, shall be given up to the sword.

73 1 'And it shall come to pass, when He has brought low everything that is in the world,

And has sat down in peace for the age on the throne of His kingdom,

That joy shall then be revealed,

And rest shall appear.

2 And then healing shall descend in dew,

And disease shall withdraw,

And anxiety and anguish and lamentation pass from amongst men,

And gladness proceed through the whole earth.

3 And no one shall again die untimely,

Nor shall any adversity suddenly befall.

4 And judgments, and abusive talk, and contentions, and revenges,

And blood, and passions, and envy, and hatred,

And whatsoever things are like these shall go into condemnation when they are removed.

5 For it is these very things which have filled this world with evils,

And on account of these the life of man has been greatly troubled.

6 And wild beasts shall come from the forest and minister unto men

And asps and dragons shall come forth from their holes to submit themselves to a little child.

7   And women shall no longer then have pain when they bear,

Nor shall they suffer torment when they yield the fruit of the womb.

74 1 'And it shall come to pass in those days that the reapers shall not grow weary,

Nor those that build be toil-worn;

For the works shall of themselves speedily advance

Together with those who do them in much tranquility.

2   For that time is the consummation of that which is corruptible,

And the beginning of that which is not corruptible.

3   Therefore those things which were predicted shall belong to it:

Therefore it is far away from evils, and near to those things which die not.

4   This is the bright lightning which came after the last dark waters.'

75. Baruch's Hymn on the Unsearchableness of God's Ways and on His Mercies through which the Faithful shall attain to a blessed Consummation

75 1   And I answered and said:

'Who can understand, O Lord, Your goodness?

For it is incomprehensible.

2   Or who can search into your compassions,

Which are infinite?

3   Or who can comprehend Your intelligence?

4   Or who is able to recount the thoughts of Your mind?

5   Or who of those who are born can hope to come to those things,

Unless he is one to whom you are merciful and gracious?

6   Because, if assuredly you did not have compassion on man,

Those who are under Your right hand,

They could not come to those things,

But those who are in the numbers named can be called.

7   But if, indeed, we who exist know wherefore we have come,

And submit ourselves to Him who brought us out of Egypt,

We shall come again and remember those things which have passed,

And shall rejoice regarding that which has been.

8   But if now we know not wherefore we have come,

And recognize not the principate of Him who brought us up out of Egypt, We shall come again and seek after those things which have been now,

And be grieved with pain because of those things which have befallen.'

76. Baruch bidden to instruct the People for forty days and then to hold himself ready for his Assumption on the Advent of the Messiah

76 1 And He answered and said unto me: ['Inasmuch as the revelation of this vision has been interpreted to you as you requested], hear the word of the Most High that you may know what is to befall you after these things. 2 For you shall surely depart from this earth, nevertheless not unto death, but you shall be preserved unto the consummation of the times. 3 Go up therefore to the top of that mountain, and there shall pass before you all the regions of that land, and the figure of the inhabited world, and the top(s) of the mountains, and the depth(s) of the valleys, and the depths of the seas, and the number of the rivers, that you may see what you are leaving, and whither you are going. 4 Now this shall befall after forty days. Go now therefore during these days and instruct the people so far as you are able, that they may learn so as not to die at the last time, but may learn in order that they may live at the last times.'

77. Baruch's Admonition to the People and his writing of two Letters—one to the nine and a half tribes in Assyria and the other to the two and a half in Babylon

77 1 And I, Baruch, went there and came to the people, and assembled them together from the greatest to the least, and said unto them: 2 'Hear, you children of Israel, behold how many you are who remain of the twelve tribes of Israel. 3 For to you and to your fathers the Lord gave a law more excellent than to all peoples. 4 And because your brethren transgressed the commandments of the Most High,

He brought vengeance upon you and upon them,

And He spared not the former,

And the latter also He gave into captivity:

And He left not a residue of them,

5   But behold! you are here with me.

6   If, therefore, you direct your ways aright,

Ye also shall not depart as your brethren departed,

But they shall come to you.

7   For He is merciful whom you worship,

And He is gracious in whom you hope,

And He is true, so that He shall do good and not evil.

8   Have you not seen here what has befallen Zion?

9 Or do you perchance think that the place had sinned,

And that on this account it was overthrown?

Or that the land had wrought foolishness,

And that therefore it was delivered up?

10 And know you not that on account of you who did sin,

That which sinned not was overthrown,

And, on account of those who wrought wickedly,

That which wrought not foolishness was delivered up to (its) enemies?'

11 And the whole people answered and said unto me: 'So far as we can recall the good things which the Mighty One has done unto us, we do recall them; and those things which we do not remember He in His mercy knows. 12 Nevertheless, do this for us your people: write also to our brethren in Babylon an epistle of doctrine and a scroll of hope, that you may confirm them also before you do depart from us.

13 For the shepherds of Israel have perished,

And the lamps which gave light are extinguished,

And the fountains have withheld their stream whence we used to drink.

14 And we are left in the darkness,

And amid the trees of the forest,

And the thirst of the wilderness.'

15   And I answered and said unto them

'Shepherds and lamps and fountains come from the law:

And though we depart, yet the law abides.

16   If therefore you have respect to the law,

And are intent upon wisdom,

A lamp will not be wanting,

And a shepherd will not fail,

And a fountain will not dry up.

17 Nevertheless, as you said unto me, I will write also unto your brethren in Babylon, and I will send by means of men, and I will write in like manner to the nine tribes and a half, and send by means of a bird.' 18 And it came to pass on the one and twentieth day in the eighth month that I, Baruch, came and sat down under the oak under the shadow of the branches, and no man was with me, but I was alone. 19 And I wrote these two epistles: one I sent by an eagle to the nine and a half tribes; and the other I sent to those that were at Babylon by means of three men. 20 And I called the eagle and spoke these words unto it: 21 'The Most High hath made you that you should be higher than all birds. 22 And now go and tarry not in (any) place, nor enter a nest, nor settle upon any tree, till you have passed over the breadth of the many waters of the river Euphrates, and have gone to the people that dwell there, and cast down to them this epistle. 23 Remember, moreover, that, at the time of the deluge, Noah received from a dove the fruit of the olive, when he sent it forth from the ark. 24 Yea, also the ravens

ministered to Elijah, bearing him food, as they had been commanded. 25 Solomon also, in the time of his kingdom, whithersoever he wished to send or seek for anything, commanded a bird (to go thither), and it obeyed him as he commanded it. 26 And now let it not weary you, and turn not to the right hand nor the left, but fly and go by a direct way, that you may preserve the command of the Mighty One, according as I said unto you.'

78–86. THE EPISTLE OF BARUCH THE SON OF NERIAH WHICH HE

WROTE TO THE NINE AND A HALF TRIBES

78 1 These are the words of that epistle which Baruch the son of Neriah sent to the nine and a half tribes, which were across the river Euphrates, in which these things were written.

2 Thus says Baruch the son of Neriah to the brethren carried into captivity: 'Mercy and peace.' I bear in mind, my brethren, the love of Him who created us, who loved us from of old, and never hated us, but above all educated us. 3 And truly I know that behold all we the twelve tribes are bound by one bond, inasmuch as we are born from one father. 4 Wherefore I have been the more careful to leave you the words of this epistle before I die, that you may be comforted regarding the evils which have come upon you, and that you may be grieved also regarding the evil that has befallen your brethren; and again, also, that you may justify His judgment which 5 He has decreed against you that you should be carried away captive—for what you have suffered is disproportioned to what you have done—in order that, at the last times, you may be found worthy of your fathers. 6 Therefore, if you consider that ye have now suffered those things for your good, that you may not finally be condemned and tormented, then you will receive eternal hope; if above all you

destroy from your heart vain error, on account of which you departed hence. 7 For if you so do these things, He will continually remember you, He who always promised on our behalf to those who were more excellent than we, that He will never forget or forsake us, but with much mercy will gather together again those who were dispersed.

79 1 Now, my brethren, learn first what befell Zion: how that Nebuchadnezzar king of Babylon came up against us. 2 For we have sinned against Him who made us, and we have not kept the commandments which he commanded us, yet he hath not chastened us as we deserved. 3 For what befell you we also suffer in a preeminent degree, for it befell us also.

80 1 And now, my brethren, I make known unto you that when the enemy had surrounded the city, the angels of the Most High were sent, and they overthrew the fortifications of the strong wall, and they destroyed the firm iron corners, which could not be rooted out. 2 Nevertheless, they hid all the vessels of the sanctuary, lest the enemy should get possession of them. 3 And when they had done these things, they delivered thereupon to the enemy the overthrown wall, and the plundered house, and the burnt temple, and the people who were overcome because they were delivered up, lest the enemy should boast and say: 'Thus by force have we been able to lay waste even the house of the Most High in war.' Your brethren also have they bound and led away to Babylon, and have caused them to dwell there. 5 But we have been left here, being very few. 6 This is the tribulation about which I wrote to you. 7 For assuredly I know that (the consolation of) the inhabitants of Zion consoles you : so far as you knew that it was prospered (your consolation) was greater than the tribulation which you endured in having to depart from it.

81 1 But regarding consolation, hear the word. 2 For I was mourning regarding Zion, and I prayed for mercy from the Most High, and I said:

3   'How long will these things endure for us?

And will these evils come upon us always?'

4   And the Mighty One did according to the multitude of His mercies,

And the Most High according to the greatness of His compassion,

And He revealed unto me the word, that I might receive consolation,

And He showed me visions that I should not again endure anguish,

And He made known to me the mystery of the times.

And the advent of the hours he showed me.

82 1 Therefore, my brethren, I have written to you, that you may comfort yourselves regarding the multitude of your tribulations. 2 For know you that our Maker will assuredly avenge us on all our enemies, according to all that they have done to us, also that the consummation which the Most High will make is very nigh, and His mercy that is coming, and the consummation of His judgment, is by no means far off.

3   For lo! we see now the multitude of the prosperity of the Gentiles,

Though they act impiously,

But they shall be like a vapor:

4   And we behold the multitude of their power,

Though they do wickedly,

But they shall be made like unto a drop:

5   And we see the firmness of their might.

Though they resist the Mighty One every hour,

But they shall be accounted as spittle.

6   And we consider the glory of their greatness,

Though they do not keep the statutes of the Most High,

But as smoke shall they pass away.

7   And we meditate on the beauty of their gracefulness,

Though they have to do with pollutions,

But as grass that withers shall they fade away.

8   And we consider the strength of their cruelty,

Though they remember not the end (thereof),

But as a wave that passes shall they be broken.

9   And we remark the boastfulness of their might,

Though they deny the beneficence of God, who gave (it) to them,

But they shall pass away as a passing cloud.

83 1 [For the Most High will assuredly hasten His times,

And He will assuredly bring on His hours.

2 And He will assuredly judge those who are in His world,

And will visit in truth all things by means of all their hidden works.

3 And He will assuredly examine the secret thoughts,

And that which is laid up in the secret chambers of all the members of mail. And will make (them) manifest in the presence of all with reproof.

4 Let none therefore of these present things ascend into your hearts, but above all let us be expectant, because that which is promised to us shall come. 5 And let us not now look unto the delights of the Gentiles in the present, but let us remember what has been promised to us in the end. 6 For the ends of the times and of the seasons and whatsoever is with them shall assuredly pass by together. 7 The consummation, moreover, of the age shall then show the great might of its ruler, when all things come to judgment. 8 Do you therefore prepare your hearts for that which before you believed, lest you come to be in bondage in both worlds, so that you be led away captive here and be tormented there. 9 For that which exists now or which has passed away, or which is to come, in all these things, neither is the evil fully evil, nor again the good fully good.

10 For all healthinesses of this time are turning into diseases,

11 And all might of this time is turning into weakness,

And all the force of this time is turning into impotence,

12   And every energy of youth is turning into old age and consummation.

And every beauty of gracefulness of this time is turning faded and hateful,

13   And every proud dominion of the present is turning into humiliation and shame,

14   And every praise of the glory of this time is turning into the shame of silence,

And every vain splendor and insolence of this time is turning into voiceless ruin.

15   And every delight and joy of this time is turning to worms and corruption,

16   And every clamor of the pride of this time is turning into dust and stillness.

17   And every possession of riches of this time is being turned into Sheol alone,

18   And all the rapine of passion of this time is turning into involuntary death,

And every passion of the lusts of this time is turning into a judgment of torment.

19   And every artifice and craftiness of this time is turning into a proof of the truth,

20   And every sweetness of unguents of this time is turning into judgment and condemnation,

21   And every love of lying is turning to contumely through truth.

22 [Since therefore all these things are done now, does anyone think that they will not be avenged? But the consummation of all things will come to the truth.]

84 Behold! I have therefore made known unto you (these things) whilst I live: for I have said (it) that you should learn the things that are excellent; for the Mighty One hath commanded me to instruct you: and I will set before you some of the commandments of His judgment before I die. 2 Remember that formerly Moses assuredly called heaven and earth to witness against you and said: 'If you transgress the law you shall be dispersed, but if you keep it you shall be kept.' 3 And other things also he used to say unto you when you the twelve tribes were together in the desert. 4 And after his death you cast them away from you: on this account there came upon you what had been predicted. 5 And now Moses used to tell you before they befell you, and lo! they have befallen you: for you have forsaken the law. 6 Lo! I also say unto you after you have suffered, that if you obey those things which have been said unto you, you will receive from the Mighty One whatever has been laid up and reserved for you. 7 Moreover, let this epistle be for a testimony between me and you, that you may remember the commandments of the Mighty One, and that also there may be to me a defense in the presence of Him who sent me. 8 And remember you the law and Zion, and the holy land and your brethren, and the covenant of your fathers, and forget not the festivals and the Sabbaths. And deliver this epistle and the traditions of the law to your sons after you, as also your fathers delivered (them) to you. 10 And at all times make request perseveringly and pray diligently with your whole heart that the Mighty One may be reconciled to you, and that He may not reckon the multitude of your sins, but remember the rectitude of your fathers. 11 For if He judge us not according to the multitude of His mercies, woe unto all us who are born.

85 1 [Know, moreover, that

In former times and in the generations of old our fathers had helpers,

Righteous men and holy prophets:

2   No more, we were in our own land

[And they helped us when we sinned],

finish

Made in the USA
Columbia, SC
07 June 2025